American Slavery

Other Books in the Turning Points Series:

The American Revolution
The Atom Bomb
The Civil Rights Movement
The Collapse of the Soviet Union
The Crusades
The Decline and Fall of Ancient Greece
The French Revolution
The Great Depression
North American Indian Wars
The Reformation
The Renaissance
The Rise of Christianity
The Rise of Nazi Germany
The Spread of Islam
Victorian England
Women's Suffrage

Turning | Points

IN WORLD HISTORY

American Slavery

William Dudley, *Book Editor*

David L. Bender, *Publisher*
Bruno Leone, *Executive Editor*
Bonnie Szumski, *Editorial Director*
David M. Haugen, *Managing Editor*

Greenhaven Press, Inc., San Diego, California

Every effort has been made to trace the owners of copyrighted material. The articles in this volume may have been edited for content, length, and/or reading level. The titles have been changed to enhance the editorial purpose.

Library of Congress Cataloging-in-Publication Data

American slavery / William Dudley, book editor.
        p.   cm. — (Turning points in world history)
     Includes bibliographical references and index.
     ISBN 0-7377-0213-3 (alk. paper) —
     ISBN 0-7377-0212-5 (pbk. : alk. paper)
     1. Slavery—United States—History. I. Dudley, William, 1964–   .
     II. Series: Turning points in world history (Greenhaven Press)

E441 .A578 2000
306.3'62'0973—dc21   99-055866
                                                                         CIP

Cover photo: Corbis/Bettmann
North Wind, 16
Library of Congress, 30

©2000 by Greenhaven Press, Inc.
P.O. Box 289009, San Diego, CA 92198-9009

Printed in the U.S.A.

Contents

Foreword   9

Introduction   11

The Rise and Fall of American Slavery: A Brief Overview   14

Chapter 1: Origins of American Slavery

1. The Atlantic Slave Trade by *Daniel C. Littlefield*   34
Slavery in what would become the United States was one
small part of a large economic system based on cash
crops raised in Brazil, Central America, the West Indies,
and southern North America. In fact, England's North
American colonies received less than five percent of the
total number of Africans shipped across the Atlantic
Ocean.

2. Establishing Slavery in the Southern Colonies   44
by John B. Boles
English settlers in Virginia and Maryland turned to slavery of blacks only after white indentured servants proved
to be an insufficient source of labor. By contrast, the
colonists who founded South Carolina immediately established a system of slavery similar to that in England's
Caribbean sugar colony of Barbados.

3. Slavery in the Northern Colonies by *Donald R. Wright*   58
Slavery was legal and played an important part in the development of American colonies north of Virginia and
Maryland. However, because the economies of New England and the Middle Colonies did not rely on plantation agriculture, slavery was different in several important respects compared to the South.

Chapter 2: Slavery and the American Revolution

**1. American Slavery: The American Revolution
(The Demise of Slavery in the North)** by *Peter Kolchin*   68
Patriot leaders took steps, both during and immediately after
the American Revolution, to bring about slavery's demise. The
northern states began the process of abolishing slavery within
their borders, but the institution remained entrenched in the
South.

2. **The Failure of Gradual Emancipation in the South**   74
by Gary B. Nash
Although several influential planters in the South supported the gradual abolition of slavery, the opportunity
to end slavery in the whole of the United States after the
American Revolution was not grasped by northern and
southern political leaders. One reason for their reluc-
tance to end slavery was a growing white racism that rejected the idea of black American citizens.

Chapter 3: A House Divided: American Slavery in the Antebellum Era

1. **The Missouri Compromise of 1820** *by Roger L. Ransom*   83
The first major political crisis related to slavery in the
1800s involved the question of whether Congress should
prohibit or permit slavery in the Louisiana Territory. In
the Missouri Compromise of 1820, Congress divided the
territory into slave and free regions and temporarily resolved the issue of slavery in the western territories.

2. **John C. Calhoun and the Southern Defense of**   92
Slavery *by Nathaniel Weyl and William Marina*
As the South expanded westward and cotton became a
dominant crop during the 1800s, the defensiveness that
many Southerners possessed about slavery was replaced
by a militant belief in slavery's social virtues. An influential individual in the changing thought on slavery was
John C. Calhoun, who argued that the human rights
listed in America's Declaration of Independence did not
apply to black slaves.

3. **The Abolitionist Movement Provokes the South**   103
by William W. Freehling
In the 1830s religious activists in the North organized a
movement calling for the immediate emancipation of all
slaves. Abolitionists' efforts to publicize the issue of slavery made them extremely unpopular in the South, where
many people called for the suppression of their activities.

4. **Social Tensions Within Southern Plantation Society**   113
by Ronald Takaki
Although defenders of slavery argued that it was a benev-
olent institution and that slaves were happy with their
condition, many whites in the South harbored doubts
about slavery and fears about slave rebellions. How slaves

behaved and what they felt about slavery did not comport with the stereotype of the childish and happy slave.

5. **Fugitive Slaves Exacerbate the Sectional Crisis over Slavery** by *James Oakes*   121
By the simple act of running away, fugitive slaves helped to intensify sectional tensions between North and South. Stories of escape were a recurring theme in abolitionist literature, including the influential novel *Uncle Tom's Cabin*.

6. **Slavery and Sectional Tensions in the 1350s**   128
by John Hope Franklin and Albert A. Moss Jr.
The decade preceding the Civil War was a tense and tumultuous period for the United States. Slavery was the underlying cause of the numerous political crises that divided the nation and ultimately led to war.

Chapter 4: Civil War and the End of American Slavery

1. **Slaves Seek Freedom in the Civil War**   137
by Merton L. Dillon
Thousands of slaves took advantage of the Civil War's disruption to escape behind Union army lines and to assist the North as spies, laborers, and soldiers. Their actions helped to undermine slavery in the South and commit the North under President Abraham Lincoln to take further steps to abolish it.

2. **Abraham Lincoln and the Emancipation Proclamation** *by James M. McPherson*   148
In the early months of the Civil War, Abraham Lincoln resisted entreaties by abolitionists to use his wartime powers to free the slaves of the Confederacy. However, a combination of events and circumstances eventually led to his decision to issue the Emancipation Proclamation, which transformed the war into an antislavery crusade.

3. **How Slaves Responded to Their Emancipation**   157
by Leon F. Litwack
Slaves demonstrated a wide variety of responses to the news of their liberation, ranging from joyful celebration to sorrow and uncertainty. Former slaves now had to determine what their new freedom meant to their daily lives.

4. **Reconstruction: The Aftermath of Emancipation and Civil War** by *David W. Blight*   171

In the period after the Civil War known as Reconstruction, the United States faced the challenge of integrating former slaves into the restored Union as free citizens and workers. During this time many schools for former slaves were founded, some political reforms and civil rights laws were passed in Congress, and a sharecropping system was developed in the South as a basis for hiring black labor.

Chapter 5: Was the Civil War Necessary to End Slavery?

1. **War Was Not Necessary to End American Slavery**   180
   by *Jeffrey Rogers Hummel*

   The United States was one of only two nations that abolished slavery in the midst of a war. The experiences of Brazil and Cuba suggest that the institution of slavery was politically moribund and could have been stopped without the bloodshed of the Civil War.

2. **The Significance of America's Civil War and Abolition of Slavery in World History**   185
   by *Robert W. Fogel*

   The abolition of American slavery following the defeat of the South in the Civil War marked a significant turning point not just for the United States, but for the world. If the Confederacy had been allowed to secede peacefully or had emerged victorious in the Civil War, it would have constituted a powerful economic and diplomatic force in preventing worldwide trends toward abolishing slavery, extending democracy, and other nineteenth-century reform movements.

Discussion Questions   194
Appendix of Documents   197
Chronology   238
For Further Research   243
Index   248

Foreword

Certain past events stand out as pivotal, as having effects and outcomes that change the course of history. These events are often referred to as turning points. Historian Louis L. Snyder provides this useful definition:

> A turning point in history is an event, happening, or stage which thrusts the course of historical development into a different direction. By definition a turning point is a great event, but it is even more—a great event with the explosive impact of altering the trend of man's life on the planet.

History's turning points have taken many forms. Some were single, brief, and shattering events with immediate and obvious impact. The invasion of Britain by William the Conqueror in 1066, for example, swiftly transformed that land's political and social institutions and paved the way for the rise of the modern English nation. By contrast, other single events were deemed of minor significance when they occurred, only later recognized as turning points. The assassination of a little-known European nobleman, Archduke Franz Ferdinand, on June 28, 1914, in the Bosnian town of Sarajevo was such an event; only after it touched off a chain reaction of political-military crises that escalated into the global conflict known as World War I did the murder's true significance become evident.

Other crucial turning points occurred not in terms of a few hours, days, months, or even years, but instead as evolutionary developments spanning decades or even centuries. One of the most pivotal turning points in human history, for instance—the development of agriculture, which replaced nomadic hunter-gatherer societies with more permanent settlements—occurred over the course of many generations. Still other great turning points were neither events nor developments, but rather revolutionary new inventions and innovations that significantly altered social customs and ideas, military tactics, home life, the spread of knowledge, and the human condition in general. The developments of writing, gunpowder, the printing press, antibiotics, the electric light, atomic energy, television, and the computer, the last two of which have recently ushered in the world-altering information age, represent only some of these innovative turning points.

Each anthology in the Greenhaven Turning Points in World History series presents a group of essays chosen for their accessibility. The anthology's structure also enhances this accessibility. First, an introductory essay provides a general overview of the principal events and figures involved, placing the topic in its historical context. The essays that follow explore various aspects in more detail, some targeting political trends and consequences, others social, literary, cultural, and/or technological ramifications, and still others pivotal leaders and other influential figures. To aid the reader in choosing the material of immediate interest or need, each essay is introduced by a concise summary of the contributing writer's main themes and insights.

In addition, each volume contains extensive research tools, including a collection of excerpts from primary source documents pertaining to the historical events and figures under discussion. In the anthology on the French Revolution, for example, readers can examine the works of Rousseau, Voltaire, and other writers and thinkers whose championing of human rights helped fuel the French people's growing desire for liberty; the French *Declaration of the Rights of Man and Citizen*, presented to King Louis XVI by the French National Assembly on October 2, 1789; and eyewitness accounts of the attack on the royal palace and the horrors of the Reign of Terror. To guide students interested in pursuing further research on the subject, each volume features an extensive bibliography, which for easy access has been divided into separate sections by topic. Finally, a comprehensive index allows readers to scan and locate content efficiently. Each of the anthologies in the Greenhaven Turning Points in World History series provides students with a complete, detailed, and enlightening examination of a crucial historical watershed.

Introduction

Historians identify two major turning points in the long history of slavery. The first is the massive expansion of the institution during European colonization of the New World, beginning in the 1500s. Spain, Portugal, England, France, and the Netherlands, seeking a reliable and cheap source of labor to develop their colonial possessions in North and South America and in the Caribbean islands, transported millions of Africans across the Atlantic Ocean as slaves. The second turning point is the movement to abolish slavery. From modest beginnings at the end of the 1700s, the antislavery movement, which included in its ranks European and American reformers, free blacks, and rebellious slaves, fulfilled its goal of outlawing slavery in the Western Hemisphere by the close of the nineteenth century.

The United States both shaped and was shaped by these two turning points. Slavery—already flourishing in the New World prior to the initial settlement of England's American colonies—played a major part in colonial development, especially in the South, where slave labor underpinned the region's agricultural economy. By 1759, one-fifth of the inhabitants of England's North American colonies were black slaves, many of them born in America.

However, during the colonial revolution against Great Britain that established the United States of America (1775–1783), some northern colonies chose to abolish slavery. Vermont, in 1777, and Pennsylvania, in 1780, became the first political entities in the Western Hemisphere to officially ban slavery. The actions of these newly independent states helped inspire the movement to end slavery worldwide, but did not spur the southern states to abolish the institution. Slavery survived and expanded in the southern United States for nearly a century as a defining feature of that region's culture and economy. American slavery finally came to an abrupt and violent end in the American Civil War (1861–

11

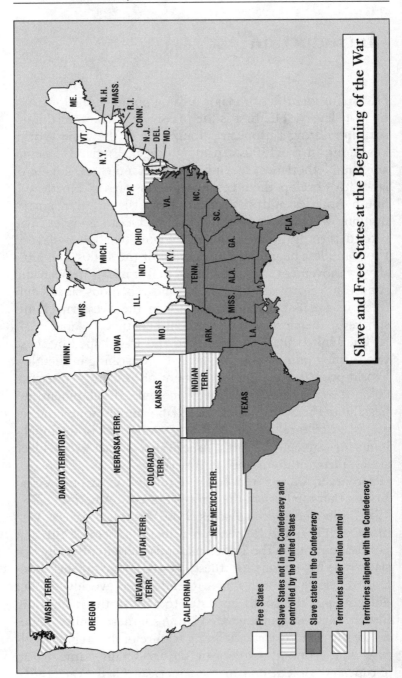

Slave and Free States at the Beginning of the War

Free States

Slave States not in the Confederacy and controlled by the United States

Slave states in the Confederacy

Territories under Union control

Territories aligned with the Confederacy

1865), liberating a slave population that had by then reached 4 million. The United States thus recorded both the earliest instance of slave abolition in the Western Hemisphere and the largest. The history of the nation between these two milestones is a story of deepening division between slave and free regions; deciding the issue essentially decided the course of American society.

American slavery has been the subject of tremendous historical research and analysis. Historians have approached the subject from many angles, examining slave culture, the economics of slavery, its effects on family life and religion, the ideological arguments of its defenders and critics, and comparing slavery in different places and eras. The historical essays presented in this volume address many aspects of American slavery, but the primary focus is how slavery divided America and how slavery became both a cause and casualty of the Civil War. An introductory overview provides background information on the rise and fall of slavery in the United States; an appendix of primary documents supports and illuminates the discussion in the essays. These readings, combined with the other research tools in this volume, give the reader insight into American slavery and its impact on U.S.—and world—history.

The Rise and Fall of American Slavery: A Brief Overview

In his annual State of the Union address delivered to Congress on December 2, 1856, President Franklin Pierce criticized abolitionists who called for the end of slavery in the United States. He stated that such a "foreign object" could only be accomplished "through burning cities and ravaged fields, and slaughtered populations, and all there is most terrible in foreign complicated with civil and servile war."[1]

Pierce's prediction turned out to be correct. Within ten years America's 4 million slaves, whose labor provided the economic and social foundation of the southern part of the United States, would be freed, but only after a civil war that left much of the South destroyed and 625,000 people dead. Historians have since debated whether the United States could have abolished slavery by any means other than such a violent and costly war. In examining this question, many have found it necessary to investigate how and why slavery came to exist in the United States, how it evolved differently in different parts of the country, how after the American Revolution slavery was extinguished in the North yet continued to flourish in the South (albeit with persistent social tensions and fears of slave revolt), and how various political compromises between the states ultimately failed to either resolve the slavery question or preserve the unity of the nation.

Slavery in the New World

Slavery—the practice in which a person is held in involuntary servitude as property (chattel) of another—of course predates the founding of the United States. It is an institution as old as recorded human history, found in the societies of ancient India and China; the Mayans, Aztecs, and other pre-European populations of the Americas; and in indigenous African civilizations. Slavery was also an integral part of the ancient civilizations of Greece and Rome.

Slavery declined in Europe following the fall of the Roman Empire in the 400s. Renaissance Europe's colonization of the New World, however, provided a major impetus to the development of what historians have called "modern slavery." Spain and Portugal led the European powers in establishing colonies in Brazil, South America, and Cuba and other islands of the Caribbean (the West Indies) in the 1500s. At first early explorers enslaved thousands of native inhabitants, but when most either died of diseases introduced by the Europeans or were able to resist or avoid enslavement, Spain and Portugal began to import African slaves instead.[2] In the 1600s England, France, and the Netherlands established their own New World colonies and greatly expanded the African slave trade. Slave labor was used in gold mining and on plantations producing cash crops such as sugar, coffee, tobacco, and other staples for European consumption. Historians estimate that between 10 and 12 million Africans were taken from their homes and shipped across the Atlantic to the Western Hemisphere between the mid-1500s and mid-1800s.

Slavery in the American Colonies

In this context slavery was introduced to England's colonies in North America. Slavery was not present when the oldest of these colonies, Virginia, was founded in 1607, and for several decades thereafter. White indentured servants,[3] bound to serve their masters for a fixed number of years, provided labor for the developing tobacco farms of Virginia and neighboring Maryland. Increasingly, however, tobacco farmers and other colonists utilized the well-established Atlantic slave trade to meet their labor needs. Historian Donald R. Wright explains:

> Black slavery began in the English mainland colonies without much questioning, perhaps inevitably, because the colonies were part of the growing Atlantic colonial economic system and provided staples for the European market and relied on the labor that best fit its needs. In the Atlantic world of the mid-seventeenth century, African chattel slavery was a recognized and increasingly preferred labor sup-

ply. Throughout tropical parts of the New World from Brazil to Cuba, black slavery was spreading rapidly. Planters could work Africans harder and control them more thoroughly than they could European servants, and because Africans were inexpensive by comparison with other laborers, they brought owners greater profits. So British colonists in Virginia and Maryland were not trying something radically different when, after 1680, they began buying large numbers of Africans to work their lands. They were following what by then had become a conventional pattern in the Atlantic colonial system.[4]

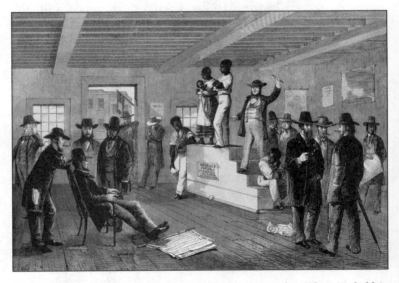

Slave owners purchased slaves at public auctions such as this one held in Virginia.

By the middle of the eighteenth century, slavery was well established in British North America. Law professor and historian William M. Wieck identifies four fundamental characteristics of American slavery:

- American slavery was racially based "in which the people subjected to it were identified by race (Negro, Indian, mulatto, and mestizo)." Converting to Christianity did not alter an African's slave status.

- A person's status as slave or free was derived from the legal status of the mother.
- Slavery was a lifelong condition (as opposed to indentured servitude, which lasted a defined period of years).
- Slaves were legally "reduced to a condition of property . . . a capitalized asset—a human being reduced to the condition of a thing."[5]

Although slavery as described was legal and accepted in all thirteen American colonies, historians have identified important differences that emerged between the northern and southern colonies. In the South, slavery more closely emulated the institution as it developed in the Caribbean and elsewhere in the New World. Slaves were used on agricultural plantations producing tobacco, rice, and other staple export crops. Agriculture became the primary economic activity of the southern colonies, and slavery formed the foundation of the region's social and economic order. North of Virginia and Maryland, where the economy was based on manufacturing and small farms, black slaves formed a much smaller proportion of the colonial population and did not fill a comparable social or economic role. Historian John Niven compares the two regions:

> Unlike the New England and Middle Atlantic colonies, where self-sufficient farming and free white labor quickly developed as the norm, the southern colonies continued their original system of one-crop plantations or farms on which black slaves performed most of the manual labor. . . . Although all of the colonies prior to the American Revolution had slave populations, northern economies were not conducive to the kind of widescale, extractive farming that made a servile labor force profitable or socially desirable.[6]

These differences would widen after the colonies became independent.

Slavery and the American Revolution

Although a few American colonists expressed moral objections to slavery, the practice did not become a serious social issue until the second half of the eighteenth century, when the colonies struggled with and eventually broke from Great Britain. The American Revolution and surrounding events challenged slavery on several levels, and marked the beginning of the end of slavery in America. It also left the nation divided between North and South.

Prior to the 1700s, few people questioned slavery. "For centuries," writes historian Peter Kolchin, "a wide range of social thinkers had seen the institution as fully compatible with human progress and felicity. . . . Largely taken for granted, the institution was simply not much of an issue for the white colonists."[7] However, the eighteenth century—giving rise to Enlightenment philosophy—was a time of intellectual ferment in which European and American thinkers questioned many traditional beliefs and practices concerning politics, religion, and society, including the venerable institution of slavery. Critics began to describe the institution as economically wasteful, cruel and inhumane to slaves, and morally corrupting to owners.

The era also gave rise to much theorizing over the meaning of freedom and the relationship between the individual and the state. Americans, inspired by the writings of Enlightenment-era thinkers such as John Locke, justified their own rebellion against England by arguing that the British government was jeopardizing their natural and inherent rights of individual freedom—most notably in America's Declaration of Independence and its assertion that "all men are created equal" and have inherent "rights of life, liberty, and the pursuit of happiness." "When these arguments gained currency as truth," writes historian Merton L. Dillon, "it became hard to believe that independence and personal autonomy were rightfully the monopoly of a master race. White Americans questioned slavery as never before."[8]

Many of the principal advocates of American independence, including Thomas Jefferson, George Washington, and Patrick Henry, themselves owned slaves. The irony of slaveholders rebelling in the name of liberty and equality was not lost on observers. "How is it," asked British author Samuel Johnson, "that we hear the loudest *yelps* for liberty among the drivers of negroes."[9] Historian and critic Benjamin Schwartz argues, however, that the intimate knowledge of slavery possessed by many of America's founders was integral to their political thought:

> It is impossible to understand how the Founders conceived of liberty, equality, and self-government without reference to slavery, which deeply and disturbingly embedded themselves

President Thomas Jefferson, who drafted the Declaration of Independence, was a slave owner.

in their consciousness. American revolutionaries voiced their determination not to become "slaves" of Britain: this topic, in fact, was the most frequent one in revolutionary discourse.[10]

Many people were quick to draw a parallel between the slave's case for freedom and the American cause of independence, not the least of whom were slaves themselves. Slaves sent their own petitions to colonial governments asking for the "natural rights" of freedom. Many took advantage of wartime conditions to escape from slavery. Some fought in the American Revolution on either the British or American side with the goal of attaining their freedom.

Though the American Revolution succeeded in attaining independence from Great Britain, it left a mixed legacy concerning slavery. Between 1777 and 1804, the states north of Virginia (where the slave population was relatively small) took legal and judicial steps to gradually abolish slavery. In some cases, slaves successfully brought suit against their masters, arguing that slavery violated the new state constitutions proclaiming the natural rights of all people. In other cases, legislative measures provided for the gradual abolition of the institution.

In the southern states, where slavery played a far more important social and economic role, proposals for general slave emancipation went nowhere. In the Upper South states of Virginia, Delaware, and Maryland, and to a lesser extent in North Carolina and the new state of Kentucky, limited emancipation did occur. Some slave owners, motivated by antislavery ideals and a slumping tobacco market, decided to free their slaves either directly or through their wills (state legislation passed in the 1780s and 1790s made it easier for masters to free their slaves). The number of free blacks in these states increased sharply, although they remained a small fraction of the total black population. In Virginia, for instance, the number of free blacks rose from about 1,800 in 1782 (less than 1 percent of the state's black population) to over 30,000 in 1810 (13.5 percent of all blacks). The manumission of slaves was much less frequent and the free black population consequently smaller in the Deep South states of South Carolina and Georgia.

Slavery ultimately survived in the South because most slave owners simply found it too difficult or costly to free their slaves. Many slave owners justified their ownership of slaves in the light of the egalitarian ideals of the American Revolution by arguing that blacks were innately inferior to whites and were not fit for freedom. "A new racism," historian Peter Kolchin concludes, "was one of the ironic byproducts of Revolutionary-era republicanism."[11]

Whether the era of the American Revolution represented a missed opportunity for Americans to totally abolish slavery is a question debated by historians. What all concede is that, despite the gradual abolition of slavery in the North and other developments, including the end of the African slave trade in 1808, the slave population in the United States doubled between 1770 and 1810. In the South the institution survived the ideological and practical challenges of the period to emerge stronger than ever. The North-South divide over slavery found in the original thirteen states was maintained as the nation expanded westward. As slavery was abolished in the rest of the United States and other parts of the world, slavery became the defining "peculiar institution" of the American South.

The Cotton Kingdom

The key to the expansion of slavery in the American South was cotton. Several factors led to the transformation of a minor crop in colonial times into the economic mainstay of the South. One was the Industrial Revolution. Textile factories in England (and, to a lesser extent, in the northeastern United States) created a tremendous demand for raw cotton. The 1793 invention of the cotton gin by Eli Whitney removed a barrier to cotton's profitable cultivation—the difficult and time-consuming task of removing seeds from the plant's fibers. Simultaneously, the development of new strains of cotton and the removal of Native American tribes from Georgia and other southern territories led to a major land and cotton boom in the South. Cotton production zoomed from 3,000 bales in 1790 to 178,000 bales in 1810; by 1820 it became more valuable to the South than all other crops combined.

Despite the invention of the cotton gin, cultivating cotton required significant labor, especially at harvest time. Slavery proved a workable system of labor for cotton growers, both large and small, many of whom used their slaves in the time between cotton-growing seasons to raise corn and hogs. In Virginia and other states on the Atlantic seaboard where cotton cultivation was limited by disadvantageous soil and climate conditions, plantation owners were able to benefit from the cotton boom by selling surplus slaves to cotton growers farther west. The growth of the "Cotton Kingdom" resulted in many new people entering the slaveholding class and many slave owners moving west. It also resulted in the forced migration of hundreds of thousands of slaves. The first federal census in 1790 counted 650,000 slaves in seven southern states. By 1830 the slave population had grown to 2 million slaves in twelve southern states.

Although slaves were used in a variety of pursuits—as domestic servants, millworkers, skilled craftsmen, and other occupations—the vast majority worked as field hands growing cotton and other crops. Slaves generally constituted about one-third of the population of the antebellum South, a ratio distinguished from that of the slave societies of the West Indies, in which black slaves formed 90 percent of the population and lived on large estates with hundreds of other slaves and absentee owners. Most slaves in the Cotton Kingdom, according to Peter Kolchin, "lived on large farms and small plantations—three-quarters on holdings with fewer than fifty slaves—with resident masters who took an active role in directing them and were committed to slavery not just as an economic investment but as a way of life."[12]

The fact that black slaves never formed an overwhelming majority of the population of the South is one reason, many believe, why the South never experienced its own version of a widespread slave revolt such as occurred in Haiti at the turn of the nineteenth century. Nevertheless, slave revolts were a consistent fear in white southern society. Southern states passed numerous laws restricting the movement and education of slaves and restricting the rights of the free black population.

"By 1830," historian Peter J. Parish writes,

Southern leaders could proudly assert their confidence in their distinctive slave society. Slavery was flourishing as a labor system, a social institution, and a device for control of one race by another. It had proven beyond a doubt its capacity for growth and its potential for further expansion. However, in other ways it was also fragile and vulnerable, and behind the confidence of its protagonists and propagandists lurked anxieties which could never be entirely suppressed. Slavery was not a sectional and no longer a national institution; it was exceptional—an unmistakably peculiar institution which set the South apart not only from the North but from almost the entire Atlantic world; it was an uneasy institution, sensitive to outside attack and disturbed by uncertainties within.[13]

The Abolitionist and Free Soil Movements

While slavery was both expanding and becoming identified with the South as a region, the movement to oppose slavery was experiencing a mirror development. As memories of slavery faded in the North, antislavery activism grew and became identified as a northern phenomenon.

Antislavery organizations were not unknown in the South in the late 1700s and early 1800s, especially in Virginia. Many shared similar goals with their northern counterparts: gradual compensated abolition through economic development and moral suasion. However, antislavery activism became increasingly rare in the South as the Cotton Kingdom grew and the Revolutionary generation of planters died out. "By the early nineteenth century," Kolchin writes, "abolitionism was virtually nonexistent in the deep South and increasingly limited in the upper South to small pockets of dissenters on the fringes of society."[14]

By the 1830s antislavery activists, or abolitionists as they were called, had adopted the more radical goals of immediate and uncompensated abolition of slavery. Abolitionists, who in most cases came from the North, worked to end slavery in several ways. In writings and lectures they attacked slavery as a sinful practice. Many activists assisted fugitive slaves in their escape or through education and charity programs. Many supported and helped enact "personal liberty laws" passed by states and communities to hinder attempts by slave owners to reclaim fugitive slaves.

While abolitionists were a focus of attention and criticism in the South, they remained a small though controversial minority in the North. However, many Northerners, while not identifying themselves as abolitionists, came to oppose slavery's continuing expansion in the federal territories. These lands, they believed, should be reserved for self-supporting farmers and free laborers found in the existing northern states. Such a policy also seemed less radical than the forced abolition of slavery where it existed in the states. "We are no abolitionists in the popular sense of the term," an editorial in Cincinnati's *Daily Unionist* took pains to emphasize, "but we would belie our convictions of democracy if we did not oppose slavery's expansion in the new lands."[15] Historian Bruce Levine examines some of the varied motives behind what came to be called the Free Soil movement:

> [A]dditional slave states meant additional proslavery votes in both Congress and the electoral college and thus greater proslavery power over the federal government. Principled abolitionists naturally opposed slavery in the new territories as well. But for many Northerners there were additional reasons for concern. Northern farmers wanted western lands for their own use as homesteads, and many urban working people shared the farmer's dream. Neither group wanted those lands preempted by slave plantations. Neither wished to dwell among slaves, compete with slave labor, or be governed locally by slave-owning politicians. Even many plebeians who expected to remain in the East wanted the West guaranteed as "free soil" for the future benefit of neighbors, children, grandchildren, and future immigrants.[16]

A Nation Divided

The United States thus became a nation divided between slave and free regions. The question facing the nation was whether these two regions could coexist as part of the same nation under the same federal government. Could northern opponents of slavery accept its continued existence as a legitimate institution in America? Could southern slave owners feel secure within the Union? For eight decades leaders of the United States attempted various political compromises aimed at resolving these questions. Their efforts at compromise foundered on two recurring issues: slavery's expansion in the western territories, and the issue of fugitive and resisting slaves and the assistance provided to them by northern governments and individuals. Both issues involved federal policy and who controlled it.

Slavery and the U.S. Constitution

The Constitution marked the first significant instance of conflict and compromise on the slavery issue. By the time leading political figures met in Philadelphia in 1787 to devise a plan of government that would strengthen and unify the new nation, a profound division already existed between states in the process of abolishing slavery and states where slavery remained strong. George Washington, who presided over the convention, had at one time confided to a visiting Englishman "that nothing but the rooting out of slavery can perpetuate the existence of our union by consolidating it in a common bond of principle."[17] However, the prevailing attitude at the Philadelphia convention held that national unity required accommodation to the interests of the southern slaveholding states, whose representatives frequently threatened to withdraw from the Union if the institution of slavery was jeopardized. Historian William D. Piersen summarizes the results:

> The limited willingness of white politicians to deal with the [slavery] issue is symbolized in the compromises of the Constitutional Convention of 1787. The word *slave* does not even appear in this distinguished document; a variety of disingenuous euphemisms are used instead, such as "person held to service" and "other persons." For instance, the Constitution prohibited Congress from ending the importation of new slaves for 20 years in these words: "The migration or importation of such persons as any of the States now existing

shall think proper to admit shall not be prohibited by the Congress prior to the year 1808." Slaves were counted as "three-fifths of all other persons" in determining the amount of representation each state received and what their proportionate share of direct taxes would be. This formulation did not mean that the Founding Fathers thought blacks were 60 percent human; the figure was based on a compromise over how to tax slave states where bondspeople were part of the wealth, but not direct taxpayers themselves. In the new Constitution, masters were also given the right to reclaim any "person held to service"—that is, fugitive slaves.[18]

These constitutional compromises had lasting social and political implications. Congress did prohibit the foreign slave trade as soon as it was allowed to, in 1808, but not before thousands of Africans were imported in a last rush to beat the deadline. The "three-fifths" clause allowing southern states to count slaves in their population gave them more representation in the House of Representatives and presidential votes in the electoral college—an advantage that enhanced the political power of southern slaveholders and that might have been the difference in some presidential elections. And finally, by empowering Congress to pass fugitive slave legislation (which Congress did as soon as 1793), the Constitution essentially harnessed the power of the federal government to support slavery. The attractiveness of the North as a refuge for fugitive slaves was a consistent source of irritation to southern slaveholders. The fact that Americans residing in northern states that had abolished slavery were still indirectly implicated in its continuation in the rest of the nation increasingly rankled Northerners in subsequent years. Abolitionist William Lloyd Garrison called the Constitution "a covenant with death and an agreement with hell."[19]

The Compromise of 1820

The next major national political crisis over slavery focused on the issue of whether it should be permitted to spread in the western territories, specifically in the Louisiana Territory purchased from France in 1803. In 1819 controversy erupted over whether Congress should admit the territory of

Missouri as a slave state—and thus give slavery interests more votes in Congress. The uneasy agreement Congress reached was to officially set a dividing line at the latitude of 36°30' dividing slave and free territories (with Missouri as a slave state exception extending north of the line).

The Missouri Compromise helped hold the Union together for more than thirty years. However, the issue of the territorial expansion of slavery rose again when the United States acquired additional territory in the 1840s through the annexation of Texas and the Mexican-American War. Both opponents and proponents of slavery opposed a western extension of the Missouri Compromise line. In 1846 David Wilmot, a Pennsylvania representative, introduced the Wilmot Proviso, a rider to a House appropriations bill that would ban slavery in territory acquired from Mexico. South Carolina senator John C. Calhoun responded by introducing resolutions asserting that Congress had no constitutional power to exclude slavery from any U.S. territory. These lands were "property of the States united; held jointly for their common use";[20] under the Constitution, he argued, citizens of any U.S. state should be free to migrate to these lands with all their property, including slaves. Historian Jeffrey Rogers Hummel writes:

> The Wilmot Proviso and the Calhoun resolutions defined the extreme northern and southern positions on slavery in the territories. In one, slavery was stigmatized at the national level and legally permitted only at the state level. In the other, slavery was a national institution sanctioned and protected by the central government. These two irreconcilable visions of the Union would continue to clash until the Civil War.[21]

Popular Sovereignty and the Election of Lincoln

In 1854 the Missouri Compromise was officially declared "inoperative and void" by the Kansas-Nebraska Act. The dividing line was replaced by the principle of popular sovereignty, under which settlers of these territories could decide themselves whether to permit slavery. In the Kansas territory, the popular sovereignty compromise resulted in violence as both opponents and proponents of slavery sought to impose their views on Kansas voters. Armed groups from both camps established residency in Kansas and clashed in an attempt to control the future of the territory.

Outside Kansas, popular sovereignty proved as unpopular as the dividing line it replaced. Slavery proponents argued that slavery could not be restricted by territorial assemblies any more than by Congress. Their views were temporarily boosted by the controversial 1857 *Dred Scott* Supreme Court decision, which denied slaves rights regardless of their resident status and undermined the Missouri Compromise dividing line. The infant Republican Party was formed largely in opposition to the Kansas-Nebraska Act and the *Dred Scott* ruling; its platform called for the federal exclusion of slavery from the territories. Though this platform virtually guaranteed the party no southern support, the Republicans succeeded in propelling their 1860 presidential candidate, Abraham Lincoln, to the White House.

Lincoln, a relatively obscure lawyer from Illinois, was no abolitionist. He was firmly opposed to the expansion of slavery in the territories, but promised not to interfere with the institution in the states. His election to the nation's highest political office was nonetheless a shock to many in the South, who viewed it as a demonstration of their loss of political control of the national government. Until then, a southern slaveholder had held the office of president for forty-nine of the nation's first seventy-two years. Twenty of thirty-five Supreme Court justices had come from the South, as had two-thirds of the past leaders of both houses of Congress. "Lincoln's election," Hummel writes, "was a bitter pill to swallow for a section of the country that had hitherto dominated the national government."[22] Many southern slaveholders argued that the survival of their peculiar institution was at risk given a federal government that was antagonistic to slavery.

Lincoln's election occurred at a time when "the white South had taken on a siege mentality" that centered on "defending slavery from alien attack," writes Kolchin. Their solution was to withdraw from the United States and form their own country, in which slavery was explicitly recognized and condoned. When Lincoln determined to use military force to prevent the dismembering of the nation, the result was war. "Ironically," Kolchin writes about the southerners who pressed for secession, "by going to war for the preservation of slavery, they took the only action that could foreseeably have led to its speedy and complete abolition."[23]

The Civil War and Slavery

The abolition of American slavery in the Civil War was the product of at least two separate, yet interrelated, developments. One was the actions of the U.S. government in prosecuting the war. When the war began, Lincoln, mindful of the constitutional limits of presidential authority and seeking the loyalty of border slave states such as Missouri and Kentucky, did not propose to abolish slavery. Preserving the Union—not ending slavery—was his official and overriding war aim. However, the Civil War gave Lincoln both the means (expanded wartime powers as commander in chief) and the motive (advancing the war effort and weakening the Confederacy) to take a series of steps making the federal government an instrument of abolition. These included military confiscation acts that employed escaped slaves in Union armies as "contraband of war," the Emancipation Proclamation declaring all slaves in states waging war against the Union to be free, the enlistment of slaves and free blacks as soldiers, and finally the passing of the Thirteenth Amendment to the Constitution, which officially banned slavery in the entire United States. These actions, obviously coupled with the North's victory in the Civil War, ended the era of American slavery.

Also instrumental in ending American slavery were the actions of slaves themselves. Many were well aware of the potential consequences of the war. Black scholar W.E.B. Du Bois, in his 1935 study *Black Reconstruction*, credited the slaves' massive "general strike" for weakening the Confederacy to the point of defeat. The term "strike" and its connotation of organization are debatable; nonetheless Kolchin writes, "By refusing to cooperate with the slave regime—by refusing to act like slaves—blacks throughout the South struck a mortal blow to slavery."[24]

In addition, thousands of slaves took advantage of the chaotic conditions of the war to escape. Their continually growing numbers among Union army camps prompted northern leaders to use their services as spies, workers, and ultimately as soldiers. "By abandoning their owners, coming uninvited into Union lines, and offering their assistance as laborers, pioneers, guides, and spies, slaves forced federal soldiers at the lowest level to recognize their importance to the Union's success," writes historian Ira Berlin. "The slaves' resolute determination to secure their liberty converted many white Americans to the view that the security of the Union depended upon the destruction of slavery. . . . With their loyalty, their labor and their lives, slaves provided crucial information, muscle, and blood in support of the federal war effort."[25] Following a change in Union military policy, slaves also provided more than 135,000 soldiers to the northern ranks. Longstanding southern fears of successful black resistance to slavery had finally materialized—not as part of a Haitian-style black rebellion, but as soldiers and adjuncts to Union armies.

Contrabands, runaway slaves, who came to the Union lines during the Civil War were often employed by the government as laborers.

Fittingly, many members of the Union cavalry and infantry units who entered the Confederate capital of Richmond, Virginia, in April 1865 at war's end were former slaves. At that time a group of slaves were waiting in a town jail to be sold at auction. When they saw a crowd of black soldiers and townspeople approaching, the prisoners began to sing:

Slavery chain done broke at last!
Broke at last! Broke at last!
Slavery chain done broke at last!
Gonna praise God till I die![26]

Notes

1. Quoted in Merton L. Dillon, *Slavery Attacked: Southern Slaves and Their Allies, 1619–1865*. Baton Rouge: Louisiana State University Press, 1990, p. 188.

2. The use of Africans as slaves in Europe dates back to between 1200 and 1400, when merchants began using black Africans (bought or captured from North African Arabs) as slaves on sugar plantations in the Mediterranean. In the 1400s Portuguese sailors exploring the coast of West Africa began to ship black African slaves back to Europe or to sugar plantations off West Africa's coast. Europeans generally did not capture slaves directly, but purchased them from other Africans.

3. Under a system devised by the Virginia Company in the 1610s, a person signed an "indenture" to work for a master for five to seven years. Servants were provided passage across the Atlantic and food, clothing, and shelter during their term of service. Unlike slaves, servants retained some legal rights against abusive masters and could own property.

4. Donald R. Wright, *African Americans in the Colonial Era: From African Origins Through the American Revolution*. Arlington Heights, IL: Harlan Davidson, 1990, pp. 46–47.

5. William M. Wiecek, in Robert A. Goldwin and Art Kaufman, eds., *Slavery and Its Consequences: The Constitution, Equality, and Race*. Washington, DC: American Enterprise Institute, 1988.

6. John Niven, *The Coming of the Civil War, 1837–1861*. Arlington Heights, IL: Harlan Davidson, 1990, pp. 3–4.

7. Peter Kolchin, *American Slavery, 1619–1877*. New York: Hill and Wang, 1993, p. 64.

8. Dillon, *Slavery Attacked*, p. 27.

9. Quoted in David Brion Davis, *The Problem of Slavery in the Age of Revolution*. Ithaca, NY: Cornell University Press, 1975, p. 275.

10. Benjamin Schwartz, "What Jefferson Helps to Explain," *Atlantic Monthly*, March 1997, pp. 64–65.

11. Kolchin, *American Slavery*, p. 91.

12. Peter Kolchin, "The Institution of Slavery," in *The Reader's Companion to American History*. Boston: Houghton Mifflin, 1991, p. 991.

13. Peter J. Parish, *Slavery: History and Historians*. New York: Harper & Row, 1989, p. 22.

14. Kolchin, *American Slavery*, p. 89.

15. Quoted in Bruce Levine, *Half Slave and Half Free: The Roots of Civil War*. New York: Hill and Wang, 1992, p. 178.

16. Levine, *Half Slave and Half Free*, p. 178.

17. Quoted in John P. Kaminski, ed., *A Necessary Evil? Slavery and the Debate over the Constitution*. Madison, WI: Madison House, 1995, p. 244.

18. William D. Piersen, *From Africa to America: African Americans from the Colonial Era to the Early Republic, 1526–1790*. New York: Twayne, 1996, pp. 139–40.

19. Quoted in Jeffrey Rogers Hummel, *Emancipating Slaves, Enslaving Free Men: A History of the American Civil War*. Chicago: Open Court, 1996, p. 21.

20. Quoted in Hummel, *Emancipating Slaves*, p. 88.

21. Hummel, *Emancipating Slaves*, p. 88.

22. Hummel, *Emancipating Slaves*, p. 131.

23. Kolchin, *American Slavery*, pp. 198–99.

24. Kolchin, *American Slavery*, p. 204.

25. Ira Berlin, "Emancipation and Its Meaning in American Life," *Reconstruction*, vol. 2, no. 3, 1994, pp. 42–43.

26. Quoted in Levine, *Half Slave and Half Free*, p. 242.

Chapter 1

Origins of American Slavery

Turning | Points
IN WORLD HISTORY

The Atlantic Slave Trade

Daniel C. Littlefield

Historian Daniel C. Littlefield describes the introduction of slavery into Britain's North American colonies. He places that development within the context of a large Atlantic slave trade that developed in the sixteenth century and flourished in the seventeenth and eighteenth centuries. Europeans came to rely on imported African slave labor for their agricultural plantations in their colonies in North and South America and the Caribbean islands, in the process creating a system of slavery based on race. Littlefield is a professor of history and black studies at the University of Illinois at Urbana and author of *Rice and Slaves: Ethnicity and the Slave Trade in Colonial South Carolina*.

Africans were among the earliest voyagers to the New World and among the first settlers in Hispaniola. Unlike the Europeans seeking wealth and adventure, most Africans came as bound servants, destined to secure wealth for others. . . .

Most blacks . . . [came] to America . . . directly from Africa as part of the Atlantic slave trade. They went primarily to sugar-producing regions in the West Indies or Latin America to fill the insatiable demands of Brazil (from the sixteenth to nineteenth centuries), Barbados (in the seventeenth century), Jamaica and St. Domingue (in the eighteenth century), and Cuba (in the nineteenth century). Before the 1830s, four times as many Africans as Europeans came to the Americas; it wasn't until the 1840s that European migration permanently surpassed African migration. 'In terms of immigration alone, then,' one scholar [David Eltis] comments, 'America was an extension of Africa rather than Europe until well into the nineteenth century.'

Excerpted from "Africans in America," by Daniel C. Littlefield, in *A History of the African People* (New York: Smithmark, 1995). Reprinted with the permission of Salamander Books, Ltd.

Africans fed an Atlantic economy based largely upon the production of tropical and semitropical staples for European consumption. Sugar was most important, but rice, indigo and coffee, and other crops like cotton and tobacco, were included. Grown on large plantations, these crops united West Africa, western Europe, and the Americas in an economic and social-symbiotic relationship. This 'plantation complex' reached from Portuguese Brazil to the English colonies on the Chesapeake Bay. French, English, Spanish, and Dutch islands in the Caribbean were focal points, but the system's grasp extended throughout the New World, even to those areas where most labor was free. Even free labor economics, like New England and the British middle colonies, contained slaves. These were not slave societies, but the presence of slaves stood as mute testimony to their participation in the slave-labor system.

Spanish Domination of the New World

Within 50 years of [Christopher] Columbus's discovery, most of the tropical New World was under Spanish control. Blacks were part of many Spanish expeditions, and 200 blacks accompanied the expedition of Pedro de Alvarado in 1520 to conquer Guatemala. By the beginning of the sixteenth century, numerous blacks were scattered throughout Spanish possessions in the Caribbean and on the mainland. As early as 1503 the governor of Cuba complained that black slaves were running away and encouraging Native Americans to revolt.

Despite the prior existence of blacks in the Spanish New World, the responsibility for black importation is usually attributed to the Spanish monk Bartolomé de las Casas. He was with Columbus in Hispaniola in 1495 when Native Americans revolted against Spanish exploitation. This threat to Spanish authority was one that Columbus could not permit, and he suppressed it ruthlessly. . . .

Las Casas was horrified, and he devoted the rest of his life to the service of the Indians, appealing for more Africans to be sent in order to spare Native Americans. Although he may not have envisioned the exploitation that slavery eventually became, he obviously expected most of the work to be done by blacks. In answer to his appeal, Emperor Charles V authorized the beginning of the *asiento*, a license or contract to import African slaves into the Spanish New World. In the 10 years between 1520 and 1530, 9,000 blacks were brought to the New World, some of them directly from the coast of Africa. But what really spurred the importation of blacks was the decline of Native American populations. . . .

Columbus brought sugar cane to Hispaniola during his second voyage in 1493. By 1526 there were reported to be 25 sugar plantations on the island, each employing 80–100 African and Indian slaves. Sugar is a very labor-intensive crop and extremely taxing to grow: many believed that only blacks could do it well. Indians were often used but they were generally considered to be too weak.

Blacks also performed skilled tasks connected with sugar production. They sometimes filled the role of sugar master,

Life on a Slave Ship

Olaudah Equiano was kidnapped from his home in Benin (now Nigeria) in West Africa and brought to Barbados when he was eleven. He later was sent to Virginia, served in the British navy, and eventually bought his freedom. In the following excerpt from his autobiography, Equiano describes some of his harrowing experiences on the "Middle Passage."

At last, when the ship we were in, had got in all her cargo, they made ready with many fearful noises, and we were all put under deck, so that we could not see how they managed the vessel. But this disappointment was the least of my sorrow. The stench of the hold while we were on the coast was so intolerably loathsome, that it was dangerous to remain there for any time, and some of us had been permitted to stay on the deck for the fresh air; but now that the whole ship's cargo were confined together, it became absolutely pestilential. The closeness of the place, and the heat of the climate, added to the number in the ship, which was so crowded that each had scarcely room to turn him-

supervising all operations of the mill. Other slaves were cartwrights, blacksmiths, press operators, carpenters, sugar refiners, and sugar boilers, but these jobs were also among the most rigorous and dangerous. It was not unusual for slaves to have their arms broken or cut off by catching them in the sugar mill. A viceroy complained in 1586 about the use of Indians in these jobs, and in 1601 the [Spanish] Crown prohibited the use of Indians on sugar plantations in any capacity whatsoever. The planters were to rely exclusively on black slaves. . . .

Colonization by Northern Europe

Northern Europeans, coming late to discovery, found most of the tropical New World in Iberian hands. Spaniards were the only European settlers in the Caribbean before the seventeenth century, and they located selectively, principally in the Greater Antilles (Cuba, Hispaniola, Jamaica, and Puerto

---

self, almost suffocated us. This produced copious perspirations, so that the air soon became unfit for respiration, from a variety of loathsome smells, and brought on a sickness among the slaves, of which many died—thus falling victims to the improvident avarice, as I may call it, of their purchasers. This wretched situation was again aggravated by the galling of the chains, now became insupportable; and the filth of the necessary tubs, into which the children often fell, and were almost suffocated. The shrieks of the women, and the groans of the dying, rendered the whole a scene of horror almost inconceivable. Happily perhaps, for myself, I was soon reduced so low here that it was thought necessary to keep me almost always on deck; and from my extreme youth I was not put in fetters. In this situation I expected every hour to share the fate of my companions, some of whom were almost daily brought upon deck at the point of death, which I began to hope would soon put an end to my miseries.

Olaudah Equiano, *The Life of Olaudah Equiano, or Gustavus Vassa the African, Written by Himself*. Boston: Isaac Knapp, 1837.

Rico), with a view to protecting and supporting their interests on the mainland. In the early seventeenth century, Dutch, English, and French colonization efforts succeeded in the Lesser Antilles, a chain of islands stretching south from Puerto Rico toward the Venezuelan coast. They raised minor crops like cotton, tobacco, and pimento.

The English and French began their plantations with white indentured servants, whose numbers were supplemented by condemned criminals and war prisoners. French policy until the 1680s was to depend on white bondsmen to populate the Antilles. But the English began a transition to sugar in Barbados in the 1640s and simultaneously switched to African slaves. In a generation, with the aid of Africans supplied by Dutch traders, Barbados went from a settlement based on white labor (6,000 Africans and 19,000 Europeans in 1643) to one where (by 1680) blacks outnumbered whites by a ratio of 2:1.

Once the switch was made, Europeans argued that Africans were superior laborers, able to stand the tropical clime where white men could not. They conveniently forgot the viable, though not as remunerative, agricultural regime that preceded sugar's sway. The physical advantage that Africans offered was their greater immunity to tropical disease, *not* their superior resistance to the sun. They offered the practical advantage that, bought and sold as chattels, they could be made to perform tasks that white men could not be compelled to do.

In fact, sugar planters forced Africans to labor far beyond the normal expectations of traditional society. West India plantations were capitalist enterprises, regarding slaves as units of production. They did not value stable, slave family life and seldom attempted to establish or maintain an equal sex ratio on their estates. They normally requested two men for every woman and viewed raising young slaves to adulthood as being bad business. Consequently, they neither encouraged women to reproduce nor supported them or their children when they did. As a result, sugar regions usually suffered a net annual slave population decrease and had to depend on the slave trade to maintain their labor force.

There were exceptions in the West Indies, but not generally until sugar production decreased or the slave trade was threatened. The big exception was North America. Africans had greater susceptibility to pulmonary diseases like pneumonia and influenza there, and in early Virginia, for example, the death rate for both black and white people was high. Nevertheless, blacks thrived on the continent in a way that they did not under slavery in the islands, because the economics of production did not permit the same thoughtless waste of life. Neither cotton, nor tobacco, nor rice was as remunerative as sugar, and planters could not totally replace their labor force every few years as they might in the Caribbean. Consequently, they learned to depend on slave conservation and reproduction. The North American slave population was the only one in the New World's major slave societies to reproduce itself. . . .

Traditional Slavery in Africa

Early European observers frequently justified enslaving Africans on the grounds that Africans engaged in their *own* form of indigenous servitude and that the European version was preferable. In fact, argues historian John Thornton, African slavery derived from a different social and legal structure from that in Europe. . . .

African institutions of slavery were more than labor systems; they were related to the issue of kinship. African lineage-based societies and state systems increased their wealth and strength by adding members to the group. This accretion could occur in a number of ways, perhaps most often by marriage—women and children being particular assets. But it could also occur in the involuntary service of war captives or other unfortunates who worked for or were adopted by the state or individual families in 'patron-client' relationships, thus according them social existence. As members of an extended family, they might in many ways be treated like other family members and yet not achieve absolute equality, based on their status as historical outsiders. The longer they were part of a community, the closer they came to absorption, even though their origin might never be forgotten. They would obtain many rights and privileges, se-cure land for cultivation, and be free from the threat of sale. They might achieve great wealth and political power, ex-ceeding even that of free people. They might even acquire slaves of their own.

Trade slaves, those most likely to be sold to Europeans, were often older war captives who were perceived as a threat to the host community. They might never adjust and always posed the risk of running away. Their greatest value to the community was the return from their sale. Their position was closest to that of chattel slaves in the Americas, though they often had more privileges, were not distinguished per-manently from their masters by skin color as an unques-tioned mark of degradation, and did not perform chores that separated them from free men. Younger people, especially women and children, had value beyond the simply pecuniary and were more often kept—adopted—to become part of the local society. Olaudah Equiano, who experienced both African and American slavery, spoke almost wistfully of the Old World experience:

> With us, [slaves] do no more work than other members of the community, even their master; their food, clothing and lodging were nearly the same as theirs, [except that they were not permitted to eat with those who were free born]; and there was scarce any other difference between them, than a superior degree of importance which the head of a family possesses in our state, and that authority which, as such, he exercises over every part of his household.

Indigenous African servitude, therefore, had similarities as well as significant dissimilarities with institutions of bondage elsewhere. . . .

The Middle Passage

The trip from West Africa to the Americas, the notorious 'Middle Passage,' took an average of 62 days and was horri-fying and costly. Initially, regular merchant vessels were con-verted to slave ships, especially fitted to hold the human cargo. By the second half of the eighteenth century, however, vessels were constructed specifically for the trade. They were sleek, narrow vessels, with special grates and portholes to direct air below deck. The space between decks was normally 4–5ft (1.2–1.5m) and slaves could not stand— and occasionally could not even sit—upright. In one remarkably objectionable and presumably atypical case, the space between decks was a mere 14in (35cm). Crowded and unsanitary conditions, poor food, inadequate supplies, insufficient drinking water, epidemic diseases, and long voyages conspired to make slave ships legendary for their foul smell and high death rate.

Seventeenth-century ships of the Royal African Company averaged a death rate as high as 24 percent. These rates decreased in the eighteenth and nineteenth centuries, reaching an average range of 10–15 percent. Of course the death rate for white sailors engaged in the trade was high too. In the second half of the eighteenth century sailors' deaths frequently exceeded that of slaves: one study found, for example, that whites died at a rate of 169 per 1000 compared to a black rate of 152 per 1000. Still, the crews, in the business for profit, had a choice, whereas the slaves did not. Because they had to care for slaves and guard against insurrection, slavers carried larger crews than merchant ships. A common measure was 1 sailor for every 10 slaves.

Despite harsh conditions, the economics of trade encouraged ship captains to have reasonable consideration for their cargo, as often their wages and commissions depended on the number of slaves delivered safely to port. They tried to obtain sufficient food for them, and of the type preferred by their particular African group. They sometimes carried peas and beans from England but usually secured food on the African coast: rice in Upper Guinea, yams or plantains in the Niger Delta, corn in Angola. They also learned to carry limes to reduce scurvy.

European profits ranged enormously, from as low as 3 percent to as high as 57 percent in the eighteenth century. . . .

Profits depended upon many things going well, and there was a great deal of luck involved. Some people made much money, but there could also be great loss. Depending on the cost of goods dispensed, the rate of mortality in passage, and the demand in America, slave voyages could be hazardous. A 10 percent return seemed to be average for the eighteenth century. . . .

Britain's North American Colonies

Because Britain's North American colonies did not grow sugar, they were economically less important to the mother country than her West India colonies and commanded less of the slave trade. The region that became the United States absorbed only about 5 percent of Africans brought into the New World. Jamaica alone absorbed more than that. South Carolina was an exception, however, and by 1715 her black population exceeded her white population by about 40 percent. In that respect, South Carolina looked more like Barbados or Jamaica than it did Virginia or Maryland. Accordingly, eighteenth-century South Carolina was the continent's leading importer of slaves.

Unlike Virginia, where slavery was developed gradually, in South Carolina slavery was envisioned from its inception in the 1660s. And while Virginia's plantation system was established and worked for most of the seventeenth century largely by white indentured servants, black slaves were important in South Carolina from the start. . . .

As early as 1698, though, the colonial government expressed alarm at the number of blacks brought in and urged that they be balanced by settlement of more whites. But well into the eighteenth century and beyond, depending on locale, South Carolina continued to look, in the words of one visitor, 'more like a negro country than like a country settled by white people.'

Virginians embraced African slavery more slowly. Determined to build an English society, they did not encourage large numbers of foreigners—even those from Scotland or Ireland—to settle in their midst, much less the exotic African. Moreover, tobacco cultivation in a temperate climate was readily accomplished by white labor. . . .

For planters, the high death rate meant that even had they changed their preference from English servants to African slaves, the initial higher outlay for a slave who might not survive made slavery an uneconomical choice. Not until the end of the century did better survival rates in the Chesapeake and an increase in slaving make African labor a viable alternative. Simultaneously, falling birth rates and greater opportunity in England produced fewer British emigrants, while acquisition of New York and Pennsylvania gave them more choice of destination in America. These conditions, and others, made African slavery more practical in the Chesapeake. . . .

By the end of the seventeenth century, then, Africans worked plantations from Brazil to the Chesapeake. In regions where there were no plantations, particularly in the Spanish empire and in English colonies north of Maryland, they worked in the country and in towns as domestic servants, farm hands, and commercial laborers. Many had gained their freedom but most were bound in an evolving system of slavery which provided the basis for economic development in an unfolding Atlantic society. Their relationships with Europeans and Native Americans produced a New World culture in which their contribution was pervasive. They brought brains as well as brawn, and African knowledge and expertise secured the survival and success of European enterprise that might otherwise have failed.

Establishing Slavery in the Southern Colonies

John B. Boles

John B. Boles recounts how slavery was established in the Chesapeake colonies (Virginia and Maryland) as well as the largely separate origins of slavery in South Carolina. He contends that slavery was not a predetermined or inevitable development when English settlers founded Jamestown, Virginia, in 1607. Viewing themselves superior to the Spanish and Portuguese who dominated the Atlantic slave trade, English colonists initially shunned slavery as a labor source, preferring to rely on white (and a few black) indentured servants. Boles examines why, beginning in the late 1600s, black African slaves gradually supplanted white indentured servants as the chief source of labor for the Chesapeake colonies and how race became a marker of slave or free status. In South Carolina, by contrast, black slavery was immediately embraced by its founders, many of whom came directly from the West Indies island of Barbados where the institution was firmly established. Boles is a professor of history at Rice University in Houston, Texas, and managing editor of the *Journal of Southern History*.

It was by no means predetermined in 1607, when England planted her first permanent settlement in the New World at Jamestown, that slavery would inevitably follow in the mainland colonies. African bondage was already a century old in the Western Hemisphere, but it was under the auspices of the Spanish and Portuguese. Plantation organization and the technological understanding of sugar manufacture had like-

wise taken root in the New World, but in semitropical islands. Along the western coasts of Africa the far-flung Dutch
maritime interests had supplanted the pioneering Portuguese
traders, and African chieftains were as eager to deal in human
beings in exchange for Dutch bars of iron, cloth, and simple
manufactures as for those of the Portuguese. The ravenous
labor demands of the sugar regions consumed the human
cargoes. The whole transatlantic system was in place, primed
to flourish as the seventeenth century unfolded. Yet this was
essentially a Mediterranean-Caribbean cultural development, with roots in a whole series of Iberian and Genoese
(and even earlier Arab) legal and economic traditions quite
alien to the English historical experience. In Europe slavery
had survived to the south while England had moved down
another path; there was no evidence that in the New World
the English experience was to be any different. The indices
for the future were mixed as the Elizabethan era in England
drew to a close at the beginning of the seventeenth century.

The English and Slavery

The English before Jamestown were certainly aware of the
existence of slavery. As part of their preening pride in being
Englishmen, they valued their own liberty and looked down
their collective noses at those southern Europeans who not
only were Catholic but also stooped to enslave with brutal
consequences both American Indians and imported Africans.
The crown even encouraged English adventurers to raid the
trading vessels of the competing nations. The English perception of being set apart from, and better than, the Spanish
and Portuguese included a tendency to downgrade slavery as
something foreign and backward, though on several occasions English adventurers like John Hawkins overcame their
scruples and traded in slaves when the opportunity presented
itself. In addition to being aware that slavery existed, the English also were prepared to accept that in certain circumstances it could be legal—when those in servitude, for example, were war captives or convicted criminals. Their choice
was a bit ethnocentric, but they simply preferred the English
system of modified serfdom that included temporary owner-

ship of the labor—not the person—of individuals who bartered their service for a certain price, in this case passage to America.

This system of indentured servitude was similar to apprenticeship, whereby servant and master had reciprocal responsibilities. When the English began establishing settlements in the New World, they brought their traditional labor systems with them. Feeling superior to the Spanish anyway and intending to avoid the genocidal horrors attributed to the Spanish in the West Indies, they felt no necessity to throw aside English practices and adopt instead the ways of their European rival. Virginia was to be peopled with and developed by Englishmen, and perhaps willing Indians and such others as wanted to escape the rigors of Spanish authority, but it was intended to be a transplanted England with only minimal concessions to imagined New World conditions. Within a century, however, English mainland colonies, especially those to the south, had made such crucial adaptations that they were unlike anything in the presettlement English experience. The history of those adaptations is the story of the emergence and evolution of a slave society in the American South.

The First Africans in America

Although there is a slight hint in some of the sources that one or more Africans arrived in Virginia several years earlier, 1619 is the date generally accepted for the introduction of blacks to the English mainland colonies. In an offhand manner John Rolfe wrote to Sir Edwin Sandys, treasurer of the Virginia Company, that five months previously a Dutch man-of-war had arrived at Point Comfort, where the James River emptied into the Chesapeake, and in exchange for badly needed provisions had paid the colony officials with "20. and odd Negroes," meaning evidently a number greater than twenty. With those four words begins the documented history of Africans in what is now the United States (except for one or more blacks who accompanied Spanish explorers in the early 1500s). Yet we know frustratingly little about that initial score of blacks—neither their immediate past before being unceremoniously introduced to Virginia nor their subsequent history. The Dutch captain no doubt sold them without a flicker of conscience, so hardened did those in the slave trade come to be; still, one wonders what thoughts occurred to the Virginia officials as they made that first ill-starred purchase. Did they simply see themselves as buying the labor of the Africans, who would thus be differentiated from countless other servants only by their complexion, or did they purposely acquire them as slaves for life, possibly justifying themselves on the grounds that the Dutch—or the Africans' original captors—had already enslaved them, and thus the Virginians were making a perfectly unexceptional commercial transaction? Did the Virginia officials harbor deep doubts about the propriety of their actions but feel that the Dutch captain's "great need" justified their selling him provisions in exchange for the only currency he had available? These questions will probably never be answered. The only sure point that can be made is that the system of black slavery did not emerge full-blown with the fateful transaction off Point Comfort in 1619.

Certainly one of the reasons Englishmen did not instantly introduce slavery to their mainland colony was their prejudice against non-English ways of doing things. In the West Indian islands, where the native populations had essentially died out as a result of exposure to Old World diseases, where the climate favored sugar cultivation, which, because of the labor demands of harvesting and processing, seemed to necessitate slave workers, and where the climate seemed to offer little hope of large-scale English settlement, the British quickly accepted what they perceived as the reality of the situation and hence began their prosperous sugar-slave empire. None of these precipitating factors worked to change their expectations for Virginia. True enough, mineral riches proved nonexistent, but John Rolfe's early discovery that West Indian tobacco grown in Virginia was sweet to the palates of English smokers changed only the source, not the prospect, of riches from Virginia. And tobacco, unlike sugar, required little capital expenditure to begin cultivation, had less rigorous labor demands, could be grown profitably in small patches, and required no expensive manufacturing process—in short, tobacco made possible an economic boom in Virginia without the necessity of jettisoning traditional English laboring practices. The Chesapeake tobacco plantation economy was founded on white indentured labor.

Race Relations

This English aversion to things non-English included peoples who were not English. Elizabethans, who disliked even the Irish, hated and were suspicious of the Spanish, and quickly grew shockingly callous toward the Indians, certainly were prejudiced against those most foreign of all, the Africans. It was almost as if the English had a scale of acceptance ranging from white English Christian (read Protestant) civilization to black heathen savagery, with each word as loaded with meaning as they sound to the modern ear. The Africans' very blackness, associated as it was in Western culture with evil, made only more visible and indelible his unflattering identity. Yet such an automatic predisposition to denigrate the African as existed among the English was more an abstract, superstitious dislike of the unknown, a generalized and passive prejudice, than a systematic racism that shaped every black-white interpersonal relationship. The existence of the prejudice surely made easier the acceptance of perpetual slavery for Africans, and toward the end of the seventeenth century it became gradually transformed into a peculiarly American racism, but it did not in the first decades after 1619 push all Africans into the despised category of slaves-for-life.

The half century or so of race relations after 1619 is very confusing. There is no doubt at all that many, quite probably most, Africans were considered slaves, or at least servants whose period of servitude was lifelong. Just as clearly, there were others who served a set number of years—at least occasionally no longer than similarly aged whites of the same sex—and then were freed. Not every black was a slave, not every slave served for life, and the treatment of black slaves/servants seems at times indistinguishable from that accorded white servants. Because the legal presumption that blackness meant slavery did not yet exist, the nature of one's bondage was subject to court decisions. The judicial records of seventeenth-century Maryland and Virginia bear testimony to freedom-seeking "slaves" who sought their liberty on such grounds as having been baptized or having already served the period of time previously contracted. On a number of occasions, proof of their Christianity or documentation of their contractual obligations having been met—in fact, often exceeded—resulted in the court's declaring them free. There are still other examples of blacks being adjudged free upon proof that one of their parents was free. Precisely because such avenues to freedom existed in the first decades, planters were sometimes troubled about the permanency of their "slave" property. . . .

The Switch to Slavery

The evidence is overwhelming that the English planters in Maryland and Virginia greatly preferred that the Chesapeake be a white man's country. By comparison, within a decade of its settlement [in 1627], Barbados [a West Indies island colony of England] was in the midst of a sugar-slave boom, and its black population skyrocketed. In the Chesapeake colonies even as late as the mid-1670s, the number of white servants far outstripped black slaves. Then, starting almost imperceptibly in the 1670s, growing in tempo in the 1680s, and rising to a torrent in the 1690s, planters began the shift to African slaves that transformed the whole society. Twice as many African slaves were imported into the Chesapeake in the first decade of the 1700s as during the whole previous century. Why was the switch to African slavery delayed for a half-century, and why did it occur when it did?

In the first place, Englishmen naturally preferred to work with people of their own kind, people whose language and ways they understood and with whom they were comfortable. Living three thousand miles from dear old England, cast among a smattering of red men and subject to the whims of an unfamiliar climate, half-fearing a Spanish attack and unsure always of disease, worrying that the thousand leagues of choppy waves separating them from their motherland might also separate them from the civilization they desperately wanted to cling to, there was scant reason to let go of a familiar labor system and import hordes of the strangest people imaginable—blacks from the dark continent—into an already threatening environment *unless they felt they absolutely had to.* And for six decades they did not have to, for more or less voluntary immigrants—the indentured servants—met the ever-increasing labor needs of the Chesapeake.

Beginning about 1450 England experienced almost two centuries of sustained population growth, which, among other changes such as the enclosure acts that drove serfs off the manor lands and into the cities, led to a fall in wages and an apparent surplus of population. Such conditions, of course, had underlain some of the original justifications for colonization, and indeed these demographic conditions had produced an ample flow of willing migrants, most of whom were young males from the middle class. At the same time as these prime workers were coming to the Chesapeake (avoiding the West Indies for reasons of climate and the reputedly bad working conditions of the sugar-slave regions), the booming sugar islands were absorbing as many prime Africans as slavers could deliver. Few Africans were left over for the mainland, their prices relative to indentured servants were prohibitive (the price differential was exacerbated by the high death rates for blacks as well as whites in the first decades), and the small size of the available market in Virginia and Maryland made large-scale trade direct from Africa unprofitable to slavers as long as the sugar island demand stayed firm and the Chesapeake demand uncertain.

A Decreasing Supply of White Servants

For reasons that are not entirely clear, but certainly including the English Civil War, the birth rate in England fell sharply in the 1640s, with the consequence that twenty years later the supply of ablebodied potential indentured servants dropped. In the mid-1660s the Great Plague resulted in changes in the population structure of England that led to a gradual rise in wages, and job opportunities there in general seem to have improved. Many, for example, were employed in the rebuilding of London after the Great Fire of 1666. Moreover, with the settlement of other colonies in America—particularly the Carolinas and later Pennsylvania—would-be migrants had alternative destinations. The sum of these social developments was a relative and then an absolute decline in the number of white indentured servants entering the Chesapeake starting at the very end of the 1660s. By the 1670s we detect more frequent complaints about the shortage of labor, and the relative price of servants increased in the 1680s, indicating that planter demand for white servants remained strong. In response to this severe labor shortage planters at first began to lower their qualifications for acceptable English servants—after the mid-1660s they were more willing to take younger males, women, Irishmen, the almost totally unskilled laboring poor, finally even convicts. In other words, the quality of the white servant working class fell in the final decades of the seventeenth century. So drastic did the labor shortage seem that planters reconsidered enslaving American Indians.

It was in the midst of this insufficiency of workers, in 1674, that the Royal African Company (the joint-stock corporation authorized to engage in the slave trade) first began direct shipments of slaves from Africa to the North American mainland. From that date on, ever-increasing numbers of slaves were sold in the Chesapeake, and, while most were probably purchased via the West Indies, a larger volume than previously estimated now appears to have been imported directly from Africa. After 1698, when the Royal African Company's monopoly was ended by a parliamentary act, and numerous enterprising merchants with smaller vessels—more appropriate to the kind of plantation-to-plantation slave peddling that existed in the Chesapeake—entered the trade, the slave imports to the Chesapeake reached flood-tide proportion. Yet the unfilled demand for white indentured servants remained high. Clearly the Chesapeake planters still preferred whites, but when for reasons beyond their control the English supply was insufficient to meet their needs, they turned to large-scale slave importations. As they came to realize that the lowered death rates now made the initially more expensive Africans more cost-efficient in the long run, and related to this, as there slowly dawned the recognition that slave offspring represented an additional permanent benefit, African slavery increasingly was accepted as the permanent solution to the labor supply of the tobacco colonies. Accommodating laws soon followed, and within a few years of 1700 the Chesapeake system of slave plantations was sustained by strong legal sanctions. Yet more had changed than the complexion of the laborers.

Changing Views on Race

The character of race relations underwent as far-reaching a change as did the nature of the plantation work force. For two generations white and black plantation laborers had related to each other as equals to a greater extent perhaps than ever since in southern history. Living and working together, sharing drudgery and a common master, whites often failed to apply to the particular blacks with whom they toiled and cavorted the generally prejudiced attitudes embedded in their English culture. But with the demographic changes occurring in the Chesapeake society in the decades on either side of 1700, the vague, implicit, abstract racism of the English was transformed into a far more concrete, legally precise, and individually applicable societal racism that would in myriad ways poison the interpersonal relations of whites and blacks for the following two and a half centuries.

As the number of blacks rose abruptly at the turn of the century, they for the first time began to be perceived as a tangible threat to whites. . . .

A far more virulent racism emerged, and an apparent repugnance toward blacks arose that had not existed earlier. The laws of the 1660s and 1670s were intended more as a convenience to slave owners than as a denigration of blacks or an outlawing of interracial relationships. An owner's property was jeopardized as long as religious conversion could be interpreted as voiding bondage, or if mixed parentage could facilitate freedom suits. Hence obliging laws were provided to ensure property "rights" in slaves. Virginia, for example, in 1662 levied a special fine on interracial fornication—all for-

nication was sinful and therefore illegal, but sex between unequal classes was especially frowned upon—yet not until
1691 was interracial marriage prohibited by law. A flurry of
statutes in the final decade of the seventeenth century fla-
grantly discriminated against blacks and sought to separate
the races as far as possible. Also in the 1690s private manumission of slaves was made more difficult. After 1700 the laws
against blacks hardened dramatically, and roughly after that
date it is accurate to speak of the Chesapeake as a chattel slave
society where blacks had few rights protected by law.

A Changing White Society

The increasing Africanization of the labor force, however,
was not the only significant social change occurring in the
1680s and 1690s, nor was it the sole cause of the rampant
white racism that emerged toward the end of the century.
The nature of the white society was changing too. Before
about 1660 those white servants who lived long enough to
complete their term of service could find cheap, easily available land, plant several acres of tobacco, eventually import a
few servants of their own, and in general share in the developing prosperity of the colony. For a variety of reasons—
overproduction of tobacco with a resultant drop in price, the
restrictions of the Navigation Act of 1660, an increase in the
cost of land because of increased population, the growing
success of farsighted and self-serving big planters in en-
grossing the best land in the tidewater regions—opportunities for new white freedmen decreased. Because of falling
death rates, the numbers of such new freedmen grew rapidly
just as their chances for land ownership and prosperity were
decreasing. The result was [a] growing population of young,
free males, landless, indigent, frustrated, increasingly es-
tranged from the planter and governing establishment. The
situation seemed to be made worse by the necessity to accept
ever-lower standards in order to attract fresh indentured servants from Britain.

Bacon's Rebellion in 1676 showed the potential of violent
social unrest posed by a lower class of free, poor whites.
While no one in the planter aristocracy seems to have de-

duced logically that lifetime black slavery was a "solution" to this problem, the drying up of the supply of new indentured recruits and the increasing availability of Africans offered an unforeseen way out of the dilemma. Slaves never became free and thereby would not be competitors for land or labor; accommodating laws made them more susceptible to control; and the rising racial antipathy to blacks—which the statutes reflected or perhaps intensified rather than caused—generated an identification on the part of even the poorest white freedman with the white establishment rather than with the despised black. Black denigration elevated the lowest white to a level above the most talented slave into a pseudo fraternity of white equals. The transformation of the Chesapeake into a racist society, possessing a virtual caste system, laid the foundation for the social myth of white equality, defusing white social tensions and allowing the growth of white democracy. Thus ironically American slavery and American freedom were both born in the temperate clime of the Chesapeake toward the end of the seventeenth century.

Slavery in South Carolina

Despite their obvious importance to American history, events in the Chesapeake do not exhaust the story of slavery's origins in this nation. The developments in South Carolina reveal a different route to bondage. While it is quite possible that the very first Africans to set foot on the North American continent were those accompanying the Spanish adventurer Lucas Vásquez de Ayllón, who planted a short-lived settlement near Cape Fear in 1526, significant colonization of the Carolinas did not begin until 1660. Newly restored to the English throne, King Charles II in that year gave to eight supporters a huge tract of land south of Virginia. A Barbadian loyalist and planter, John Colleton, led the group of royalists, who successfully requested of the thankful king an empire of American territory in reward for their steadfast support. The eight proprietors upon whom Charles II so bountifully bestowed the Carolinas were all familiar with slavery, and most of the early settlers—white and black—came from Barbados. This tiny speck of an island was already in the midst of its sugar boom, with a surging slave population and several hundred large planters quickly expanding their land holdings. Hundreds of less prosperous white planters, feeling opportunity slipping away from them in England's first plantation society, were eager to seek the greener pastures of Carolina. Consequently they moved to the newly opened mainland colony, bringing their families, their property (including bondsmen), and their commitment to a slave plantation economy. For the pioneers of Carolina, which was practically a colony of Barbados, no special decision to enslave Africans was required once they arrived on the mainland. The acceptance of slavery had been an earlier Barbadian development; the institution was simply transferred to Carolina.

From the very beginning then, Negroes came with white Barbadians to Carolina, and, though their legal status as slaves may not have been precisely established, they were treated much as chattel slaves later came to be treated. Barbadian custom dictated that blacks served for life, children followed the status of their mother, and they could be sold as property in payment of debt, while their legal status was left purposely ambiguous to avoid any possible conflicts with the officials in England. Less concerned with definitions of status than with controlling the behavior of the slaves, the Fundamental Constitutions of Carolina, drafted in 1669 and perhaps influenced by John Locke, provided that "Every freeman of Carolina, shall have absolute power and authority over his negro slaves, of what opinion or Religion soever." A South Carolina statute in 1690 expanded the police functions of masters, but it was disallowed by the proprietors in London. However, the local economy—cattle, lumber products, and increasingly rice—expanded so rapidly that by 1696, with approximately two thousand slaves in the provinces (a far higher proportion than in the Chesapeake colonies), the South Carolina assembly passed its first truly comprehensive slave code, based on the Barbadian code of 1688.

Except that they could be used for payment of debt, slaves in South Carolina were not legally chattel property until 1740. During the first generation after its founding, in the colony's pioneer period, white-black relations were less rigid than they later became. Slaves pursued a variety of occupations, often worked with whites—either [as] indentured servants, hired laborers, or even their owners—in ways that suggested a degree of equality. But the quickly achieved prosperity of the colony, and the rapid increase in the number of slaves, soon brought a close to this first age of relative racial harmony. As the preface to the 1696 Act for the Better Ordering and Governing of Negroes and Slaves (often mistakenly dated 1712) vividly indicates, the evolution from befriended co-worker to feared black slave was as complete in Carolina by about 1700 as it was in the Chesapeake, and the process had taken less than half the time in Carolina.

> Whereas, the plantations and estates of this Province cannot be well and sufficiently managed and brought into use, without the labor and service of negroes and other slaves [Indians]; and forasmuch as the said negroes and other slaves brought into the people of this Province for that purpose, are of barbarous, wild, savage natures, and such as renders them wholly unqualified to be governed by the laws, customs, and practices of this Province; but that it is absolutely necessary, that such other constitutions, laws and orders, should in this Province be made and enacted, for the good regulating and ordering of them, as may restrain the disorders, rapines and inhumanity, to which they are naturally prone and inclined, and may also tend to the safety and security of the people of this Province and their estates; to which purpose. . . . [The assembly went on, in thirty-five sections, to outline measures to control the rapidly growing black segment of the population.]

The Chesapeake planters, having come directly from Britain and having no direct prior experience with slavery, turned to bondage only when white laborers were no longer plentiful; the Carolina planters, having accepted boom-time slavery in Barbados, instantly established bondage and bought slaves as soon as they could. The joint result, by 1700, was full-fledged slave plantation economies in both regions primed for unprecedented growth in the next century.

The coming decades saw a dramatic increase in the number of African imports, the beginning of population growth among American-born blacks, and the resultant rise of an Afro-American people with a distinct culture. The rise of the black community was to be the most important development in black history in the eighteenth century.

Slavery in the Northern Colonies

Donald R. Wright

Donald R. Wright provides a description of slavery as it developed in the seventeenth and eighteenth centuries in the American colonies north of Maryland. Slavery in both New England (Massachusetts, Connecticut, New Hampshire, and Rhode Island) and the Middle Colonies (New York, New Jersey, Pennsylvania, and Delaware) differed in several important respects from the institution found in the southern colonies. New England and the Middle Colonies did not develop a plantation system; most slaves worked on small farms, households, or in urban areas. Laws regulating slavery were generally less stringent than in the southern colonies, in part because blacks remained a small fraction of the northern colonies' total population. Wright, who teaches history at the State University of New York College at Cortland, has done historical research and writing on both African history and on African Americans.

When examining the development of slavery in the mainland colonies, it is important to bear in mind what Ira Berlin emphasizes in "Time, Space, and the Evolution of Afro-American Society in British Mainland North America," *American Historical Review*, 80 (1980). Black slavery came into being at different times in various mainland regions; it began for different reasons (though some factors were similar); and through the seventeenth and eighteenth centuries various forms of slave systems developed in different mainland areas. Berlin recognizes three such systems: one in the Chesapeake region with smaller plantations; one in the Carolina and Georgia low country with larger plantations; and one in the northern colonies without plantations at all. These separate regions had different economies and particular labor needs; so over the years they developed different demographic characteristics, especially in the proportion of blacks to whites and native-born Africans to persons of African descent born in the colonies (commonly referred to as creoles). This interplay of factors determined the nature of the slave system and the African American society that evolved in each of the regions. . . .

Slavery North of Maryland

After considering black slavery in the Chesapeake and low country, one tends to think of the much smaller number of blacks in New England and the Middle Colonies as relatively insignificant. After all, in 1770 there were barely fifty thousand individuals of African descent north of Maryland (not quite 4.5 percent of the total population) whereas in the same year from Maryland southward some four hundred thousand blacks made up 40 percent of the total. Blacks were only 2.5 percent of the New England population and 6.5 percent of the people in the Middle Colonies on the eve of the American Revolution. But figures alone fail to give an accurate picture of the importance of slavery to the economy of the area north of the Chesapeake and especially to particular regions of the area. In some of the most agriculturally productive rural areas of Connecticut, Long Island, and the lower Hudson River valley, blacks made up as much as half the work force. Certain industries—ironworking in Pennsylvania or tanning in New York, for instance—relied heavily on slave labor, and slaves worked in the carrying trade and around shipyards in Rhode Island and Massachusetts. In New England, blacks were concentrated near coastal urban centers along river systems. There was a particularly heavy concentration in Rhode Island. The Middle Colonies had black urban populations of considerable size. Thus, in certain areas the black population was a significant proportion of the total. In these areas blacks did not live in isolation from others of African descent and the demands and customs of whites did not totally dominate their lives.

In addition to sheer numbers, slavery in New England and the Middle Colonies was different in other obvious ways from the institution found on the mainland from the Chesapeake southward. Plantations never formed from Pennsylvania northward. If the typical southern African American lived and worked with a fair-sized group of other slaves on a large tobacco or rice plantation, the typical northern slave lived alone or with one or two other slaves, perhaps in a dwelling with the family of the owner, and worked on a small farm, in a small industry, as a domestic, or at a trade in an urban area. The origin of most northern slaves was different, too. Before 1740 it was rare for captives to arrive in a northern port immediately after the voyage from Africa. Most came from the West Indies or the southern colonies. Only between 1740 and 1770 was there direct importation of Africans into northern markets, and then the numbers of imports never approached those of the plantation colonies.

Reasons for the considerable differences of slavery in the northern colonies have to do with the northern economy. New England and the Middle Colonies never devoted most of their resources to production of a major staple to export. There was simply not one in demand they could produce. Instead, over time, northerners became efficient at a variety of tasks that, when combined, brought them the export credits they needed to keep in check their balance of trade. These tasks included grain and livestock farming, whaling and fishing, and the carrying trade. None of these tasks involved the same economy of scale that southern planters exercised. Even those producing food for export did so efficiently on family farms. There were exceptions, of course, but most producers relied on their own and their families' labor, and they tended not to gain the extraordinary wealth that would enable them to buy more laborers and expand operations.

Participation in the Slave Trade

But why, then, did settlers of the northern colonies get involved with black slavery in the first place, even in the small numbers they did? Part of the reason has to do with their early and extensive participation in the carrying trade of the Atlantic world.

Dutch colonists rather than the English were the first to import slaves north of Maryland. The Dutch West India Company, which carried out settlement of New Netherland along the Hudson River, established posts in the mid-1620s for the fur trade. The company may have desired development of a stable, agriculture-producing colony along the lower Hudson, but it refused to invest enough to prompt colonizers from the Netherlands to go there. Instead, it brought in workers before farmers. Always eager to introduce chattel slavery to New World colonies so it could enhance its brisk carrying trade in slaves, the company began in 1626 to import blacks into its own mainland colony. Most came from Curaçao in the Dutch West Indies. In addition to building roads and forts and raising food for the Dutch garrison in New Amsterdam, the slaves cleared lands along the Hudson. By midcentury enough slaves had entered the colony and rendered enough land arable to alter the nature of New Netherland. Only then did Dutch colonists begin coming to settle permanently, using the cleared lands for growing grain and keeping livestock. Farming replaced fur-trading as the principal colonial activity. The new farmers preferred slaves to free laborers largely for reasons of cost. In the 1640s a "seasoned" slave from the West Indies cost about the same as the wages, provisions, and lodging for a free worker for a single year.

The takeover of New Netherland by the English in 1664 did not alter the slaves' status. The earliest English laws in New York recognized slavery as a legal institution at the same time they placed restrictions on white servitude. As a consequence, demand for slaves increased, the slave trade from the islands and other colonies flourished, and New York's black population grew. By 1700 the colony had two thousand slaves in a population of about nineteen thousand and by 1750 the number had grown to ten thousand out of seventy-five thousand total—more than any other mainland colony north of the Chesapeake. Many of these were in the vicinity of New York City, where 43 percent of whites in a rough 1703 census owned one or two slaves. Because of their use as domestics, there were as many black women as black men among the slave population.

New York was not the only Middle Colony to which the Dutch West India Company brought slaves. Its ships carried small numbers of blacks to settlements along the Delaware River after 1639 and to the west bank of the Hudson that became part of New Jersey in 1664. English proprietors of New Jersey eventually authorized slavery and encouraged importation with offers of up to sixty acres for each slave brought to the colony. By the end of the century, Perth Amboy became one of the main ports of entry for northern slaves.

If Pennsylvania did not have slaves at the arrival of its Quaker founders in 1681, it did soon after. William Penn preferred black slaves to white servants "for then," Penn reasoned, "a man has them while they live," and he used slaves on his own estate. Philadelphia carriers in the Caribbean trade soon were bringing black men and women with return cargoes. The presence of Quakers there and in Delaware did not preclude slave imports. Philadelphia Quakers bought 150 Africans in 1684 to work clearing trees and erecting houses. By 1700 one Philadelphia family in fifteen owned slaves.

New England Colonies

New England had fewer African Americans than any other region of the mainland colonies. Black slaves had been in New England since before 1640, however, and in some places they were important elements of the economy and society. Most black men and women came there because of coastal New England's interdependence with the West Indies and its heavy participation in the Caribbean trade. Ships arriving in New England ports from the British West Indies often carried half a dozen slaves. Some were "refuse" slaves (the infirm or ailing, who could not be sold profitably in the island markets), exiled offenders of various sorts, or those purchased to work the voyage northward and then sold upon its termination. More New England slave imports were African by birth than this implies, however. A slaver sometimes used the Caribbean islands as way stations, selling some of its captives and then passing on to New England with a partial load of Caribbean produce and the remainder of its slaves. New England masters seemed to care less than Tidewater planters about receiving the "bad lot" of slaves from the Caribbean, just as they showed less concern for place of origin of Africans. They believed they could train blacks individually and instill proper Yankee traits in the most reluctant slave. Thus, although most ships carrying slaves to the region came from the West Indies, probably three of four slaves imported into New England once had a home in Africa.

Nowhere in the northern colonies was the uneven distribution of blacks more evident than in New England. Because of the ties of slave imports to colonial shipping, major ports held concentrations of African Americans. In 1754 three-quarters of Massachusetts's black population of twenty-seven hundred lived in coastal towns in only three counties. At the same time, blacks made up good portions of the population of Rhode Island's Narragansett ports— 20 percent of Newport, 30 percent of South Kingston, and 40 percent of Charlestown.

Urban and Rural Slaves

Slavery in northern towns and cities from Salem to Philadelphia was different from most other forms of slavery in the colonies. Gary B. Nash's "Slaves and Slaveowners in Colonial Philadelphia" in his *Race, Class, and Politics: Essays on American Colonial and Revolutionary Society* (1986) provides a picture of who owned slaves in a northern colonial city and what the slaves did. In 1767 most Philadelphia masters (521) owned only one or two slaves (905 total). For many owners the bondsmen were a symbol of status. Merchants and shopkeepers owned one-third of the slaves; professionals owned 10 percent; innkeepers or tavern owners about 5 percent; and widows and "gentlemen" another 5 percent. Nearly all slaves from this last group were household servants. Artisans and craftsmen or men involved in maritime ventures owned the other half of the city's slaves. Bakers, ropemakers, brewers, millers, shipwrights, blockmakers, sailmakers, goldsmiths, and ferrymen used slaves in their work. A surprising number of ship captains and mariners (10 percent of all owners) purchased slaves with the intention of having them work on board ship as sailors.

None of this should give the impression that northern slavery was primarily an urban experience. As elsewhere, the vast majority of northern blacks lived and worked in the countryside. Most were agricultural workers on small farms, with the heaviest concentrations in Connecticut and Rhode Island, on Long Island, and in northern New Jersey. These farms raised provisions and draft animals primarily for export to the West Indies. Even here, white laborers made up a majority of workers on the seasonal crops. Through most of the year, African Americans worked around the masters' houses and stables. As in the cities, owning a slave was a mark of wealth and status.

Slavery Laws

Because African Americans were in much smaller proportion to the total northern population, control of slaves in most locales was less of a problem than it was in the southern colonies. Absence of laws regulating slavery did not reflect this so much as did lax enforcement. Slave codes in New England were probably the least stringent of all. There, slaves walked a fine line between being persons with certain rights on the one hand, and being pieces of property on the other. The result was ambivalence in colonial statutes. Massachusetts taxed slaves as persons *and* as property; Connecticut and Rhode Island taxed them as they did livestock. New England slaves could own, transfer, and inherit property at the same time their masters could sell and bequeath them. Puritan masters were especially inconsistent in dealings with their bondsmen. To them the slave was part of the master's family, so Massachusetts Puritans saw to it that slaves had "all the liberties and Christian usages which the law of God, established in Israel concerning such persons, doth normally require." However, Puritans regarded persons of African descent in Biblical terms, too, which meant, in the words of Cotton Mather, they were "miserable children of Adam and

Noah." Strict in their response to all sexual matters, Puritans held particular abhorrence of miscegenation. The Massachusetts law banishing—usually to the West Indies—blacks guilty of fornication with whites was the most severe of such laws in any continental colony.

The Middle Colonies, where larger numbers of African Americans tended to congregate in cities, had more difficulty controlling their slave populations. Curfews and laws forbidding serving of alcohol to blacks were common; punishments were severe. New York had the most difficulty of northern cities. It had slave conspiracy panics in 1712 and 1741. The latter led to the arrest of fifty-four blacks and execution of thirty-one.

In spite of the body of legislation that governed northern slaves, their lives were not so proscribed as those of slaves in southern colonies. It was difficult in a town or city, where slaves worked as deliverymen, runners of errands, or hired artisans, to restrain movement and assembly. So authorities grew tolerant of curfew violations and gatherings of African Americans that did not appear to presage trouble. Still, lack of enforcement did not reduce the total effect of the northern slave codes. "They cast a shadow everywhere," writes Edgar J. McManus in *Black Bondage in the North* (1973), "reminding slaves they were a caste apart, living on sufferance in a system amply geared for their destruction."

Beyond jurisdiction of the slave codes was a body of African Americans in the North who were free. Numbers of free blacks in the northern colonies were small, not much different from the numbers of free blacks in the southern colonies. In material ways, their existence was not considerably better than slaves in their midst. In some ways the existence of slavery hindered free blacks. Slaves who rose to responsible positions under their masters' employ posed no threat to white society, but free blacks who achieved important positions by themselves did. So whites took care to see that northern free black persons remained in menial jobs. Free black shopkeepers had difficulty getting credit; free black artisans were not always welcome in shipyards or at building sites. For those who were destitute it was more difficult in freedom than in slavery. In Boston of 1742 there were 110 free blacks in the almshouse and 36 in the work-house out of the city's total black population, slave and free, of only 1500. If other immigrants to the mainland received rewards for hard work, thrift, and steady movement toward assimilation, Africans in colonial America suffered for such behavior at the hands of a white population that saw African American advancement as a threat to the established order.

Chapter 2

Slavery and the American Revolution

Turning|Points

IN WORLD HISTORY

American Slavery: The American Revolution

Peter Kolchin

Many of America's Founding Fathers who spearheaded the American Revolution were uncomfortable with slavery and took steps to bring about its gradual demise following independence, writes historian Peter Kolchin. In the northern states, where slaves formed a relatively small proportion of the population, legislative and judicial actions in the three decades following the American Revolution brought about the abolition of legalized slavery. However, while some slave owners in the South, including George Washington, privately freed their slaves, the institution remained firmly in place in the region. This discrepancy resulted in a nation increasingly divided over the continuing practice of slavery. Kolchin is a professor of history at the University of Delaware and author of the prizewinning *Unfree Labor: American Slavery and Russian Serfdom.*

The Revolutionary era saw an increasing gap between the South as a whole, where slavery survived the challenge to its legitimacy and remained firmly entrenched, and the North, where slavery gradually gave way to freedom, albeit a severely restrictive freedom. Because the Revolution was waged for "liberty," and generated an enormous amount of rhetoric about despotism, tyranny, justice, equality, and natural rights, it inevitably raised questions about slavery, questions that seemed all the more pertinent in view of the determined efforts of slaves to gain their own freedom, and it is no accident that the United States was the first country to take significant (although ultimately limited) action against the peculiar in-

Excerpted from "The American Revolution," by Peter Kolchin in *American Slavery, 1619–1877.* Copyright ©1993 by Peter Kolchin. Reprinted with the permission of Hill and Wang, a division of Farrar, Straus, and Giroux, LLC.

stitution. Patriots commonly denounced the "slavery" they suffered at the hands of the British, and insisted that they would rather die than remain slaves; although there was considerable hyperbole in this rhetoric—clearly Patriots did not believe that they were slaves in the same sense their own chattels were—the irony of fighting a war for liberty at the same time that they held one-third of their own population as slaves was not lost upon them. They might not have liked the way British Tory author Samuel Johnson phrased the matter when he asked rhetorically, "How is it that we hear the loudest *yelps* for liberty among the drivers of negroes?" but they were acutely aware of the problem.

Whites in the Revolutionary era were by no means united on the question of slavery. A few Americans became abolitionists, arguing for the immediate and unconditional freeing of all slaves; although abolition societies emerged in the South as well as the North, they were heavily dominated by Quakers and became progressively rarer as one moved farther south. Others took action to end their own association with what they regarded as an immoral practice, providing freedom for their slaves either immediately or (like George Washington) in their wills. Even among the great majority of slave owners who never freed their slaves, however, there was widespread unease about an institution that seemed backward and unenlightened. Many agreed with Thomas Jefferson that slavery was wrong, both for moral and practical reasons, and would if properly curtailed suffer a gradual and peaceful death.

Indeed, the Founding Fathers took a series of steps designed to bring about slavery's gradual demise. As children of the Enlightenment, they typically abjured hasty or radical measures that would disrupt society, preferring cautious acts that would induce sustained, long-term progress; rather than a frontal assault on the peculiar institution, they favored a strategy of chipping away at it where it was weakest. Still, there seemed reason to believe—although time would ultimately prove otherwise—that these acts had contained American slavery and put it on the road to gradual extinction.

Much of the action on slavery during the Revolutionary

era occurred at the state level. In the upper South, the state legislatures of Virginia, Maryland, and Delaware revised their laws on manumission, making it easier during the 1780s and 1790s for masters to free their bondspeople. (From 1723 to 1782, private acts of manumission had been illegal in Virginia.) In those states (and to a lesser extent in North Carolina and in the new state of Kentucky), prompted by both principled opposition to slavery and a reduced demand for labor stemming from the downturn in tobacco cultivation, growing numbers of slave owners took advantage of the new laws to free some or all of their slaves. Some masters manumitted only a few select favorites; others, such as George Washington, John Randolph, and Robert Carter III, provided in their wills for the freedom of all their slaves, thereby securing emotional benefit without suffering financial loss. (Legal complications, however, prevented most of Randolph's and Carter's slaves from ever receiving their freedom, and Washington lacked the legal authority to free the numerous "dower Negroes" belonging to his wife, Martha, from a previous marriage; of 277 Washington slaves, 124 belonged to George at the time of his death in 1799, while 153 belonged to Martha.) A smaller number of slaveholders— often Quakers—followed to the end the logic of their antislavery convictions and freed all their slaves immediately. Acts of private manumission freed thousands of blacks in the upper South following the Revolution, and for the first time, especially in Delaware and parts of Maryland, seemed to threaten the very survival of slavery; in Delaware, three-quarters of all blacks were free by 1810.

Farther north, state action was more decisive. Because slaves in the Northern states formed only a small proportion of the population and constituted a minor economic interest, abolishing the peculiar institution in an era that celebrated liberty and natural rights proved relatively easy, although often painfully slow. During the three decades following the outbreak of the Revolutionary War, every Northern state initiated complete slave emancipation. The process varied considerably. In some states, emancipation was immediate: the Vermont constitution of 1777 prohibited slavery, and soon thereafter Massachusetts courts, reacting to a series of freedom suits brought by blacks themselves, interpreted that state's constitution as outlawing slavery, too; as the state's chief justice put it in 1781, "there can be no such thing as perpetual servitude of a rational creature." In most Northern states, however, especially those with a significant slave population, emancipation was gradual, so as to provide as little shock to society (and the masters' pocketbooks) as possible. According to Pennsylvania's law of 1780—the first of five gradual-emancipation acts passed by Northern states— all future-born slaves would become free at age twenty-eight. New York's law of 1799 freed future-born boys at age twenty-eight and girls at twenty-five; New Jersey's act of 1804 (the last emancipation act of a Northern state) was similar, but provided that boys would receive freedom at age twenty-five and girls at twenty-one. Because these gradual-emancipation laws freed no one actually in bondage at the time of their passage, and freed children subsequently born into slavery only when they reached adulthood, the North contained a small number of slaves well into the nineteenth century. By 1810, however, about three-quarters of all Northern blacks were free, and within a generation virtually all would be.

Complementing the abolition acts of individual Northern states was legislation by Congress to restrict the geographical scope of slavery. Because the western territories were largely unsettled (except by Indians), the movement to prohibit the spread of slavery there did not challenge vested interests in the same way that the movement to abolish slavery in existing states did, and received considerable support from those convinced that slavery, although wrong, could not be immediately ended in the South. In 1784, a bill drafted by Jefferson, which would have barred slavery from all the western territories after 1800, was defeated by a single vote. Three years later, the Northwest Ordinance did abolish slavery in a vast area north of the Ohio River known as the Northwest Territory, including the present states of Ohio, Indiana, Illinois, Michigan, and Wisconsin.

The African slave trade, viewed as deplorable even by

many defenders of slavery, was also the object of considerable legislation, at both the state and the national level. Widespread opposition to the trade in the North and upper South led the second Continental Congress to pass a resolution opposing slave imports in 1776, and a number of states (including Virginia in 1778) banned such imports on their own. In the upper South, economic depression sharply reduced the demand for new slaves, and the happy convergence of economic interest with principle easily carried the day. Farther south, however, in South Carolina and Georgia, planters suffered from an acute shortage of labor and bitterly resisted what they considered the hypocritical efforts of those who now had enough slaves suddenly to force others to do without.

Although advocates of the slave trade represented a small minority among the Founding Fathers, they were powerful enough to force a compromise on the question at the Constitutional Convention of 1787: the new Constitution prohibited Congress from outlawing the slave trade for twenty years. During this period, labor-hungry planters in the lower South imported tens of thousands of Africans; indeed, more slaves entered the United States between 1787 and 1807 than during any other two decades in history. Still, the general understanding among those who were politically active was that Congress would abolish the slave trade at the end of twenty years, an expectation that was borne out by congressional legislation passed in 1807 and taking effect in 1808. In their usual cautious, roundabout manner, the Founding Fathers succeeded in ending the importation of Africans to the United States; many believed, incorrectly, that this ending would doom slavery in the United States as well.

The Constitutional Convention showed the Founding Fathers at their most cautious with respect to slavery. In drafting the Constitution, they carefully avoided the word "slavery," resorting to a variety of euphemisms such as "other persons" and "person[s] held to service or labor." At the same time, they acceded to slaveholding interests by recognizing the right of masters to reclaim fugitives and by unanimously accepting a compromise formula whereby for purposes of congressional representation a slave would count as three-fifths of a free person, thereby substantially augmenting the political power of the Southern states. In the future, both supporters and opponents of slavery would wrap themselves in the Constitution and claim to be expressing the views of the Founding Fathers. In fact, although most of the decisions taken by the delegates at the Constitutional Convention represented compromises rather than clear-cut victories for pro-slavery or anti-slavery forces, on balance the Constitution bolstered slavery by throwing the power of the federal government behind it.

Still, to many informed Americans in the 1790s, time seemed to be on the side of reason, reform, and progress. The Northern states were in the process of abolishing slavery within their borders. Congress had acted to guarantee that the Northwest would be forever free. The laws of several Southern states had been changed to facilitate private manumissions, and hundreds of slave owners in the upper South were taking advantage of these laws to free some or all of their chattels. And although importation of new slaves remained legal in South Carolina and Georgia, a compromise had been worked out that would end such importation in 1808. In short, a moderate opponent of slavery—like many of the Founding Fathers—had good grounds for being cautiously optimistic. Slavery appeared to be in full retreat, its end only a matter of time.

The Failure of Gradual Emancipation in the South

Gary B. Nash

In the 1790s, in the wake of the American Revolution, several prominent political leaders in Virginia proposed the gradual abolition of slavery in their state. According to historian Gary B. Nash, these plans reveal the widespread desire of many slaveholders to abolish slavery—and also to rid their society of all blacks through a program of colonization or resettlement. Their proposals, Nash writes, ultimately failed to come to fruition in part because northern politicians and antislavery activists failed to exercise leadership in pushing for a national abolition of slavery. Northern whites proved as unwilling as their southern counterparts to contemplate the creation of a biracial republic. They thus share responsibility for the continuing existence of slavery and the resulting sectional divide between North and South that bedeviled the nation until the Civil War. Nash is a professor of history at the University of California at Los Angeles.

In 1790 . . . at a time when the North and South had learned to reconcile their differences over the management of the western lands, a prominent Virginian published a plan for a gradual emancipation. Ferdinando Fairfax, a protege of George Washington and a man with many ties to Virginia's planter aristocracy, argued that many slaveholders were ready to release their slaves voluntarily and many others could be induced to do so with compensation. But Virginians, argued Fairfax, vehemently resisted the idea of having freed slaves in their midst and would never admit of equal privileges for those whom they emancipated. Hence, gradual abolition must be accompanied by recolonization in Africa, Fairfax suggested (as had Thomas Jefferson in 1776) under the auspices of the federal government. Fairfax's plan was notable not only in pointing to a widespread desire among Virginians (who represented about half of the nation's slave-owners) to be quit of slavery but the simultaneous desire to be quit of blacks. It was a desire, as it turned out, widely shared by northerners.

It is telling that no discussion in the North found its way into public prints after this southern proposal for a federally sponsored gradual abolition. Fairfax's plan was not unknown to northerners, for he published it not in Virginia but in Philadelphia, in Mathew Carey's *American Museum*, the most widely subscribed magazine of the early federal period. Fairfax's conclusions about the sentiment against free blacks living among whites was ominous, for thousands of Virginia slaves had by now been liberated, and white sentiment, in the North as well as the South, was beginning to turn against them. A general emancipation, northerners had reason to believe, would bring free blacks churning northward in search of economic opportunity and some measure of social justice.

St. George Tucker's Proposal

Six years later, in 1796, another prominent Virginian laid before the legislature of his state another plan for the gradual abolition of slavery. Much had transpired since the first Congress had buried the issue of slavery. But two occurrences weighed with special force upon the mind of St. George Tucker, a prominent lawyer and state officeholder. First, was the emerging knowledge of a demographic explosion revealed by the first federal census in 1790; the second was a political explosion that had erupted in the Caribbean shortly after the census of 1790 was taken. Both frightened Tucker, for together they seemed to spell the ruination of the South.

Tucker reported that the first federal census showed that nearly 293,000 slaves resided in Virginia—roughly a 250 percent increase since 1755 and an increase of more than a third since 1782, despite the flight of thousands of slaves to the British during the Revolution, the migration of many freed slaves to the North after the war, and the sale of a large number of slaves southward in the 1780s. In the Tidewater, enslaved blacks now constituted more than 50 percent of the population. Alarmingly, instead of withering, as many expected after Virginia had halted slave importations in 1774, slavery was growing rapidly.

Tucker clothed his appeal for gradual abolition on precisely the point that had been made repeatedly during the revolutionary period—that the institution was incompatible with republican government and was a monstrous stain on the national escutcheon. But the timing of his proposal—and his hopes for its success—rested far more on the widespread fear that black rebellion on the French sugar-producing island of St. Domingue [Haiti] had aroused throughout the South. Partly inspired by the American Revolution, a black revolt had broken out on the French island in 1791. In the next few years it produced spiraling racial violence and wholesale killing and had sent thousands of French planters fleeing to the American mainland, many with slaves in tow. The volcanic fury of the enslaved Caribbean masses shook many whites to their boots, including some abolitionists. In Virginia, where many refugees came with their slaves, fear spread that the revolt might touch off a sister insurrection. "The calamities which have lately spread like a contagion through the West India islands," Tucker wrote to a friend in Massachusetts, "afford a solemn warning to us of the dangerous predicament in which we stand. . . ."

Certain that the demographic history of Virginia was paralleling that of the French West Indies in a way that made massive black rebellion a near certainty, Tucker summoned history and the principles of the Revolution to convince his countrymen of the need for immediate action. Tucker began by quoting Montesquieu's powerful words from the title page of *Spirit of the Laws:* "Slavery not only violates the Laws of Nature, and of civil Society, it also wounds the best Forms of Government; in a Democracy, where all Men are equal, Slavery is contrary to the Spirit of the Constitution." Then

Tucker provided readers with a capsule history of slavery in the New World, organized around the point that "Whilst America hath been the land of promise to Europeans, and their descendants, it hath been the vale of death to millions of the wretched sons of Africa. The genial light of liberty, which hath here shone with unrivalled lustre on the former, hath yielded no comfort to the latter, but to them hath proved a pillar of darkness."

Tucker excused the men of '76 for their inability to deal with the wretched institution "during the convulsions of a revolution," but he argued that now, in a state of "constitutional health and vigour," Americans must remove the "stigma" of slavery in order to uphold "the principles of our government, and of that revolution upon which it is founded." That such a "horrid practice" as the slave trade could be "sanctioned by a civilized nation" was a national disgrace; "that a nation ardent in the cause of liberty . . . can continue to vindicate a right established upon such a foundation" was a national disgrace; "that a people who have declared, 'That *all men* are by nature *equally free* and *independent*,' and have made this declaration the first article in the foundation of their government, should in defiance of so sacred a truth, . . . tolerate a practice incompatible therewith" was a national disgrace.

Like Ferdinando Fairfax, Tucker designed his publication with northerners as well as southerners in mind and may have even designed it as an invitation to the North. While preparing his plan for gradual abolition, Tucker had corresponded with Jeremy Belknap, one of Boston's leading Congregational ministers, regarding the ending of slavery in Virginia. Belknap had queried a number of prominent friends in trying to help Tucker find a formula for abolition. Tucker judged that an abolition of slavery in Virginia was by no means impossible. "A large majority of slave-holders among us," he told Belknap, "would cheerfully concur in any feasible plan for the abolition of it [slavery]." That this was no wild opinion is indicated by Tucker's willingness to state publicly in the pamphlet of the following year that it is "unquestionably true, that a very large proportion of our fellow-citizens lament [slavery] as a misfortune." Within a few months, echoing Tucker, Jefferson wrote that "if something is not done, and done soon, we shall be the murderers of our own children . . . ; the revolutionary storm, now sweeping the globe, will be upon us."

A Plea to the North

Tucker's plan is important because it was, in its way, another plea to the North to assist in the work of dismantling slavery and because it went beyond Fairfax's plan in offering more concrete proposals for eliminating the two obstacles that had heretofore impeded progress on this issue—the economic interest of slaveholders and the deeply rooted feeling among whites that blacks were so inferior that they could not be incorporated into white society on an equal footing. Tucker specifically pointed to these as the most important objections of "most others [plans] that have been submitted to the consideration of the public. . . ." Tucker thought he could overcome the economic question by granting liberty to female slaves born after a certain date only after they had reached 28 years of age, thus allowing masters to recapture their investment, and by requiring even the male and female children of these black women born free to serve 28 years. His plan, in other words, would be cost-free to the present generation of slaveowners and required not a penny of northerners in taxes or appropriations from the government's general fund.

To the second problem Tucker had a harsh solution, though less harsh than the forced colonization in Africa that Fairfax had proposed. Spreading abolition over nearly 100 years, he argued, would allow blacks to acquire skills and behavioral patterns that would make them more acceptable to whites; but even so he doubted that white Virginians would find them acceptable, and so they were to be excluded from most civil rights or liberties, including voting, officeholding, owning land, keeping arms, intermarrying with whites, serving as witness or juror in cases involving whites, and even making a will or testament. Thus would blacks, given legal freedom but kept in social bondage, be driven to emigrate voluntarily to uninhabited western lands or to the Spanish territories in Florida and Louisiana.

Tucker's *Dissertation on Slavery* could not have escaped the attention of northern political leaders because it too was published in Philadelphia where Congress was now sitting; it is even possible that Tucker chose to have it published in that city in order to put it squarely before their view. But Tucker, like other prominent Virginians concerned to find a way of disengaging from slavery, could evoke no response from northern leaders. Even the Quaker-led Pennsylvania Abolition Society, perhaps stung by the failure of their attempts in 1790 to get congressional action, failed to suggest or promote a plan of emancipation carried out under the auspices of the national government. In fact the PAS, when it had the opportunity, refused even to seek the judicial abolition of slavery in Pennsylvania, though precedent for this had been provided in Massachusetts in 1786. . . .

A Fading Opportunity

As the Jeffersonian presidency proceeded after 1800, it became apparent that the time had nearly passed when a gradual but general emancipation might have worked. The environmentalist belief of the Revolutionary period posited that circumstances, not inborn qualities, accounted for the degradation of Africans in America was weakening, with the old view that blacks were innately inferior making a resurgence. Free blacks were more and more regarded as a dangerous element, to be controlled or excluded from society. Moreover, the economic viability of slavery had suddenly been greatly enhanced by Eli Whitney's famous invention [of the cotton gin]. As before, no northerners came forward with emancipation schemes, nor did they tender support for those that southerners continued to put before the public.

In 1803, the year that the St. Dominguan revolution culminated in the final defeat of white French colonialism, St. George Tucker republished his plan, again in Philadelphia. A New Jersey congressman proposed gradual emancipation for slaves in the District of Columbia in the same year. In 1810, two southerners, the Maryland Quaker John Parrish and the abolitionist Lewis Dupre put forward plans, both variations on the formula of emancipation followed by removal. [James] Madison would make a last-ditch attempt, as the question of extending slavery into Missouri and Kansas heated up, with his gradual emancipation proposal in 1819, by which time he estimated that $240 million would be required to settle freed blacks on western lands. In 1824, two years before he died, Jefferson proposed a federally financed plan for gradual abolition, and in the next year the English reformer Fanny Wright put forward another plan.

White Racism

And by this time, opinion had turned strongly against the thousands of free blacks who had sought a life of freedom in the northern cities. Any ember of northern desire to participate in a national plan for abolition, gradual or immediate, had ceased to glow. Instead, a belligerent white supremacism was manifesting itself throughout the North. As early as 1805, white Philadelphians drove their black neighbors from the traditional Fourth of July celebrations in Independence Square. Within another decade the first burning of a black northern church took place in the City of Brotherly Love.

The rampaging white racism that developed in the aftermath of the War of 1812 took institutional form in the American Colonization Society, founded in 1817 and dedicated both to Christianizing slaves and to shipping free blacks back to Africa. At a lower level, in urban streets, hostility against free blacks took the form of bloody attacks on black neighborhoods. Northern whites began demonstrating militantly that they had little commitment to a biracial republic. The republican edifice they were constructing would provide little shelter to those who were black—free or slave. Slavery would remain a national problem, not a southern problem, but northerners, with few exceptions, acknowledged no responsibility for solving the problem. In fact, many within the northern intellectual elite, including such titans of northern academic training as Timothy Dwight and Samuel Stanhope Smith, president of Yale and Princeton respectively in the early nineteenth century, helped to forge "a new framework for the discussion of slavery"—a framework, as [historian] Larry Tise has shown, upon which an "antebellum proslavery tradition" could be built. Conservative northern Federalists, not southerners, "were the first Americans to revive the defense of slavery in public" in the second decade of the nineteenth century. With northerners becoming increasingly involved in the booming cotton economy of the South, such former officers of the Pennsylvania Abolition Society as Tench Coxe were publishing virulently racist essays denying that free blacks, as well as Native Americans and other people of color, were genetically endowed for citizenship.

From failing to support abolition plans put forward by southerners in the 1780s and 1790s to their emergence in the first quarter of the nineteenth century as contrivers of an intellectual defense of slavery, northern leaders—political, academic, and clerical—consistently ducked the issue that the Revolutionary leaders had insisted must be solved if the nation was to be united and true to the sacred texts enunciated during its birth. Slavery would continue to grow in the South and the problem of slavery would continue to require a national solution. When it came, the solution was so costly that the casualty rate was more than five times as great as Americans sustained in World War II. The North has always blamed the South for that carnage from 1861 to 1865, but in truth the North was equally blameworthy.

A House Divided: American Slavery in the Antebellum Era

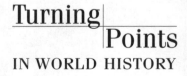

Turning Points

IN WORLD HISTORY

The Missouri Compromise of 1820

Roger L. Ransom

Historian Roger L. Ransom provides an account of the background, enactment, and legacy of the 1820 Missouri Compromise. This first major slavery-related political crisis that the United States faced in the 1800s centered on slavery in the western territories. Congress had first dealt with this problem shortly after the American Revolution when it passed laws that divided up the western lands ceded by Great Britain into slave and free regions. By prohibiting the introduction of slavery in territory north of the Ohio River and permitting it south of the river, a numerical balance between slave and free states was maintained as territories were settled and became states. President Thomas Jefferson's 1803 purchase of the Louisiana Territory from France doubled the size of the country, but left open the question of whether slavery would be introduced into the newly acquired area. In 1819 Congress deadlocked over whether Missouri—part of the Louisiana Territory—should be admitted to the Union as a slave state. The following year a compromise was narrowly approved in which Missouri was admitted as a slave state and the rest of the Louisiana Territory was officially divided into future free and slave territory. Ransom, a professor of history at the University of California at Riverside, argues that because Americans were not ready to "go to the wall" on slavery, they were willing to fashion a compromise that put to rest the issue of slavery in the territories for the next three decades.

Excerpted from *Conflict and Compromise: The Political Economy of Slavery, Emancipation, and the American Civil War,* by Roger L. Ransom. Copyright © 1989 by the Cambridge University Press. Reprinted with the permission of the Cambridge University Press.

The issue of slavery remained relatively quiet for the three decades following the ratification of the Constitution. The slave trade was banned in 1809 with relatively little opposition from North or South. As [Thomas] Jefferson had observed in 1776, only two states—South Carolina and Georgia—really favored a continuance of the trade at that time; in the rest of the South, a growing number of slaveholders favored putting an end to the flow of slaves from abroad. The question of allowing importation of slaves had always produced some ambivalence among slaveholders. Although imported slaves obviously represented a cheap source of labor for those wishing to purchase slaves, their presence also depressed the price of slaves. Those owning slaves realized that the value of their investment would be depressed by continuing imports. On balance, the slave interests were content to let the external slave trade disappear.

With the arrival of what promised to be a lasting peace in Europe and the settlement of our quarrel with England [following the War of 1812], the United States turned its attention with renewed vigor toward economic expansion. That meant western settlement. The years immediately following 1815 witnessed the first great land boom in the United States. Settlers pushed westward into both the Northwest Territory and the Southwest Territory.[1] With the admission of Alabama in December 1819, nine new states had been formed and admitted into the Union. That brought the total to twenty-two states, evenly balanced between eleven slave and eleven nonslave. All this was in accordance with the guidelines of the Ordinance of 1787; each of the slave states had been south of the Ohio River, and each had been regarded as a slave territory from the outset of settlement. Thanks to the agreement of 1787, the process of settlement and organization had proceeded peacefully. That was about to change. As the Sixteenth Congress of the United States convened in the spring of 1820, the question of slavery and

---

1. These areas refer to the land between the Appalachians and the Mississippi River ceded by Great Britain to the United States in the 1783 Treaty of Paris and divided by the Ohio River. Congress in the Ordinance of 1787 prohibited slavery in the Northwest Territory.

the western territory had suddenly been thrust to the fore-front of national politics once again.

Crisis over Missouri

The immediate source of the problem was a difficulty in Congress over the request of Missouri to be admitted as a slave state. The roots of controversy went back to 1803, when President Thomas Jefferson obtained the Louisiana Purchase. At the time, it seemed a masterful stroke. For a mere $15 million, the nation's land area was almost doubled and the use of the Mississippi was secured for Americans. The issue of settling the new land (with or without slavery) was hardly on anyone's mind. Apart from New Orleans, most of the Louisiana Purchase was far beyond the limits of settlement in 1803. But as people began to think more seri-ously about settling in the new territory, they realized that most of that land lay north of the area defined in the North-west Ordinance as being free from slavery. Of the land west of the Mississippi River, only Louisiana (admitted as a state in 1812) and the Arkansas Territory were clearly marked as territories that would have slavery if the boundaries implic-itly laid down by the compromise of 1787 were to be applied to the Louisiana Purchase.

The problem that arose in 1819 began in 1817 with the establishment in Missouri of a territorial government in preparation for statehood. The situation is evident in Map 1. The proposed state of Missouri lay only slightly south of Illi-nois; the Ohio River joins the Mississippi River in the south-eastern corner of the territory. By the terms of the compro-mise of 1787, the new state would clearly be free territory. Slaveholders, however, were determined that Missouri would have slaves, and a substantial number of settlers pushed north into the territory bringing their slaves with them. In November 1818, the Legislative Council and the House of Representatives of Missouri petitioned Congress for statehood. Speaker of the House Henry Clay presented the memorial from the citizens of Missouri to the House on December 18, 1818. There was no question but that Mis-souri would eventually enter as a slave state under the

Map 1. The Missouri Compromise

FREE STATES
AND
TERRITORIES

UNORGANIZED
FREE
TERRITORIES

MISSOURI
COMPROMISE

SLAVE
TERRITORY

SLAVE STATES
AND
TERRITORIES

N

0   500 MI.

arrangements existing in 1818.

Just prior to the Missouri request, Illinois and Alabama had each petitioned Congress for statehood. Although there was little controversy over the admission of these two states, Representative James Talmadge of New York created a minor crisis when he argued that the petition of Illinois to form a government should be rejected on the grounds that the proposed constitution of that state did not explicitly prohibit slavery. Talmadge's opposition did not carry the day, but his efforts signaled a warning that the case of Missouri might not be so simple.

The Talmadge Amendments

Missouri's petition for statehood represented the first attempt to allow slavery in a state that lay north of the implicit line of the Ohio River established by the Land Ordinances of 1787 and 1790. On February 13, 1819, as the House took up the bill for Missouri statehood, Talmadge renewed his efforts to exclude slavery north of the Ohio. He offered the following amendment to the bill admitting Missouri to the

Union: "That the further introduction of slavery or involuntary servitude be prohibited . . . and that all children of slaves, born within the said state, after the admission thereof into the Union, shall be free, but may be held to service until the age of twenty-five years."

The House split Talmadge's amendment into two parts. The clause dealing with prohibition of slavery passed by a vote of 87 to 76; the clause for gradual emancipation passed by 82 to 78. The amended bill was then sent to the Senate. By a rather substantial margin, that body refused to accept Talmadge's clause and passed a bill admitting Missouri with no restrictions regarding slavery. Efforts to resolve differences between the bills passed by the House and the Senate failed, and the Fifteenth Congress adjourned without acting on Missouri's application for statehood. Talmadge had created a crisis in Congress that reached a critical juncture just as Congress adjourned.

The votes on the Talmadge amendments made it clear that opponents of slavery in the House of Representatives had enough votes in the House to hold up statehood for Missouri indefinitely. Encouraged by their success, antislavery forces redoubled their efforts during the Congressional recess to solidify the opposition to the admission of Missouri with slavery. Two issues were at stake here. The first was the importance of maintaining a balance between slave and nonslave states. This was largely a problem of timing and was clearly of greater concern to the South than to the North. Everyone could see that at least two more free states were going to be formed from existing territories in the Old Northwest, and there was the added possibility that Congress would act on the application of the newly formed territory of Maine [previously part of Massachusetts] for statehood. The second issue was more difficult: How could the territories of the Louisiana Purchase be kept free from slavery in the future?

The Compromise of 1820

As the Sixteenth Congress began debate on the Missouri question, it became apparent that the Senate would continue to oppose the Talmadge amendment adamantly and that the House was equally determined to force the issue of eliminating slavery in Missouri. The resolution of this stalemate is known as the Compromise of 1820. It was ultimately fashioned by tying together three related actions:

1. Admit Missouri as a slave state in accordance with the initial request for statehood.
2. Approve the application for statehood of Maine as a free state.
3. Define the territories in the Louisiana Purchase, which henceforth would be free and slave.

The first two parts of the compromise "package" were obvious enough; the applications for statehood from Maine and Missouri were combined into an omnibus bill. The third part of the bargain was the crucial element to get passage in the House. The solution, offered by Senator Jesse Thomas of Illinois, was to take the language used in the Northwest Ordinance of 1787 and apply it to the Louisiana Territory. What became known as the Thomas Proviso was attached to the bill approving statehood for Missouri and Maine:

> That, in all that territory ceded by France to the United States, under the name of Louisiana, which lies north of thirty-six degrees and thirty minutes north latitude, excepting only such part thereof as is included within the limits of the State contemplated by this act, slavery and involuntary servitude . . . shall be and is hereby forever prohibited: *Provided always*, That any person escaping into the same, from whom labor service is lawfully claimed in any State or Territory of the United States, such fugitive may be lawfully reclaimed and conveyed to the person claiming his or her labor or service as aforesaid.

In the Senate there was little problem putting the pieces together, although the vote on the omnibus Missouri-Maine bill with the Thomas Proviso was uncomfortably close: 24 in favor and 20 opposed. In the House the task was not so easy. As [historian] Glover Moore observes, "One of the noticeable things about the passage of the Missouri Compromise was that the House never voted yea or nay on the compromise as a whole." Instead, Speaker Henry Clay masterfully guided the various parts of the package through the legislature piece by piece. The closest call came on the vote to eliminate the Talmadge clause from the Missouri bill and allow slavery in the new state, an action that passed by only 3 votes. The Thomas Proviso was then approved by an overwhelming majority, 134 to 42. The result of the compromise can be seen in Map 1, which shows the demarcation line established by the Thomas Proviso.

A Significant Achievement

Although it has received relatively little attention from historians in recent years, the Missouri Compromise was a pathbreaking achievement on the part of those who fashioned it. The narrowness with which it passed suggests a fragility that belies the robustness of the contract once it was struck. In fact, for the next three decades, the line defined in the Missouri Compromise clearly established the limits of slavery in the United States. One reason it worked so well was that it was based on the precedent established by the Northwest Ordinance in 1787. A majority of Southerners actually favored the Thomas Proviso when it came to a vote in the House. Although Northerners were more truculent in agreeing to the admission of Missouri as a slave state, it is easy to exaggerate the force of their opposition. Slavery, after all, was firmly established in Missouri by the time the issue came to a head in Congress. However distasteful opponents of slavery might find this fact, they could not reverse the pattern of settlement. Moreover, by the time the issue came to a vote, the outcome was assured. This meant that those strongly opposed could vote negatively so long as their vote did not jeopardize the agreed-upon outcome. They then overwhelmingly approved the Thomas Proviso. This was a compromise in the classic sense of the term: Each side got something and each side gave up something they deemed important. The slave interests got approval of Missouri as a slave state; opponents succeeded in permanently extending the ban on slavery in the Louisiana Territory north of the line thirty-six degrees thirty minutes.

Over the long term, the most important development of the Missouri Compromise turned out to be even more basic than the details of the bargain itself. The Missouri Compromise established the right of Congress to pass legislation allowing or prohibiting slavery in the western territories. This was not universally applauded; indeed a few people saw in the Thomas Proviso a threat to their long-term interests. Nathaniel Macon of North Carolina was one of only two southern senators to vote against the omnibus bill in the Senate. "To compromise," he wrote a friend shortly before the vote, "is to acknowledge the right of Congress to interfere and to legislate on the subject, this would be acknowledging too much." Future generations of southern representatives in Washington would tend to agree with Macon's assessment, while Northerners, many of whom resisted the compromise, gradually came to see the limitations to slavery contained in the Thomas Proviso as the cornerstone upon which a resistance to expansion of slavery could be built.

Emotions ran high during the debates over slavery in Missouri and the Louisiana Territory. Yet almost as quickly as it arose, the tension subsided. The country, as it were, heaved a collective sigh of relief and went back to work. Why was the compromise so successful? In part, because it reflected the fact that both sides could point to tangible gains from the legislation. But in a larger sense it was because, despite the rhetoric that proclaimed a willingness to fight for the principles at stake, the fact remained that most Americans were not prepared to "go to the wall" on the slavery issue in 1820. The specter of a slave system that was a genuine threat to northern interests had not yet appeared on the political scene. Slavery was a moral indignity; and some Southerners had pressed a step too far in allowing slavery to take hold in Missouri. But for most people living outside the south in 1820, slavery was a distant and relatively quiescent institution. Patience, not force, was needed to deal with the problem. The slave trade had been eliminated and a clear line of demarcation between slave and free territory had been established by the terms of the Thomas Proviso. Even if it could not be eradicated, slavery had been contained.

The political situation added to the sense of consensus rather than sectionalism. "Republicanism," the political movement launched by Thomas Jefferson with his presidential victory in 1800, was just reaching its zenith at this point. There was, for all practical purposes, only one effective political party. In the elections of 1820 the Federalists [a rival political party] captured only 7 of 42 seats in the Senate, and 27 of 183 seats in the House. The absence of party rivalries made the quest for a compromise much easier. The other side of that coin was that the crisis over slavery between 1819 and 1821 had a profound effect on the development of the two-party system that was to emerge a decade later.

Unresolved Issues

That was all in the future. For the time being, the deal that had worked in 1787 had worked again in 1820. Both sides had been given some territory; both sides had some assurances about the future. A few could look ahead to see that a troubling question remained: What would happen when there was no longer any land to give away? The issue of slavery and territories was put to rest for the time being, but for how long? The man who drafted Article 6 of the Northwest Ordinance thirty-four years earlier [Thomas Jefferson] was uneasy over the solution of 1820:

> But this momentous question, like a fire bell in the night, awakened and filled me with terror. I considered it at once as the knell of the Union. It is hushed, indeed, for the moment. But this is a reprieve only, not a final sentence. A geographical line, coinciding with a marked principle, moral and political, once conceived and held up to the angry passions of men, will never be obliterated; and every new irritation will mark it deeper and deeper.

The passage has been quoted often, perhaps because no one since has said it any better. Jefferson understood where the crux of the conflict lay. The line that had resolved the dispute of 1820 would become the basis of an even more bitter fight thirty years later.

John C. Calhoun and the Southern Defense of Slavery

Nathaniel Weyl and William Marina

At the beginning of the nineteenth century many Southerners such as Thomas Jefferson believed that slavery was
morally objectionable and economically obsolete. As the
nineteenth century advanced, however, the South's fore-
most thinkers and leaders increasingly began to extol slavery as a "positive good" that was necessary for the region's
prosperity. Nathaniel Weyl and William Marina describe
some of the political and economic developments of the
region that contributed to this change of view. These factors include the westward expansion of the South with the
addition of Alabama, Mississippi, and other states, and the
emergence of cotton as the region's dominant cash crop.
Political leadership of the region moved south and west
from Virginia to the "Cotton Kingdom." Weyl and Marina argue that John C. Calhoun of South Carolina was the
South's most influential leader and political theorist, and
they examine his beliefs in some detail. Calhoun rejected
the doctrines of human equality and natural rights found
in America's Declaration of Independence. He instead insisted that blacks were inferior to whites and that slavery
provided a stable and desirable foundation for society that
avoided the exploitation of workers and class conflict
found in the North. Weyl is a former government official
and author of numerous books and journal articles. Marina is a history professor at Florida Atlantic University.

The year 1825 marks a turning-point in the political and intellectual history of the South. In that year James Monroe,

after having served two terms, relinquished the Presidency to John Quincy Adams, thus terminating an uninterrupted twenty-four years of government by Thomas Jefferson and his two chosen successors. In the third of a century that was to elapse before the outbreak of the Civil War, leadership of the South would pass from the Virginia dynasty to more dynamic and aggressive spokesmen from the newer and more fertile cotton lands of the Black Belt.

Of these, John C. Calhoun of South Carolina towered above the rest in genius and iron determination, in breadth of outlook, in intellectual creativity and in his ability, not merely to argue a case, but to build a novel political philosophy. The successors to Calhoun, men who adopted his ideas with scarcely any original contributions of their own, were also primarily politicians of the new cotton lands. They included Alexander H. Stephens, Robert Toombs and William Lowndes Yancey of Georgia, Judah P. Benjamin of Louisiana and, of course, Jefferson Davis of Mississippi.

To suggest that Virginians contributed nothing to the emerging political philosophy, which asserted that slavery was both necessary and a positive good when two races of widely disparate abilities occupied the same territory, would be false. John Taylor of Caroline County, Virginia, initiated this revaluation of moral concepts when he suggested that Jefferson's attacks on slavery were merely a reflection of the intellectual environment of the American and French Revolutions. Professor Thomas Roderick Dew of the College of William and Mary was one of the first American intellectuals to defend slavery as a desirable institution. His 1833 work *An Essay in Favor of Slavery* had an enormous impact on the Southern mind. Finally, George Fitzhugh, the Richmond lawyer and writer, went beyond Calhoun to the extremist position that slavery is a more just and desirable relationship than wage labor even among white people. . . .

He compared the slave and the free laborer in these terms:

> Slavery without domestic affection would be a curse, and so would marriage and parental authority. The free laborer is excluded from its holy and charmed circle. Shelterless,

naked, and hungry, he is exposed to the bleak winds, the cold rains, and hot sun of heaven, with none that love him, none that care for him. His employer hates him because he asks high wages or joins strikes; his fellow-laborer hates him because he competes with him for employment. . . . As a slave, he will be beloved and protected. Whilst free, he will be hated, despised, and persecuted.

An Economic Revolution

An economic revolution caused the new Southern imperialism and the displacement of the Jeffersonian philosophy. The development of a modern cotton spinning and weaving industry in England, coupled with the invention of the cotton gin by Eli Whitney, laid the foundations for the transformation of the South into a monocultural agrarian society. Machine-made cotton textiles and clothes progressively supplanted home-made woolens throughout Europe. As cotton textiles fell in price until they were within reach of the masses, the demand for raw cotton rose. During the decades before the Civil War, there was a rapid increase in the cost of slaves since, with the African slave trade outlawed, cotton cultivation was expanding faster than the slave labor force could be bred and raised to working ages. The price of an able-bodied male slave for field work was $350 to $500 in 1800 and double that twenty years later.

Cotton cultivation, like sugar cane cultivation, involved an enormous expenditure of hard, back-breaking labor. Unlike the diversified family farming of the North and West, cotton agriculture consisted primarily of the repetition of simple manual operations, requiring physical strength, the ability to work under intense heat, and practically no exercise of intelligence or judgment. Chopping and picking were operations which could be performed by gang labor, in which entire families participated, and in which normal daily performance per worker could be estimated with a fair degree of accuracy. All of these characteristics made cotton cultivation well adapted to Negro slave labor and shunned, wherever possible, by free white labor. Thus, as the South became transformed from the diversified agricultural economy of Jefferson's age to the cotton monoculture of Calhoun's, Negro slavery ceased to appear as an obsolete and morally obnoxious institution and seemed rather to be the cornerstone of the entire Southern economy. This transformation of economic fundamentals made a philosophical and ethical justification of slavery urgently needed as a prop for the morale and self-respect of the slaveowning class.

The Cotton Kingdom

As the 19th Century advanced, the Southern Cotton Kingdom acquired a peculiar dynamism of its own. Under the prevailing methods of tillage, cotton quickly exhausted soils. Loss of soil fertility spread southward from Virginia to the Carolinas and westward to the Piedmont and beyond. The South opened up new lands to cotton to meet rising European demand. Planters from the exhausted lands of Virginia and the Carolinas moved westward with their slaves in search of better soil or else stayed behind and sold off the natural increase in their Negro population. Despite all efforts to encourage Negro reproduction, the demand for slave labor increased faster than the supply. The consequent increase in the cost of slave labor was accompanied by marked and significant improvements in the working conditions, diet, housing and medical care of the latter. Since Negroes were neither cheap nor easy to replace, it was to the masters' interest to keep them at peak working efficiency as long as possible.

The Southern theory of the dynamics of slavery was predicated on continuous expansion into new lands propitious for Negro labor. This expansion was putatively necessary to counteract falling soil fertility, to meet rising world demand for cotton, and to maintain the balance of power in Congress. As each new State was admitted to the Union, two new members were added to the Senate. As existing States increased in population, the balance in the House of Representatives changed. The basis of Southern political power was threatened by the torrent of European immigration into the free States of the North and the free States and territories of the West. The Southern power position was visibly menaced in the House of Representatives as the 1840's drew toward a close. Immigration had increased from 84,000 in 1840 to 370,000 in 1850. At this rate, immigration was adding 1½ percent per annum to the United States population and virtually the entire stream was directed toward free States.

The South's last power stronghold within the Union seemed to be the Senate, where representation was not based on population. Hence, it was no accident that the most able and brilliant political leaders of the South, its professional military men excepted, served as Senators. Even here, the South found itself in an impasse after the annexation of Texas. Within the territorial limits of the United States, there were no other present or prospective candidates for statehood which seemed climatically propitious for Negro slavery or likely to request admission as slave States. In desperation, as the crisis of secession and civil strife approached, the political leaders of the South sought to expand slavery by purchase, subversion or conquest of potential slave lands in the West Indies, Mexico and Central America.

Calhoun and the Inequality of Man

That admirable commentator on American political thought, Vernon Louis Parrington, considered Calhoun "the greatest figure" in the long controversy over slavery, the intellectual superior of Henry Clay and Daniel Webster, "the one outstanding political thinker in a period singularly barren and uncreative," a man of tenacious logic and "apostolic zeal," a pervasive influence on his age, "the master political mind of the South," and its uncrowned king.

After this unstinted praise, Parrington made the extraordinary comment: "Born and bred in South Carolina, he was enveloped from infancy in the mesh of southern provincialisms." Actually, Calhoun was less provincial than most of his contemporaries. He spent two years at Yale, where he graduated with distinction and was elected to Phi Beta Kappa. After studying law in Connecticut for another year and a half, Calhoun entered politics, where he served as Congressman, Senator, Secretary of War (in which post his record was outstanding), Vice President of the United States, and Secretary of State. He lived in Washington as much as in South Carolina and travelled all over the United States.

The owner of anywhere from 30 to 90 slaves, Calhoun was generally conceded to be a kind and just master. He believed that every planter should be "the parent as well as the master of his Slaves; that is, let the Slaves be made to do their duty as well as to eat, drink and sleep; let morality and industry be taught them, and the Planter will have reason to be satisfied; he will always obtain seven or eight per cent upon the value of his Slaves; and need never be compelled to the distressing alternative of parting with them unless he allows them by overindulgence to waste his substance."

Calhoun refused to separate slave families. He once freed a Negro shoemaker who with his family went North, where, as a free Negro, he starved. Returning to the plantation, the shoemaker begged Calhoun to take him back into slavery, where his wants and those of his family would be satisfied. Calhoun obliged. The incident made a deep impression on him and fortified his conviction that the natural state of the Negro was slavery. . . .

Even when the planters were just, kindly and good managers, Calhoun recognized that they were perched on the rim of a volcano. "We are surrounded by invisible dangers, against which nothing can protect us, but our foresight and energy." The obstacle to concord was "the diversity of the races," a difficulty which "no power on earth can overcome."

Calhoun rejected Jefferson's statement in the Declaration of Independence that "all men are created equal," stating that "there is not a word of truth in it." Strictly speaking, they were not created men, but infants. Infants and children are subordinated to their parents; wives to their husbands. When they grow to manhood, their inequality persists and may even be intensified. The poor are not equal to the rich, the weak to the strong, the stupid to the intelligent, or, Calhoun added, the black to the white. . . .

Calhoun [also] discussed the relationship between liberty and security. Of the two, the latter was the more important, because security was essential to survival, liberty merely to progress. A society can survive without progress, but it cannot progress without survival. As Calhoun put it [in *A Disquisition on Government*]:

> Liberty, then, when forced on a people unfit for it, would, instead of a blessing, be a curse; as it would, in its reaction, lead directly to anarchy,—the greatest of all curses. No people, indeed, can long enjoy more liberty than that to which their situation and advanced intelligence and morals fairly entitle them. If more than this be allowed, they must soon fall into confusion and disorder,—to be followed, if not by anarchy and despotism, by a change to a form of government more simple and absolute; and, therefore, better suited to their condition. And hence, although it may be true that a people may not have as much liberty as they are fairly entitled to, and are capable of enjoying,—yet the reverse is unquestionably true,—that no people can long possess more than they are fairly entitled to.
>
> Liberty, indeed, though among the greatest blessings, is not so great as that of protection; inasmuch, as the end of the former is in the progress and improvement of the race,—while that of the latter is its preservation and perpetuation. And hence, when the two come into conflict, liberty must and ever ought, to yield to protection; as the existence of the race is of greater moment than its improvement.

These general principles constitute the foundation for Calhoun's views on slavery and the Negro. . . .

Views on Race and Slavery

Like most Americans of the day, Calhoun believed the Negro to be mentally and morally inferior. Seizing on statistics derived from the Census of 1840, the accuracy of which was dubious, Calhoun replied to a formal British request that slavery be outlawed in Texas with the assertion that "in all instances in which the States have changed the former relation between the two races, the condition of the African, instead of being improved, has become worse. They have invariably sunk into vice and pauperism, accompanied by the bodily and mental inflictions incident thereto—deafness, blindness, insanity, and idiocy—to a degree without example." By contrast, in the slave States, the Negroes had shown improvement in "intelligence, and morals." Calhoun added that Britain's action "under the plausible name of the abolition of slavery" would either destroy the Negro race or relegate it to "vice and wretchedness.". . .

In a more formal and considered defense of slavery, Calhoun observed,

> In the present state of civilization, where two races of different origin, and distinguished by color, and other physical differences, as well as intellectual, are brought together, the relation now existing in the slave-holding States between the two, is, instead of an evil, a positive good. . . . There has never yet existed a wealthy and civilized society in which one portion of the community did not, in the point of fact, live on the labor of the other. . . . I fearlessly assert that the existing relation between the two races in the South, against which these blind fanatics are waging war, forms the most solid and durable foundation on which to rear free and stable political institutions.

Calhoun's vision of the South was based on Athenian democracy as he understood it. At the time of Pericles [who ruled the ancient Greek city-state from 443 to 429 B.C.], Athens had had 43,000 citizens, who alone were entitled to vote and discharge political functions, 28,500 *metics*, or resident aliens, and 115,000 slaves. A century and a half later, Demetrius of Phalerum took a census of the city and counted only 21,000 citizens, 10,000 *metics*, and 400,000 slaves. The presence of this large slave class to do menial and manual work gave the citizens leisure to cultivate their minds, defend their city and help guide its policies.

Calhoun accepted Aristotle's views concerning the distinction between natural and artificial slaves and the social necessity of keeping the former in a state of bondage. Just as Aristotle believed that servitude was beneficial to the natural slave, because the man who was merely an instrument needed a directing brain, so Calhoun deemed slavery beneficial to the Negro as a school in which he could advance from barbarism toward civilization.

In Plato's ideal society, depicted in *The Republic*, the population was distributed on the basis of ability among four great classes: the guardians, who ruled the city; the warriors, who defended it; the merchants and artisans, who provided it with goods and services; and the slaves, who did the unskilled menial work. The existence of a slave class, in Calhoun's view, gave the white population the leisure necessary for cultural and political development.

Moreover, a slave society was, not an arena of class conflict, but a community. The whites were unified by a common interest and harmony. The slaves were cared for by responsible masters, creating a reciprocal relationship of interdependence and trust, in contrast to the harsh, impersonal relationship of the capitalist labor market. . . .

Southern Harmony vs. Northern Discord

In the free society of the North, there was an incessant struggle between the haves and the have-nots. Since both classes were citizens, the region was faced, not only with incessant economic class war, but with a sort of electoral politics, which was also class war under a thin disguise.

"The Southern States," Calhoun wrote, "are an aggregate, in fact, of communities, not of individuals. Every plantation is a little community, with the master at its head, who concentrates in himself the united interests of capital and labor, of which he is the common representative. These small communities in the aggregate make the State, in all whose action, labor, and capital is equally represented and perfectly harmonized. Hence the harmony, the union, the stability of that section, which is rarely disturbed, except through the action of their Government. The blessing of this state of things extends beyond the limits of the South. It makes that section the balance of the system; the great, conservative power which prevents other portions, less fortunately constituted, from rushing into conflict.

On the basis of this somewhat idealized picture of Southern harmony and Northern discord, Calhoun hinted at a grand strategy to save both the South and the Union. His concept was an alliance between the South and the propertied classes of the North, based on the guarantee of slavery below the Mason and Dixon Line and stability above it. The South was permanently secure against revolution because her black proletariat were not citizens. The North, on the contrary, would, "with the increase of its population and wealth, be subject to all the agitation and conflicts growing out of the divisions of . . . capital and labor. . . ." Because of the "conservative nature" of slavery, its permanence in the South would prevent class war there and provide the propertied classes of the North with a stable and powerful ally.

Chattel Slavery or Wage Slavery

During the four years Calhoun lived in New England as a student, he probably saw "the paupers of the Town. . . . sold at auction to those who keep them cheapest. . . ." For these paupers were "slaves as long as they lived." He knew that Alexander Hamilton had championed child labor as a means of keeping minors out of mischief and that he had ordered small looms from England for the use of child workers. In the Providence area, entire families above the age of five often worked twelve to fourteen hours a day in the mills. . . .

Having observed some of these conditions and read about others, Calhoun was perhaps understandably unimpressed by those Abolitionist orators who bled for the wrongs suffered by the enslaved Negroes in the South, but were often unconcerned about the bestial oppression of women and children of their own race nearer to home. Calhoun saw the social order as inevitably based on arrangements between an owning class and a propertyless working class, in which the former utilized a variety of coercive devices to compel the latter to labor for it.

"I hold," he wrote,

> that there never has yet existed a wealthy and civilized society in which one portion of the community did not, in point of fact, live on the labour of the other. The devices to accomplish this are almost innumerable, from the brute force and gross superstition of ancient times to the subtle and artful contrivances of modern times. I might well challenge a comparison between them and the more direct, simple and

patriarchal mode by which the labour of the African race is, among us, employed. I may say with truth that in few countries is so much left to the share of the labourer, and so little exacted from him; or where there is more kind attention paid to him in sickness or in the infirmities of age.

Calhoun's Legacy

. . . Calhoun achieved what few men have. He created a logical, comprehensive and self-contained system of political philosophy. This justified slavery for the Negro within a much broader context of history and sociology. Yet, as a political achievement, Calhoun's work was merely the harbinger of catastrophe for his beloved South. Its repudiation of the dominant doctrines of human equality and natural rights was emotionally unacceptable to the North. Once the Southern States were irrevocably committed to Calhoun's philosophy of aristocracy, of the natural inequality of men, of the inevitability of class oppression, of the institution of slavery as a positive good and of the expansion of slavery as a virtual necessity, the coming of the Civil War was made both more probable and more imminent.

The Abolitionist Movement Provokes the South

William W. Freehling

A significant force in America's debate over slavery in the years leading up to the Civil War was the abolitionist movement. William W. Freehling traces the origins of the movement to religious revivals that swept over the North in the 1820s, led by evangelist Charles G. Finney and others. Many of Finney's Christian converts embarked on various social reforms; some, including Theodore D. Weld and William Lloyd Garrison, took up the cause of the immediate emancipation of all slaves. Freehling goes on to examine how abolitionism—a movement centered in the North—quickly became a leading cause of unrest in the South. Southern leaders responded to the abolitionists' attempt in 1835 to disseminate antislavery literature through the mail by demanding that U.S. postal officials censor the mails and that the northern states outlaw all antislavery speech, arguing that such speech and writings may provoke slave insurrections. According to Freehling, such demands provoked white Northerners who were generally unwilling to accede to such restrictions on their civil liberties to take up an antislavery position even though many strongly disapproved of abolitionists and their cause. Freehling is a professor of history at Johns Hopkins University in Baltimore, Maryland.

In the mid-1830s, the key new Yankee zealot was a tepid extremist on slavery. Charles Grandison Finney, northern evangelical revivalist extraordinaire, demanded a religious conversion with a political potential more radical than the

Excerpted from *The Road to Disunion*, vol. 1, *Secessionists at Bay, 1776–1854*, by William W. Freehling. Copyright ©1990 by William W. Freehling. Reprinted with the permission of the Oxford University Press.

preacher necessarily intended. Finney's was the gospel that disinterested benevolence should declare holy war on interested selfishness.

Disinterested benevolence. That concept fired Finney's preaching and his reform empire. The revivalist armed with those "mere" words was no wild-eyed screamer. He was a cool ex-lawyer, who presented hell's horror with deathly quiet. He would stand still under the tent, before multitudes from the prairies. He would quietly portray a selfish people defying their selfless Lord. Come to Christ, Finney would almost whisper, and rise up from personal selfishness. Here a slowly rising finger would break the spellbinder's motionlessness. Ascend to the anxious seat, demanded Finney. Then crusade benevolently for a disinterested world.

Cleansed converts streaming from Finney's tents generally matched the revivalist's unprovoking manner. For every Finneyite who demanded antislavery, thousands worked for less unsettling causes—for starting Sunday schools or for spreading Bibles, for curbing drunkards or for colonizing free blacks, for eating graham crackers or for establishing manual labor schools. Finney himself wished converts who marched against slavery would trod more softly.

Attacking Slavery

But Finney could not control his zealots. Among millions who would cleanse Christ's democracy, a few souls attacked the most apparent sin against republicanism. The leading Finneyite assaulter was Theodore Dwight Weld, who in the mid-1830s briefly vied with William Lloyd Garrison for the title of Mr. Abolitionist.

Garrison's agitations were rooted in old New England in general and Boston in particular. Theodore Dwight Weld, though son of a New England preacher, pushed the movement where Finney was most effective, across midwestern prairies where Yankees were migrating. Weld followed the typical Finneyite migration. After conversion under the master, he joined Finney's so-called Holy Band, worked the western New York frontier's so-called Burned Over District, fought for manual labor schools, and sometimes raised his sweet voice for nothing more controversial than mnemonics (memory improvement).

In 1833, Weld departed from holy conservatism. The new abolitionist's wild hair, sprouting in every direction as if the mane of a porcupine, epitomized the unruly West. Weld consolidated his reputation as wild man by marrying the abolitionizing feminist, South Carolina's Angelina Grimké.

Weld condemned America as democracy's laggart. England, in 1833, had abolished slavery in the British West Indies. Could America do less? Charles Stuart, Weld's friend in the Holy Band and an English reformer come to unreformed prairies, asked the question especially effectively. Weld's answer, his midwestern antislavery lectures, spread antislavery past London, past Boston, towards becoming even more of a trans-Atlantic crusade.

Spiritual conquests need materialistic ammunition. Weld and Garrison, like Kentucky's James Birney, drew on the Tappan fortune. Benjamin and Louis Tappan's previous philanthropies had fostered little more radical than searching streets for prostitutes to reform. Under Weld's influence, the brothers used part of their dry-goods fortune to help form and finance the American Antislavery Society in 1833. By 1835, the swiftly growing society possessed hundreds of local branches and tens of thousands of followers. The question was now, very suddenly, whether a fringe American antislavery movement could convert the American mainstream, North and, yes, South too.

Controversial Mailings

Conversionists aimed first at the South. The newest Finneyite plea took the form not of quiet lawyer touring unsettled provinces. Rather, silent mailings descended on slaveowners. On July 29, 1835, when Charleston Postmaster Alfred Huger opened mail sacks, he uncovered antislavery appeals addressed to South Carolina citizens.

Abolitionists' notion of converting slaveholders was hardly zany in the context of the early 1830s. No intransigent slaveholding class, determined to keep slavery forever, had developed beyond South Carolina. Instead, Maryland

and Virginia legislative debates had revealed slaveholders wistfully hopeful about diffusing blacks away. Perhaps peaceable persuasion might fortify the tremulous.

Fearing that result and more, many South Carolinians demanded repression of persuasive, alias incendiary, pamphlets. Postmaster Alfred Huger termed abolitionists' appeal to white consciences a call for black revolution. Delivering such mail, Huger noted, would strew antislavery around Charleston's houses, where blacks could see it. The postmaster locked up the insurrectionary sheets until President Jackson could send instructions.

Charlestonians would not wait. Within 24 hours, "respectable" slaveholders led a mob into the post office. The gang confiscated the letters, then used the mail to fuel a public bonfire. This time, Southerners copied South Carolina. During the long hot summer of 1835, several mobs cleansed post offices.

As for the slaveholding President responsible for delivery of mails, his instructions to Postmaster General Amos Kendall revealed the despot struggling with democracy. Andrew Jackson neither demanded that ideas circulate nor insisted on censorship. The President instead told the Postmaster General to lock up suspicious-looking letters, unless and until recipients demanded delivery. Before dispatching mail, the local postmaster should take demanders' "names down, and have them exposed thru the Publick journals as subscribers to this wicked plan of exciting the negroes to insurrection and to massacre." All "moral and good" Southerners would ostracize the fiends. Few who had asked for their mail would be "so hardened in villainry as to withstand the frowns of all good men."

Jackson here expressed a classic southern mixture of consent and coercion. Just as slaveholders called coercive slavery legitimate in part because [slaves] allegedly consented to be controlled, so Jackson would coercively censor only until some citizen dissented. Then, just as southern communal pressure and community vigilance, not state repression, customarily controlled dissenting citizens and overly harsh slaveholders, so neighbors' ostracism would deter those wishing incendiary mail. Jackson would thus edge public democracy towards coercion while still struggling to retain consent. It was all an unforgettable lesson on how this precariously poised world ideally remained in balance.

Postmaster General Amos Kendall, practical Kentuckian, knew that Southerners were not on ideal behavior. Vicious mobs were the alternative to government censorship. Jackson's instructions to Kendall thus were changed in Kendall's instructions to Huger to read that "circumstances of the case justified detention of the papers." In other words, Huger could censor without Jackson's machinery for ending censorship. Armed with Kendall's instructions. Huger and other southern postmasters cleansed the mail in the fall of 1835, unless mobs seized the task.

Abolitionists Become Scapegoats

Southerners hoped to spread censorship beyond the South. Meetings in southern communities and resolutions in southern legislatures urged Northerners to sanitize the North. Southerners called on northern states to outlaw antislavery appeals and to extradite fanatics to the South for trial.

Slaveholders deployed their usual excuse for such repression. Liberty to speak does not include license to cry fire in crowded theatres. Antislavery agitators would doubly set the social order afire. Slaves would rise in revolt. Slaveholders would erupt from the Union.

Abolitionists answered by denying intention or power to incite slaves. They sent letters to whites, not blacks. They sadly knew black noncitizens could not read. Slaveowners could keep alleged incendiary material away from slaves. Who was master down there?

Slaveowners answered that they meant to master a *Domestic* Institution. Some slaves were literate. Illiterate blacks could see provoking woodcut illustrations enclosed in supposedly peaceful propaganda. Such provocations undermined domesticity and delayed reform. Slavery could be paternalistic only if slaveholders could control servants without frightful repression. Reformers could ease blacks out only if outside agitators ceased frightening southern communities.

Abolitionists here became scapegoats for every southern trouble. Southern apologists moved against slavery too slowly? That was Yankee fanatics' fault. Domestic patriarchs whipped too often? Outsider meddlers were responsible. The upshot of this argument was that Southerners could never end a moral miasma unless Northerners stopped consolidating slavery's most immoral tendencies.

If all that sounded like hypocrisy, the self-serving cant demonstrated something more important: souls needing soothing. . . . To the old notion that a sin could be morally abolished only tomorrow was added the new notion that outside meddlers only further delayed insiders' actions.

A less convoluted defensive postulate would have declared the institution holy and forever to be perpetuated. South Carolinians proclaimed for holy perpetuation in the 1830s and before. That was not the customary southern proclamation elsewhere until the 1850s. Southerners who would exploit slaves while yearning to diffuse them away could only deploy an awkward defensiveness. The awkwardness indicated that more than fear of slave insurrection impelled demands that antislavery attack cease.

A Fear of White Dissent

Slaveholders admitted they feared white no less than black dissent. The "great and terrible danger" of insurrection, South Carolina's [state legislator] Arthur P. Hayne explained to Andrew Jackson, has little to do with white life and death, much to do with white morale and commitment. Southern whites outnumbered blacks two to one. Life was more in danger on New York and Philadelphia streets. But "a restless feeling" pervaded "the South, and not without just cause, in relation to the Question of Property at the South, and unless this feeling be put at rest, who would desire to live in such a community?"

Southerners would desert a slaveholder community, continued Hayne, because black insurrection would remind white democrats that republican consent was the holy conception of the century. The idea of abstract liberty, once agitated in the North and mailed to the South, would turn some slaves' heads, trouble some slaveholders' consciences, inspire liberty-loving nonslaveholders North and South to turn against liberty's curse. Only "if the Non-Slave-holding States . . . will come forward patriotically, generously, and fairly and unite with the South to prevent Insurrection and to organize a moral power in favour of the South—*then and only then will the South be safe.*"

In early 1836, Professor Henry Nott of Thomas Cooper's South Carolina College explained why northern moral power might overwhelm southern moral power. "Europe is against us, & the North is against us," Nott wrote privately to his representative in Congress, James Hammond. "How do we stand at home? Every town & village is full of northern people, many of whom are feebly with us & many in secret decidedly against us." In "many" of the rural districts too, "the great body of the poor people . . . would on the ground of republicanism as well as religion either be inefficient friends or decided opponents."

"Incendiary publication," continued Henry Nott, would escalate anxiety by encouraging slaves "to escape" and slaveholders to fear "open rebellion and secret poison." In this atmosphere, any slave revolt would be the beginning of the end. "Remember the serious discussions in the Virginia Legislature after the petty affair of Northampton [Nat Turner's failed 1831 slave rebellion]," concluded Professor Nott, and "think what would have been the effect had there been a revolution more extensive, well concerted & bloody at its outset."

Important molders of southern opinion publicly echoed Professor Nott's private opinion that free and open debate would contaminate whites' viewpoints. Duff Green's *United States Telegraph*, published in Washington, D.C., was dedicated to John C. Calhoun's interests. Duff Green's messages in the fall of 1835 reiterated conceptions Calhoun and other Carolinians had advanced since nullification times. The unsteady Upper South, ran the main theme, wished and believed that blacks would someday diffuse elsewhere. Those who speculated about moving blacks out would not stand firm for keeping slaves forever.

Duff Green scoffed at the notion "that the South sleeps on a volcano—that we are afraid to go to bed at night."

Green instead feared "the gradual operation of public opinion among ourselves." "Insidious and dangerous invaders" come "in the guise of friendship," seeking "to persuade us that slavery is a sin, a curse, an evil." Green's "greatest cause of apprehension" was that the "morbid sensitivity of our own people" will "make them the voluntary instrument of their own ruin." Green wished to outlaw all talk, North and South, proclaiming slavery an evil.

Northern Anti-Abolitionism

Northerners, although too democratic to outlaw talk, reassured Southerners that debate could lead nowhere. In the summer of 1835, public meetings in New York, Philadelphia, Boston, and several smaller cities condemned so-called fanatics as "nigger-lovers" and worse. Freedom for "inferior" blacks, so most Northerners conceived, was not worth a smashed white republic or a deranged national economy.

These sentiments ushered in three decades of northern anti-abolitionism. Northern membership in antislavery societies peaked at around 200,000 in 1840, a figure swollen with females who could not vote, in a year when almost nine times that many Yankee males voted in the presidential election. Abolitionists agitating in the North often received a non-lynching version of a southern reception—rotten tomatoes aimed at the face, red pepper thrust under the nose, violent epithets drowning out the fanatic's voice. Once, in the notorious case of Elijah P. Lovejoy's murder in Illinois in 1837, these distractions escalated into a southern-style lynching.

Precisely this widespread northern opposition to antislavery, deeply rooted in Yankee anxiety about blacks, Union, and commerce, makes explaining the road to disunion difficult. If the North was never committed to abolitionism, why should the South have felt compelled to secede? Troubled by that question, an important group of historians, the so-called Revisionists of the 1930s, revised away slavery as a cause of Civil War. These scholars urged that irresponsible agitators must have used delusive propaganda to whip up a needless combat.

Those 1835 northern meetings, like Yankees' assault on the Slavepower's three-fifths extra power in Missouri Controversy times,[1] supply a better explanation of Northerners' anti-southernism. While most Yankees were not fanatical about liberty for blacks, they demanded egalitarian republicanism for whites. According to prevailing opinions "on the subject of liberty and freedom," explained a Bostonian, and "according to the letter of the Constitution, the States *cannot* prevent by legislation the printing and distribution of pamphlets." Southerners must consider it "enough that the great body of the people in this quarter" condemn "any interference with the internal policy of the slaveholding states." Southerners must not "require of us a course of conduct which would strike at the root of everything we have been taught to consider sacred."

Sacred. That word lay behind Charles Grandison Finney's preaching and Theodore Dwight Weld's crusade. But few Yankees thought blacks' right to liberty so sacred as to chase a holy war with righteous Southerners. Whites' democratic rights, on the other hand, were as precious as the sacrament. The three-fifths clause already provoked northern egalitarian republicans. If Southerners now piled on insistence that Northerners jail dissenters, abolitionists might become more popular.

South Carolina Extremists

Fortunately for the Union, South Carolina extremists alone insisted that the North become a closed society. The northern majority, James Henry Hammond of South Carolina wrote the editor of the *New York Evening Star* on August 19, 1835, must not allow abolitionists "an asylum from which to hurl their murderous missiles." Fanatics "can be silenced in but one way—*Terror—death*." Northern states "must pass laws," dispatching incendiaries "on demand to those whose laws and whose rights they have violated." Unless Northerners extradited incendiaries down South for trial, "we shall dissolve the Union, and *seek by war* the redress denied us."

There echoed Carolina's advanced consciousness. There

1. Many Northerners objected to the Constitution's clause counting three-fifths of southern states' slave population in apportioning congressional seats and electoral college votes.

screeched a zealot out of touch with the southern mainstream. Few Southerners demanded abolitionists' scalps or
else. The southern mainstream plea for repressive northern
action came down to a request. The irritated northern mainstream was at liberty to reject southern calls to turn the
North into a Slavepower jail.

With northern extremists free to agitate, the southern
mainstream had to learn to live with a permanent antislavery
crusade. The learning was distressing and never complete.
Southern edginess about new Yankee extremists swiftly altered the region's political discourse, particularly in Middle
and Deep Souths.

The omnipresent new southern issue in 1835 was northern antislavery agitation. The new tone of stridency, omnipresent only in South Carolina previously, yielded period-
ically ugly debates over which southern politician was most
"soft on slavery" and secretly anxious to collaborate with antislavery Northerners.

Social Tensions Within Southern Plantation Society

Ronald Takaki

Responding to the arguments of slavery opponents, southern slave owners in the antebellum era defended slavery as humane and asserted that slaves were happy in their condition. Historian Ronald Takaki paints a darker and more complex picture in his following description of southern plantation society. He contends that the stereotype of slaves being childish, lazy, and satisfied with their lot does not accurately describe most slaves, many of whom ran away or engaged in acts of defiance. In addition, many white Southerners, both slaveholders and non-slaveholders, had moral misgivings about slavery and harbored fears of violent insurrection. Takaki is a professor of history and ethnic studies at the University of California at Berkeley.

In the South, four million blacks were slaves, representing 35 percent of the total population in 1860. . . . They constituted the essential labor force in southern agriculture for tobacco, hemp, rice, sugar, and especially cotton cultivation. The majority of the slaves worked on plantations, agricultural production units with more than twenty slaves.

Work Routines

Work on the plantations, according to historian Kenneth Stampp, began early in the morning when a horn awakened the slaves an hour before daylight. "All work-hands are [then] required to rise and prepare their cooking, etc. for the day," a plantation manual stated. "The second horn is blown

Excerpted from *A Different Mirror: A History of Multicultural America*, by Ronald Takaki. Copyright ©1993 by Ronald Takaki. Reprinted with the permission of Little, Brown and Company.

just at good day-light, when it is the duty of the driver to visit every house and see that all have left for the field." Work was highly regimented. A glimpse of plantation labor was captured by a traveler in Mississippi:

> First came, led by an old driver carrying a whip, forty of the largest and strongest women I ever saw together; they were all in a simple uniform dress of a bluish check stuff, the skirts reaching little below the knee; their legs and feet were bare; they carried themselves loftily, each having a hoe over the shoulder, and walking with a free, powerful swing, like *chasseurs* [hunters] on the march. Behind came the cavalry, thirty strong, mostly men, but a few of them women, two of whom rode astride on the plow mules. A lean and vigilant white overseer, on a brisk pony, brought up the rear.

A slave described the routine of a workday: "The hands are required to be in the cotton field as soon as it is light in the morning, and, with the exception of ten or fifteen minutes, which is given to them at noon to swallow their allowance of cold bacon, they are not permitted to be a moment idle until it is too dark to see, and when the moon is full, they often times labor till the middle of the night." After they left the fields, they had more work to do. "Each one must attend to his respective chores. One feeds the mules, another the swine—another cuts the wood, and so forth; besides the packing [of cotton] is all done by candle light. Finally, at a late hour, they reach the quarters, sleepy and overcome with the long day's toil."

To manage this enslaved labor force, masters used various methods of discipline and control. They sometimes used kindness. "Now I contend that the surest and best method of managing negroes, is to love them," a Georgia planter explained. "We know . . . that if we love our horse, we will treat him well, and if we treat him well, he will become gentle, docile and obedient . . . and if this treatment has this effect upon all the animal creation . . . why will it not have the same effect upon slaves?" But masters also believed that strict discipline was essential and that power had to be based on fear. South Carolina's Senator James Hammond, owner of more than three hundred slaves, fully understood the need for the absolute submission of a slave to his master: "We have to rely more and more on the power of fear. We are determined to continue masters, and to do so we have to draw the reign [*sic*] tighter and tighter day by day to be assured that we hold them in complete check." Employing psychological reins, masters tried to brainwash their slaves into believing they were racially inferior and racially suited for bondage. Kept illiterate and ignorant, they were told they were incapable of caring for themselves.

Were Slaves Happy?

To many white southerners, slaves were childlike, irresponsible, lazy, affectionate, and happy. Altogether, these alleged qualities represented a type of personality—the Sambo.

"Slaves never become men or women," a traveler in the South commented. Slavemasters frequently referred to adult blacks as "grown up children," or "boys" and "girls." Regarding themselves as guardians, they claimed their slaves had to be "governed as children." Unable to plan for their future, slaves would not "lay up in summer for the wants of winter" and "accumulate in youth for the exigencies of age."

Slavemasters repeatedly complained about the problem of laziness, saying their black laborers had to be supervised or they would not work. If slaves were freed, they would become "an insufferable burden to society." Slavemasters insisted that blacks had to be kept in slavery; otherwise they would surely become "indolent lazy thievish drunken," working only when they could not steal.

But slavemasters also cherished the bonds of affection they claimed existed between themselves and their childlike slaves. In his *Black Diamonds Gathered in the Darkey Homes of the South*, Edward Pollard exclaimed: "I love to study his affectionate heart; I love to mark that peculiarity in him, which beneath all his buffoonery exhibits him as a creature of the tenderest sensibilities, mingling his joys and his sorrows with those of his master's home." Slaveholders described their slaves as the happiest people in the world, working little and spending the rest of their time "singing, dancing, laughing, chattering, and bringing up pigs and chickens." "At present we have in South Carolina," one slaveholder boasted, "two hundred and fifty thousand civilized and peaceable slaves, happy and contented. . . ." In their private journals, masters recorded moments of closeness with their slaves. One of them scribbled into his diary on January 1, 1859: "The hands as usual came in to greet the New Year with their good wishes—the scene is well calculated to excite sympathies; notwithstanding bondage, affections find roots in the heart of the slave for the master."

But the boast betrayed nervousness. The image of the slave as Sambo had special significance: the whole Western world was ideologically opposed to southern slavery, and therefore masters felt compelled to justify their peculiar institution as a "positive good." If they could show that their slaves were happy and satisfied with their condition, then perhaps they could defend themselves against their moral critics. They insisted that "ours is a patriarchal institution now, founded in pity and protection on the one side, and dependence and gratitude on the other."

White Nonslaveholders

The planter class also had to persuade the white nonslaveholders of the South that slavery was right. In 1860, only 5.5 percent of the southern white population were slaveholders. In fact, the vast majority of whites had no vested economic interest in slavery. One of them, an Alabama farmer, was asked by a northern visitor what he thought about emancipating the slaves, and he replied:

> Well, I'll tell you what I think on it; I'd like it if we could get rid on 'em to youst. I wouldn't like to hev 'em freed, if they was gwine to hang 'round. They ought to get some country and put 'em war they could be by themselves. It wouldn't do no good to free 'em, and let 'em hang 'round, because they is so monstrous lazy; if they hadn't got nobody to take keer on 'em, you see they wouldn't do nothin' but juss nat'rally laze 'round, and steal, and pilfer, and no man couldn't live, you see, war they was—if they was free, no man couldn't live—and this ere's the other. Now suppose they was free,

you see they'd all think themselves just as good as we, of course they would, if they was free. Now, just suppose you had a family of children, how would you like to hev a niggar steppin' up to your darter? Of course you wouldn't, and that's the reason I wouldn't like to hev 'em free; but I tell you, I don't think it's right to hev 'em slaves so; that's the fac—taant right to keep 'em as they is.

Thus, there were moral misgivings among white southerners themselves. "We must satisfy them that slavery is of itself right," the defenders of the institution declared, "that it is not a sin against God." Time and again they insisted that the slavemaster was "enlightened," "humane," and "Christian," and that the slave was "submissive," "docile," "happy," "conscious of his own inferiority and proud of being owned & governed by a superior."

Doubts About Slavery

Many masters had doubts about the morality of the peculiar institution. "Slavery," admitted the governor of Mississippi, "is an evil at best." Similarly, a white Virginian anxiously confessed: "This, sir, is a Christian community. Southerners read in their Bibles, 'Do unto all men as you would have them do unto you'; and this golden rule and slavery are hard to reconcile." One slaveholder jotted in his diary: "Oh what trouble,—running sore, constant pressing weight, perpetual wearing, dripping, is this patriarchal institution! What miserable folly for men to cling to it as something heaven-descended. And here we and our children after us must groan under the burden—our hands tied from freeing ourselves." Few slaveholders could "openly and honestly look the thing [slavery] in the face," a European traveler in the South observed. "They wind and turn about in all sorts of ways, and make use of every argument . . . to convince me that the slaves are the happiest people in the world."

Fear of Rebellion

While claims that slaves were Sambos helped to comfort anguished consciences, they also offered the masters psychological assurances that their slaves were under control.

Surely happy slaves would not come at night and slit the throats of their masters. In reality, slaveholders were terrified by the specter of slave rebellion. Aware of the bloody slave revolts in Santo Domingo in the 1790s, they were warned by an American official in Haiti: "Negroes only cease to be *children* when they degenerate into *savages.*" After the brutal suppression of the 1822 Denmark Vesey slave conspiracy in Charleston, a worried South Carolina slaveholder warned that blacks were "barbarians who would, IF THEY COULD, become the DESTROYERS of our race."

Holding what Thomas Jefferson had called the "wolf by the ears," masters lived in constant dread of slave insurrection. Southern newspapers frequently reported news of slave unrest and "evidences of a very unsettled state of mind among the servile population." Married to a Georgia planter, Frances A. Kemble reported that slaves were "a threatening source of constant insecurity" and that "every southern *woman*" lived in terror of her slaves. A Louisiana slaveholder recalled tense times "when there was not a single planter who had a calm night's rest," and when every master went to bed with a gun at his side.

Here was a society almost hysterically afraid of a black "giddy multitude." The master-slave relationship was dynamic, contradictory, and above all uncertain. Sambo existed and did not exist. What was the reality? How did the slaves themselves view their own behavior?

There were slaves who appeared to be Sambos. Asked about whether he desired freedom, a slave replied to a curious visitor: "No, massa, me no want to be free, have good massa, take care of me when I sick, never 'buse nigger; no, me no want to be free." In a letter to his master who was away on a trip, a slave ended his report on plantation operations: "The respects of your affec. Svt. unto D[eath] in hopes ever to merit your esteem. Your most dutiful servant. Harford."

Masks of Docility

But slaves who behaved like Sambos might not have actually been Sambos: they might have been playing the role of loyal and congenial slaves in order to get favors or to survive, while keeping their inner selves hidden. Masters themselves sometimes had difficulty determining a slave's true personality. "So deceitful is the Negro," a master explained, "that as far as my own experience extends I could never in a single instance decipher his character. . . . We planters could never get at the truth." For many slaves, illusion protected them from their masters. "The only weapon of self defence that I could use successfully, was that of deception," explained fugitive slave Henry Bibb. Another former slave explained that one had to "know the *heart* of the poor slave—learn his secret thoughts—thoughts he dare not utter in the hearing of the white man."

Indeed, many slaves wore masks of docility and deference in order to shroud subversive plans. Every year thousands of slaves became fugitives, making their way north to freedom, and many of these runaways had seemed passive and cheerful before they escaped. . . .

After his flight north, fugitive J.W. Loguen received a letter from his former owner. "You know that we reared you as we reared our own children," wrote Mrs. Sarah Logue; "that you was never abused, and that shortly before you ran away, when your master asked you if you would like to be sold, you said you would not leave him to go with any body." In his reply, Loguen caustically remarked: "Woman, did you raise your *own children* for the market? Did you raise them for the whipping-post?" The ex-slave boldly proclaimed his love for liberty: "Wretched woman! Be it known to you that I value my freedom . . . more, indeed, than my own life; more than all the lives of all the slaveholders and tyrants under heaven."

Sometimes a slave would play the role of Sambo and then strike directly at his tyrant. Slavemaster William Pearce told one of his erring slaves that he would be whipped after supper. When the slave was called out, he approached Pearce submissively. As soon as he was within striking distance, the slave pulled out a concealed ax and split his master's head. Nat Turner, according to historian Stampp, was "apparently as humble and docile as a slave was expected to be." In Virginia on August 22, 1831, he led seventy fellow slaves in a violent insurrection that lasted two days and left nearly sixty whites dead. After his arrest, Turner made a statement to the authorities. His master, he acknowledged, was "kind": "in fact, I had no cause to complain of his treatment to me." But Turner had had a religious experience: "I had a vision—and I saw white spirits and black spirits engaged in battle . . . and blood flowed in streams. . . ." A voice told him to wait for a sign from heaven: "And on the appearance of the sign, (the eclipse of the sun last February) I should arise and prepare myself, and slay my enemies with their own weapons." Turner carried out his mission, and a white Virginian nervously observed: "It will long be remembered in the annals of our country, and many a mother as she presses her infant darling to her bosom, will shudder at the recollection of Nat Turner." The slave rebel's action was a frightening revelation to white southerners: smiling and holding his hat in hand, Sambo could be planning their destruction.

The reality for many slaves may have been even more complex and subtle than a duality of roles. Some Sambo-like behavior may have been not so much a veil to hide inner emotions of rage and discontent as a means of expressing them. Lying, stealing, laziness, immaturity, and ignorance all contained within them an aggressive quality: they constituted, in effect, resistance to efficiency, discipline, work, and productivity.

Fugitive Slaves Exacerbate the Sectional Crisis over Slavery

James Oakes

Thousands of slaves over the course of the antebellum era ran away and became fugitives; many successfully escaped to the North. In the following excerpt from his book *Slavery and Freedom: An Interpretation of the Old South*, historian James Oakes states that these individual acts of slave resistance had significant political repercussions for the South. Oakes argues that while southern slaveholders were determined to prevent the federal government from enacting legislation restricting slavery, they were paradoxically reliant on the same federal government in recapturing fugitive slaves. However, federal laws such as the 1850 Fugitive Slave Act not only paved the way for federal government's increasing involvement in the slavery issue, but also forced white Northerners who were apathetic toward abolitionism to confront the issue of slavery. Oakes also examines how stories of escape provided a powerful theme for antislavery literature. Works such as Harriet Beecher Stowe's novel *Uncle Tom's Cabin*, Theodore Dwight Weld's antislavery tract *American Slavery as It Is*, and numerous fugitive-slave autobiographical narratives helped to make the act of running away become a national political controversy. Oakes is a professor of history at Northwestern University at Evanston, Illinois, and author of several books on the South and slavery.

By the 1850's the expansion of slavery once again raised the ever-present specter of the federal government's power to

Excerpted from *Slavery and Freedom: An Interpretation of the Old South*, by James Oakes. Copyright ©1990 by James Oakes. Reprinted with the permission of Alfred A. Knopf, Inc.

legislate on the South's "peculiar" institution. The Compromise of 1850 had scarcely settled the question of how the spoils of the war with Mexico were to be divided when the struggle over Kansas and Nebraska once again brought slavery expansion into the heart of national politics. By then, however, a second issue—slave resistance—had burst its sectional confines, seriously undermining the slaveholders' capacity to control its political consequences.

The problem for slaveholders was that they themselves had always relied on the federal government to sustain their power. In 1787 they had fought hard and with great success for constitutional provisions recognizing and protecting slavery in a variety of different ways. Since three out of five slaves were counted for purposes of representation, free Southerners held extra seats in Congress, which they repeatedly used to protect the slaveholders' interests. For seventy-five years slaveholders dominated the Presidency. Holding the fugitive-slave clause paramount, the Supreme Court consistently upheld the masters' interests by striking down the personal-liberty laws [statutes designed to prevent slave owners from reclaiming escaped slaves] of one northern state after another. From the American Revolution through the outbreak of the Civil War, the slaveholders successfully pressed their case in the legislative, executive, and judicial branches of the federal government.

But in their reliance on the power of the federal government the slaveholders laid the groundwork for their eventual destruction. As the legal and political consequences of slave resistance extended beyond the borders of the southern states, the slaveholders found themselves in a political universe whose assumptions were antithetical to their own. If slave resistance created excruciating problems within the South, in Washington, D.C., the master class eventually lost all control of its subversive consequences.

Fugitive Slaves

Consider the problem of fugitive slaves. As resistance went, running away was a modest but consequential act. Its political significance could be direct—as in the fugitive-slave crisis of the 1850's—or indirect, as when abolitionists used escapes for propaganda purposes. And in some contexts, as we shall see, the political significance of running away could reach revolutionary proportions. In each of these ways, running away contributed to the crisis that divided the United States by forcing the federal government to take up an issue that the slaveholders wanted left out of national politics altogether. Whatever it was that frightened southern jurists about the state's recognition of the slave's legal personality paled by comparison with the potential consequences of the federal government's increasing involvement in the slavery issue. To the extent that runaway slaves compelled such involvement, slave resistance helped destroy the political power of the master class.

At the heart of the fugitive-slave controversy rested a "conflict of laws" that could have political significance only if slaves actually ran away. Northern law presumed that black people, however "inferior" and however much discriminated against, possessed the basic rights of life, liberty, and property. Southern law presumed the opposite. To protect free blacks from kidnapping by fugitive-slave catchers, northern states established legal procedures for determining whether or not a slaveholder's claim of ownership was valid. These "personal-liberty laws" necessarily extended the presumption of freedom to fugitive slaves, flatly contradicting southern law. They thereby created a potential for sectional conflict every time a slave set foot on northern soil. Nor could such conflicts be confined to relations between individual states, for the United States Constitution and the Fugitive Slave Act of 1793 together guaranteed slaveholders the right of "recaption."

So long as no slave ever set foot in a free state, this conflict of laws was a matter of mere theoretical interest. The personal-liberty laws posed no direct threat to slavery, for while they may have discouraged some masters from claiming their runaways, the laws never prevented a single fugitive slave from being returned to the South once a master's claim was validated. By the 1850's runaways had become a major source of sectional antagonism solely because of the political conflict they both exposed and provoked. Far more directly than abolitionist propaganda, fugitive slaves forced both the North and South into ever-hardening defenses of their conflicting social structures.

The Somerset Principle

The North's extension of the Somerset principle posed a more direct threat to slavery than did the legal protection of fugitives. As originally enunciated in England by [British Chief Justice] Lord Mansfield in 1772, the Somerset principle extended to slaves certain protections against arbitrary seizure by masters. As interpreted by many contemporaries, the Somerset principle held that in the absence of positive laws establishing slavery, all persons standing on English— and perhaps American—soil were presumed to be free. Massachusetts jurists invoked this interpretation of the principle a few years after it was declared, and it was subsequently adopted by other northern states as sectional tensions increased. The Somerset principle held out the prospect of freedom to anyone who set foot in the North, including slaves who were merely in transit with their owners. By contrast, the personal-liberty laws simply established procedures regulating the capture of fugitive slaves, but they could do little more than delay the eventual return of runaways. Like the personal-liberty laws, however, the Somerset principle was more significant for its political consequences than for the number of slaves it could possibly free. When Dred and Harriet Scott rested their famed lawsuit on the claim that they had once resided on free soil with their master, the political threat proved far more consequential than the prospect of two slaves being emancipated.

Dred Scott's case [decided by the Supreme Court in 1857] was only one of a climactic series of incidents that politicized the issue of slavery to the point where sectional animosities gave way to civil war. In many of those cases the precipitating action was taken by slaves who claimed their freedom, often without militant intentions. Margaret Morgan simply assumed her freedom to move from Maryland to York County, Pennsylvania. This put her putative owners in a precarious legal position after they recaptured the slave and returned her to the South. For in so doing they violated Pennsylvania laws against kidnapping and found themselves tied up in a lawsuit that went all the way to the Supreme Court. And while the captors won their case in *Prigg v. Pennsylvania*, the precedent they established subsequently proved as useful to abolitionists as to slaveholders. For although Chief Justice Joseph Story's "opinion of the court" recognized Congress's right to legislate on the subject of slavery in free states, it also exempted states from having to enforce the Fugitive Slave Law of 1793. Thanks to Margaret Morgan's successful lawsuit, a half-dozen northern legislatures passed statutes prohibiting state officials from enforcing the fugitive slave clause of the U.S. Constitution. By contrast, George Latimer ran away claiming a former master had promised him freedom, but with full knowledge that his claim was in dispute. Regardless of his motives, however, the controversy generated by Latimer's escape led directly to the passage of the Massachusetts personal-liberty law of 1843.

Abolitionist Propaganda

The abolitionists were quick to use these and other acts of slave resistance to build their case against slavery. Theodore Dwight Weld's famous antislavery tract *American Slavery as It Is* could hardly have been written had the slaves been a compliant and tractable work force. Weld's polemical effect was achieved by his documentary style: a deceptively straightforward litany of fugitive-slave advertisements, many of them gruesome in their details of physical abuse and mutilation. Since slaveholders were not a peculiarly barbaric people, it is safe to assume that the brutality Weld exposed was less a function of sadistic masters than of resisting slaves. Nor was Weld's rhetorical strategy diminished by arguments that his evidence was selective. The point is that he could never have made his selections had there been no fugitive slaves with their identifying scars.

Propagandists used slave resistance in more direct ways to make their political points. One need not have been an abolitionist to sympathize with Harriet Beecher Stowe's Eliza [a

character in Stowe's novel *Uncle Tom's Cabin*] as she crossed
the perilously icy waters of the Ohio River in a desperate effort to keep her child from being sold away. Yet how many
readers who held their breath until Eliza's escape was secure
could temper their sympathies with the knowledge that in
crossing that river Eliza was committing a crime for which
she could legally be killed, or that those who assisted the
slave mother in her effort to save her child were liable to federal prosecution under the terms of the Fugitive Slave Act of
1850? Stowe's genius lay precisely in her ability to evoke a
sympathetic response to criminal acts of resistance.

Stowe's point was made all the more effective by the fact
that Eliza was clearly not a habitually rebellious slave, that
she was motivated by no overpowering desire for freedom
nor by any festering hatred of her master. What Stowe
demonstrated, instead, was that the master-slave relationship inescapably pitted Eliza against her owner in spite of
the warm feelings each had for the other. Eliza's motives did
not change the fact that her behavior directly thwarted her
master's will, violated state and federal law, and still won the
sympathies of hundreds of thousands of northern readers.
Abraham Lincoln is said to have greeted Stowe as "the little
lady who made this big war," but he might just as easily have
blamed the Civil War on the author's sympathetic character,
the fugitive slave Eliza.

Slave Resistance and the Sectional Crisis

In such subtle but powerful ways, slave resistance redefined
the ideological battle lines in the sectional crisis. The racism
of white Northerners and their widespread animosity toward abolitionists are well established. But slaves who ran
away or sued for freedom did not compel Northerners to re-
pudiate their racism, to support abolition, or even to interfere in the southern slave system. Such cases did require
Northerners to decide whether they were willing to jeopardize their own liberties by reenslaving those who claimed
their freedom without observing the minimal rights of due
process. Many citizens who were perfectly prepared to defend the masters' right to own slaves were increasingly un-

prepared to let the slaveholders exercise their privileges as masters at the expense of northern liberties and safeguards.

Runaways themselves contributed immeasurably to the propaganda war throughout the decades that preceded secession. Fugitive-slave narratives are well known—and sometimes criticized—for their formulaic quality: the slave too often seethes under the weight of his or her oppression. Gradually, the slave's determination to be free becomes all-consuming. There are unsuccessful escapes, but recapture only strengthens the slave's determination. And finally, often unexpectedly, an opportunity arises, and the dramatic climax is reached. The slave escapes and, once secure, works tirelessly to advance the cause of freedom for all slaves—beginning with a published autobiography. Such narratives were indeed formulaic, which is precisely why they were so effective. By pressing the issue in the most categorical terms of slavery and freedom, runaways helped transform the simple act of running away into a politically explosive fugitive-slave controversy.

Slave resistance thus contributed to the ideological war that was forcing the slaveholders into ever more explicit defenses of their social order. The long period of "agitation" over the slavery issue, a New Orleans newspaper noted in late 1860, "has evolved the true principles on which the institution of slavery is based. It has convinced all Southern men of the moral right, the civil, social and political benefit of slavery."

Slavery and Sectional Tensions in the 1850s

John Hope Franklin and Albert A. Moss Jr.

John Hope Franklin and Albert A. Moss Jr. in the following essay provide an overview of the 1850s, a decade they contend was marked by one political crisis after another. These crises stemmed from one issue—slavery—which defied all attempts at political or judicial resolution. In the Compromise of 1850, Congress tried to determine the slave or free status of new territories acquired in the 1846–1848 Mexican War, but its attempt to replicate the success of the 1820 Missouri Compromise in placating both proslavery and antislavery forces fell apart within a few years. Supreme Court Chief Justice Roger B. Taney's attempt at a final pronouncement on slavery in the territories in the 1857 *Dred Scott* case worsened political strife over the issue. John Brown's abortive bid in 1859 to lead a slave insurrection in Harpers Ferry, Virginia, shocked and worried many slave owners in the South. The election of Republican party candidate Abraham Lincoln in 1860—who won the presidency with no southern support and on a platform opposing slavery's expansion in the territories—was, Franklin and Moss write, the last step that led South Carolina and other southern states to attempt secession from the Union. Franklin, a celebrated black historian, has taught at Duke University and the University of Chicago. Moss is a professor of history at the University of Maryland at College Park.

Perhaps no decade in the history of the United States has been so filled with tense and crucial moments as the ten years leading to the Civil War, and closely connected with most of these crises was the problem of slavery. The period was ushered in by the controversy over slavery in the newly acquired territory in the Southwest. With the discovery of gold in California in 1848 and with the rapid peopling of many areas in the Mexican cession, a policy had to be decided upon. Some leaders held that the new territory should be divided into slave and free sections as in the Missouri Compromise. The abolitionists, of course, and many others in the North, wanted a total exclusion of slavery from the territories, a point of view expressed in the Wilmot Proviso. Still others were of the opinion that the question should be decided by the people who lived in the new territories, an approach to the problem which was popularized by Stephen A. Douglas. Finally, there were those who insisted that slavery could not be legally excluded anywhere, a view vigorously advanced by John C. Calhoun. The question of fugitive slaves, moreover, was very much alive. Southern owners had never had too much luck in recovering them. In 1842, in the case of *Prigg v. Pennsylvania*, the Supreme Court ruled that state officials were not required to assist in the return of fugitives, and the decision did much to render ineffective all efforts to recover slaves.

The Compromise of 1850

In 1850 these questions were thoroughly aired in Congress, and a desperate effort was made to work out a solution that would diminish intersectional strife. After considerable debate by [Henry] Clay, Calhoun, Douglas, [William] Seward, and [Salmon P.] Chase, an agreement was reached which provided that (1) California should enter the Union as a free state; (2) the other territories would be organized without mention of slavery; (3) Texas should cede certain lands to New Mexico and be compensated; (4) slaveholders would be better protected by a stringent fugitive slave law; and (5) there should be no slave trade in the District of Columbia. The Compromise of 1850 was by no means satisfactory to all, and Georgia, Mississippi, Alabama, and South Carolina seriously considered secession. Southerners said they would remain in the Union only as long as there was strict adherence to the compromise, especially in enforcing the fugitive slave act.

It soon became clear that neither section was seriously reconciled to the Compromise of 1850 as a final settlement of the slavery question. Militant abolitionists were still determined to assist runaways, and new federal legislation could not deter them. In 1851 they went so far as to rescue a slave, Shadrach, from a United States marshal in Boston who was preparing to return him to his owner. It was the zeal of the slaveholders that especially irritated the abolitionists. With the new law against fugitives, slaveholders put on intensive hunts, determined to drive back into slavery even those fugitives who had lived free for years. For example, they seized Jerry McHenry, who had lived in Syracuse for several years and was regarded as a substantial citizen; but members of the Liberty party convening there were led by Gerrit Smith and William Seward to rescue McHenry and send him on his way. These are merely two examples of what came to be open defiance of the law on the part of militant abolitionists. Their attitude convinced the South that the North was not willing to abide by the Compromise of 1850.

The appearance of *Uncle Tom's Cabin* in 1852 increased the strain on intersectional relations. This novel by Harriet Beecher Stowe sold more than 300,000 copies in the first year of publication and was soon dramatized in theaters throughout the North. Its story of abject cruelty on the part of masters and overseers, its description of the privation and suffering of slaves, and its complete condemnation of Southern civilization won countless thousands over to abolition and left Southern leaders busy denying the truth of the novel. The damage had been done, however, and when Southerners counted their losses from this one blow, they found them to be staggering indeed.

Trends Toward Disunion

The sectional truce brought about by the Compromise of 1850 was at an end, but if it needed a legislative act to destroy it, the Kansas-Nebraska Act of 1854 was precisely the thing. Introduced into the Senate by Stephen A. Douglas of Illinois, the act provided that Kansas and Nebraska should be organized as territories and that the question of slavery should be decided by territorial legislatures. Whatever the motives of Douglas may have been, the passage of the act precipitated a desperate struggle between North and South for the control of Kansas. The Missouri Compromise had been in effect repealed, and those forces that mustered the greatest strength in Kansas could win it. In the ensuing years abolitionist and proslavery factions fought and bled for Kansas, and the land became a preliminary battleground of the Civil War. No longer was there much semblance of intersectional peace. Although the climate of Kansas would have prevented any extensive development of plantation slavery there, the principle was important to both sides, and they conducted themselves accordingly.

The Kansas-Nebraska Act persuaded many antislavery leaders that political action was necessary to combat the relentless drive of proslavery forces to extend slavery. Northern Whigs, Free Soilers, and Democrats who had fought the passage of the act came together, and out of their discussions arose the Republican party. This new political organization, unalterably antislavery in its point of view, profited by the mistake of earlier antislavery parties and evolved a program broad enough to attract voters who were indifferent to slavery. Southerners, meanwhile, sought to counteract this new party by demanding further extension of slavery and the reopening of the African slave trade.

The significance of these trends had hardly become apparent when the Supreme Court in 1857 handed down a decision in the case of *Scott v. Sanford* that had the effect of widening the breach between North and South. Dred Scott was a Missouri slave whose master had first taken him to live in free Illinois and subsequently to a fort in the northern part of the Louisiana Purchase, where slavery had been excluded by the Missouri Compromise. Upon his return to Missouri, Scott sued for his freedom on the ground that residence on free soil had liberated him. The majority of the Court held that Scott was not a citizen and therefore could not bring suit in the courts. Chief Justice Roger B. Taney, speaking for the Court, added that since the Missouri Compromise was unconstitutional, masters could take their slaves anywhere in the territories and retain title to them. The decision was a clear-cut victory for the South, and the North viewed it with genuine alarm. With the highest court in the land openly preaching the proslavery doctrine, there was little hope that anything short of a most drastic political or social revolution would bring an end to slavery. All abolitionists were not as optimistic as Frederick Douglass, but they hoped with him that "The Supreme Court . . . [was] not the only power in this world. We, the abolitionists and colored people, should meet this decision, unlooked for and monstrous as it appears, in a cheerful spirit. This very attempt to blot out forever the hopes of an enslaved people may be one necessary link in the chain of events preparatory to the complete overthrow of the whole slave system."

John Brown's Raid

Indeed, only two more links were needed to bring on the bitter war that gave freedom to the slaves: one was the raid of John Brown, and the other was a Republican victory at the polls in 1860. Brown had worked in the cause of freedom for many years. He had done his part to aid the antislavery forces in Kansas, and he had worked on the Underground Railroad [helping slaves to escape] out of Missouri. By 1859 he was anxious to strike a more significant blow for the freedom of slaves. He traveled through the North raising money and talking with white and black abolitionists. Finally, he laid his plans to attack slaveholders and liberate their slaves. On Sunday night, October 16, with a small band of less than fifty men he seized the federal arsenal at Harpers Ferry, Virginia, in the hope of securing sufficient ammunition to carry out a large-scale operation against the Virginia slaveholders. Immediately the countryside was alerted, and both federal and state governments dispatched troops which overwhelmed Brown and his men. Among those with Brown were several blacks, including Lewis Sheridan Leary, Dangerfield Newby, John Anthony Copeland, Shields Green, and Osborn Perry Anderson. Leary and Newby were killed; Copeland and Green were hanged; and Anderson escaped. The effect of this raid on the South was electrifying. It made slaveholders think that abolitionists would stop at nothing to wipe out slavery. No one felt secure because there were rumors of other insurrections to come and widespread complaints that slaves were insolent because they knew their day of liberation was near. The whole South was put on a semi-war footing, with troops drilling regularly as far south as Georgia and with increasing demands for arms and ammunition by the militia commanders of most states.

On December 2, 1859, John Brown was hanged, but not before he had dazzled the country by his words and his conduct after the trial. He told a reporter from the *New York Herald*, "I pity the poor in bondage that have none to help them; that is why I am here; not to gratify any personal animosity, revenge or vindictive spirit. It is my sympathy with the oppressed and wronged, that are as good as you and as precious in the sight of God. . . . You may dispose of me easily, but this question is still to be settled—the negro question—the end of that is not yet." Upon hearing his sentence he calmly said, "Now, if it is deemed necessary that I should forfeit my life for the furtherance of the ends of justice, and mingle my blood further with the blood of my children and with the blood of millions in this slave country whose rights are disregarded by wicked, cruel, and unjust enactments, I say, let it be done."

Some people said that Brown was a madman, but few who saw him and listened to him thought so. Governor [Henry A.] Wise of Virginia said, "They are themselves mistaken who take him to be a madman. . . . He is a man of clear head, of courage, of fortitude and simple ingenuousness." He terrified the South and captivated the North by his deed. Many had died fighting for freedom, but none had done it so heroically or at such a propitious moment. The crusade against slavery now had a martyr, and nothing wins followers to a cause like a martyr. Literally thousands of people who had been indifferent were now persuaded that slavery must be abolished. There can be no doubt that many voted for the Republican ticket in 1860 because of this conviction.

Lincoln's Election

When it became clear that the Republican candidate would stand on an antislavery platform, the South began once more to utter threats of secession. But with the nomination of Abraham Lincoln, instead of a pronounced abolitionist like Seward of New York or Chase of Ohio, it was the abolitionists who were worried. They were not sure how far Lincoln would go to put an end to slavery. And yet, as [historian] Dwight Dumond has pointed out, his words and deeds for twenty years had clearly been antislavery. He had said many times that slavery was hostile to the poor man. During his one term in Congress he had done what he could to keep the territories free, so that poor people could feel secure there. He had said that blacks should be protected in their right to the enjoyment of the fruits of their own labor, and he had vigorously denounced the Dred Scott decision. Nevertheless, . . . abolitionists were skeptical of him because he was not one of them.

Lincoln's election, which many Democrats conceded after they split into factions at the Charleston and Baltimore conventions, marked the elevation to power of a party whose philosophy was, from the Southern point of view, revolutionary and destructive. There was no place in the Union for states unalterably committed to the maintenance and extension of slavery. The November election returns, which gave victory to the Republicans, were the signal for calling conventions in the South to take the step that fire-eaters and proslavery leaders had already decided upon.

It was in an atmosphere of slavery that the weapons for waging the Civil War were sharpened. It was the question of slavery that sundered the sections and forced them to settle the question by a bloody war. The humanitarian reform movement would have proceeded apace had there been no slaves, for temperance, women's rights, and the like would have received generous support in communities where there was a tendency to assume civic responsibility. It was the question of slavery, however, that intensified the reform crusade and brought the country to the impasse of 1860. Without slavery the question of the extent of federal authority in the territories would have remained academic and could have been debated openly and peaceably. Without slavery the South would have remained a land where freedom of thought could command respect and where all institutions would not feel compelled to pursue a course of action prescribed by the planting aristocracy. Just as the antislavery movement had its roots deep in the liberal philosophy of the Revolutionary period, so intersectional strife and the Civil War itself had their roots in the question of the future of black people in the United States.

Chapter 4

Civil War and the End of American Slavery

Slaves Seek Freedom in the Civil War

Merton L. Dillon

Merton L. Dillon, a professor of history at Ohio State University, examines how slaves responded to and were affected by the Civil War. He argues that its designation as the "War of the Rebellion" is fitting because it was not only a rebellion of the southern states against the nation, but also encompassed a rebellion of slaves against slavery. Slaves took advantage of the disruptions of war to escape behind Union lines. Many assisted the North as spies, laborers, and (eventually) as soldiers. Northern political and military leaders, including President Abraham Lincoln, were slow to accept the help of blacks or to make the Civil War an antislavery crusade, but this did not prevent the conflict from undermining the institution of slavery.

The war that began with the Confederate shelling of Fort Sumter on April 12, 1861, was designated three days later by Abraham Lincoln as rebellion, and so by official usage it would be known. Union authorities chose not to view the conflict as a civil war, a "war between the states," or a "war for southern independence." Instead, according to them, it resulted from a combination of dissident individuals rebelling against the authority of the United States. But despite official sanction, the name never caught on—even Lincoln would speak of a "great civil war" in his Gettysburg Address of November 19, 1863. Yet "War of the Rebellion" acquires aptness extending beyond its origin in Lincoln's political theory when the conflict is viewed in its other, less familiar aspect. The war was not only a rebellion of white

Excerpted from *Slavery Attacked: Southern Slaves and Their Allies, 1619–1865*, by Merton L. Dillon. Copyright ©1990 by the Louisiana State University Press. Reprinted with the permission of the Louisiana State University Press.

southerners against the Union. It also was a rebellion of slaves against masters or, more exactly, a rebellion of slaves against bondage.

The war assumed the character of a slave uprising, not at all in the horrific manner some had predicted, but gradually, with little overt violence on the part of slaves, and with such inevitability as rarely to provoke comment outside the Confederacy. Indeed, few in the North equated the conduct of blacks during the Civil War with insurrection. The lack of remark became the equivalent of popular acceptance of a great folk movement that occurred spontaneously without need for prompting or direction.

Slave revolt was more or less expected to follow withdrawal of federal authority from the South, or if not at that moment, then surely as soon as invading Union armies appeared. For obvious, prudential reasons, Confederate leaders chose not to dwell on this danger but simply denied its possibility: "Of themselves—moving by themselves—I say history does not chronicle a case of negro insurrection," Jefferson Davis had told the United States Congress on January 10, 1861. Northerners, however, and especially abolitionists, made much of the perilous situation secessionists created for themselves when they decided to dispense with federal protection. "Well, the time has come to expect a slave insurrection at any moment," wrote [abolitionist William Lloyd] Garrison, and he promised it his "warmest sympathies."

Resistance Without Violent Insurrection

No doubt Garrison envisioned secession as producing an upheaval similar to the one that long ago had devastated Saint-Domingue.[1] But Garrison would have trouble identifying slave behavior during the Civil War with his notion of revolt, for no blood-drenched uprising followed hard upon secession. From first to last, the slaves' response to war and invasion produced little of the lurid drama and practically none of the insurrectionary horror that for so long had been predicted.

---

1. A French colony in the Caribbean, St. Domingue became the independent Republic of Haiti in 1804 after a long and violent slave revolt.

Yet the conflict was hardly under way when slaves began to take advantage of the situation by shaking off white control and setting themselves free. Some did not join the movement until late in the war, and as happens in all revolutions, some took no part at all. The process of self-emancipation was most evident wherever Union armies appeared; it was least evident far from military action. In such places, slaves were likely to continue their usual routine almost as though a revolutionary war was not under way. Many remained in their master's service until the very end (thus providing basis for the "loyal Negro" tradition), while others, willingly or under coercion, aided the Confederate war effort as military laborers or in other capacities. However much longed for, emancipation seemed to some an unreachable goal. "Us heard talk 'bout de war, but us didn't pay no 'tention," one former slave remembered. "Us never dreamed dat freedom would come." The maintenance of traditional patterns of behavior while society crumbled and distant armies decided their fate no doubt in some instances reflected ignorance as much as it did lethargy and unconcern. But except in areas reached by the Union army, even slaves who desperately wanted to be free and who understood the import of the war could not easily find a practical alternative to remaining in bondage. Although gravely weakened by invasion, the same forces that maintained slavery in peacetime continued to operate in wartime.

Local Concerns over Slavery

As war began, southern state governments moved to lessen the disruptive impact hostilities were expected to have on master-slave relationships. Despite urgent requests from Confederate headquarters for additional men and arms, some state governors early in 1861 decided to retain a home guard and a store of arms and ammunition under their exclusive control for use within the state, much as had been done during the [American] Revolution and the War of 1812. So extensive was this precautionary policy during the first months of war that it produced shortages in the Confederate armies and weakened their fighting capacity.

Even though state officials probably understood the military consequence of their decision, they nevertheless had to balance local exigencies with national needs. Pressure to yield to local concern was hard to resist. Nervous citizens in Mississippi urged the governor not to allow Confederate authorities to remove militia or volunteers. In Georgia, citizens planned to request officials to leave enough forces at home "as will be sufficient to keep our colored population under supervision and control. . . . And also a force sufficient to give assurance and confidence of protection." The same considerations may have hindered recruitment as well. Confronted by the dual threats of slave unrest and Yankee invasion, one Mississippi resident set "to thinking where I could be of the most service to my County *at home* or *in the army* you will see nothing but eternal Vigilance will keep down the enemy at home as well as *at* our frontier."

As white citizens became soldiers, civilians believed, slavery perceptibly changed. A warning reached the Mississippi governor from Jackson in August, 1861, that if more men were taken from the county, "we may as well give it to the negroes . . . now we have to patrole every night to keep them down." Even patrols did not always prove effective. In July, 1862, at Harrisonville, Georgia, citizens petitioned the governor to quarter soldiers in the county. Fifty-one slaves— "traitors . . . the worst of spies"—had run to the Federals. The petitioners understood why: "The temptation of *cheap goods, freedom, and paid labor* cannot be withstood."

Despite such disruption, means still were at hand in most places for maintenance of the slave system. Especially during the first half of the war, soldiers sometimes remained temporarily in camps within the state while they were being assembled prior to transfer to the field. Since these men now were organized in military units and were armed, their capacity to maintain order was enhanced rather than diminished by their absence from home. While soldiers could not punish the slaves' ordinary day-to-day infractions, they could be deployed as needed to crush any coordinated outbreak.

Regular slave patrols for the most part ceased to function in the summer of 1861, when the men who filled their ranks joined the armies. Thus the principal force that always had impeded free movement of slaves disappeared, but the efforts of very young men and of men beyond military age partly made up the deficiency. In plantation regions such persons, organized as home guards, mounted pickets, and vigilance committees took the place of slave patrols and helped prevent unauthorized movement and assembly of slaves. While evidence was plentiful that slave dissidence increased, the white population generally succeeded in containing it within manageable limits, even resorting to ruthless means to do so. Brutal reprisals against defiant slaves continued as before the war, thereby restating the old lesson that white power was not to be flouted. "There is a great disposition among the Negroes to be insubordinate, and to run away and go to the federals," reported a Confederate official at Natchez in 1862. "Within the last 12 months we have had to hang some 40 for plotting an insurrection, and there has been about that number put in irons." A Louisiana planter wrote: "Things are just now beginning to work right—the negroes hated to go to work again. Several have been shot and probably more will have to be." Those slaves had tested the planters' power and determination and found them still strong. Thus, except in places where the presence of Union armies effectively counterbalanced southern military power, slaves remained under coercion. They had little more chance of freeing themselves than before war began. Not until outside support appeared could revolt in the form of mass desertion occur.

Slaves Help the Union Army

The presence of a foreign foe always had provided the acid test of slavery, as southerners learned during the Revolution and again in the War of 1812. The effect of invasion proved no less severe in 1861. With the advance of Union armies, thousands of slaves, often in family units, deserted their owners to seek protection in the camps of the invaders, thereby becoming, in General Benjamin F. Butler's odd phrase, "contraband of war." Distance from Union forces was a powerful obstacle to flight but not an insuperable one, as a slaveholder in the hills of northwestern Georgia revealed when he advertised for three runaways who he believed were heading west to join the Yankees at Corinth. Most slaves located so far from Union lines risked no such perilous journeys. Instead, they stayed where they were, though they still might manifest disloyalty by performing their prescribed duties reluctantly or not at all. Uncle Tom in Alabama provided an example of such behavior. When Union soldiers arrived at the plantation, he first led them to the horses and mules he had helped his master hide and then joined the soldiers in ransacking the plantation house. "He hadn't been much good to massa since de war commenced," a former slave remembered. "Lay off in de swamp mos' of de time."

The mass flight of slaves from plantations to Union lines, an acceleration of the folk movement that abolitionists and

---

Making Themselves an Issue

The thousands of slaves who deserted their masters and escaped behind Union army lines helped transform the character of the Civil War, argues historian and former civil rights activist Vincent Harding in this excerpt from his 1981 study There Is a River: The Black Struggle for Freedom in America.

In the South the major black resistance and struggle was focused in the relentless movement of the self-liberated fugitives into the Union lines. Without speeches, laws, or guns, literally, insistently, with bold force, often organized and led by the trusted black slave drivers, they inserted their bodies into the cauldron of the war. All the denials of Lincoln and his government, all the doggerel of the white Northern population, could not stop them from their own dramatic proclamation, their own announcement that they were at the heart of this conflict. By the end of the spring of 1862, tens of thousands were camped out in whatever areas the Northern armies had occupied, thereby making themselves an unavoidable military and political issue.

Vincent Harding, *There Is a River: The Black Struggle for Freedom in America.* New York: Harcourt Brace Jovanovich, 1981.

northern free blacks had encouraged for years, was in itself rebellion, even though little violence accompanied it. Blacks in effect declared themselves free and, usually without raising a hand against their owners, simply walked away from slavery. The significance of this movement—its equivalence to rebellion—was not lost on slaveholders The Reverend Charles C. Jones in Georgia speculated on a possible remedy in the form of harsh legal sanctions: "Could their overt rebellion in the way of casting off the authority of their masters be made by construction insurrection?" he asked. Perhaps it was at Jones's urging that a committee in Liberty County, Georgia, requested officials to extend martial law to runaway slaves. "The negroes constitute a part of the body politic in fact," they reasoned, "and should be made to know their duty; that they are perfectly aware that the act which they commit is one of rebellion against the power and authority of their owners and the Government under which they live." But such proposals were at best quixotic, for the time had nearly passed when law or even the threat of summary punishment could do much toward maintaining in blacks the attitudes essential to slavery. Paternalism had had its day.

By their willingness to serve the invaders as guides, spies, informers, laborers, and—as soon as Union policy allowed—soldiers, the contrabands left no doubt about their rejection of their former owners and their owners' government. By the third summer of war, southern white soldiers found themselves facing armed blacks, most of them former slaves, wearing uniforms of the Union army At the moment northern blacks and southern contrabands took up arms against the military forces of their former masters, the Civil War unquestionably assumed the character of controlled, black insurrection.

Union Slow to Accept Help

All this happened, it must be noted, almost solely at the initiative of slaves themselves. The Union government designed no policies aimed at producing such a response. At the start of hostilities, Lincoln's administration had drawn no plan to deprive planters of their labor and property, to incite social disorder within the South, or to arm slaves. But by the summer of 1862, it found itself doing each of these things, if only by indirection.

Every earlier enemy—the French, the Spanish, the English—had been quick to exploit slave discontent as a weapon to hamper and embarrass American military effort. Among all the foes American slaveholders ever faced, only the Union, as a matter of policy, declined to do this. The self-denial appears the more remarkable because, of all the planters' enemies, the Union was the only one with an anti-slavery reputation, the only one headed by the leader of an antislavery political party, the only one whose professed ideology might have been expected to produce an emancipationist policy as a matter of course.

Contradictions early became apparent. The decades of intersectional discord that preceded secession and war vested the northern invaders with an ideological quality absent from the South's earlier enemies. Southerners, black and white alike, viewed the Yankees as antislavery agents. But by no means did all Yankees view themselves that way. When Union commanders prepared to launch their first incursions into the Confederacy, Generals George B. McClellan and Robert Patterson undertook to remove any impression that they commanded armies of liberation. They issued proclamations assuring slaveholding Unionists of their lack of revolutionary purpose and of their readiness to put down the revolt their presence might encourage. They renounced any plan to forge political and military alliances with slaves, though the expediency of doing so must have been obvious to them. When General Butler marched his army from Annapolis to Washington in April, 1861, he, too, made his intent unmistakably clear. He informed the governor of Maryland of his readiness to help suppress slave uprisings in the state.

With no trace of gratitude, Governor Thomas Hicks reported himself fully capable of controlling the situation without Yankee aid. Butler's message to Hicks produced intense editorial controversy in the North, thereby revealing support in some quarters for the instigation of slave revolt. Predictably, Garrison preached his customary editorial sermon in the *Liberator*—this time a reprimand—with Butler supplying the text. "General Butler supposes himself to be better than a negro slave," wrote Garrison. "He is no better. He assumes to have a better right to freedom: he has none. . . . Men who glory in Bunker Hill and Yorktown must not deny to the oppressed any of the means necessary to secure their freedom, whatever becomes of their oppressors."

Lincoln's Priorities

Such statements, though consistent with abolitionist principle, ignored long-standing and widely shared dread of black insurrection, but more important, they also ignored Lincoln's declared purpose in waging the War of the Rebellion. Lincoln had issued his call for seventy-five thousand volunteers to restore the Union, not to free the slaves or to ruin the planters. Although a dynamic element in the North long had sought any opportunity to end slavery and eliminate planter influence from national affairs, only slowly did Lincoln come to share its revolutionary intent.

Lincoln earlier had voiced a commitment to place slavery on the road to ultimate extinction; yet the war he conducted bore in its first phase little relation to that end. War was an accident. It had been forced on the Union by the planters' rebellion and their subsequent aggression. Union armies in 1861 drove into the South with no further political aim than to suppress white Rebels and thereby make the Union operable. Had slaves at that time misunderstood Union policy and managed to rise in open revolt, Union forces, it is possible to believe, would have joined Confederates in restoring order, as Butler in fact had promised to do in Maryland. "The forlorn hope of insurrection among the slaves may as well be abandoned," wrote the northern black journalist Robert Hamilton in the summer of 1861. "They are too well informed and too *wise* to court destruction at the hands of the combined Northern and Southern armies."

The limited goal of political restoration could be achieved more quickly and at less cost, administration leaders supposed, if in the process race relations were left undisturbed. In particular, slaveholding Unionists in border states—who had committed no political offense—should not be further alienated and perhaps driven to join the secessionists. Lincoln hesitated for a long time to accept the logic of the Union's position with respect to both planters and slaves. "What I do about slavery, and the colored race," he would write in 1862, "I do because it helps to save the Union; and what I forbear, I forbear because I do *not* believe it would help to save the Union." Unacceptable as black and white abolitionists found that statement, it accurately expressed the president's priorities and his assessment of political necessity.

A war against slavery was politically impossible in 1861. Lincoln understood the complexities of public opinion better than did most antislavery radicals, who were prone to ignore or simplify them. Secession drew a political line between the sections; yet the line imperfectly demarked contrasting interests and ideologies. Lincoln could never ignore the sizable body of states' rights, antiabolitionist, anti-Negro thought that flourished in the North. Its presence must be taken into account when determining policy, and nothing must be done that might mobilize its influence against the war for the Union. Garrison, too, had grasped this fact well before the war began, though he did not allow that insight to compromise his antislavery zeal. "If we fight with actual slaveholders in the South," he had written in January, 1859, "must we not also fight with proslavery priests, politicians, editors, merchants, in the North? Where are we to begin?" The Union's long delay in acknowledging emancipation as a war aim was the practical consequence flowing from the problem Garrison had identified.

Abolitionist War Aims

With their hostility to slavery in no way compromised by political necessity, abolitionists held to a far different conception of the war and its revolutionary possibilities than did Lincoln. The slaveholders' decision to dissolve the Union had added to their numbers and determination. "Lawyers and laymen who have never been willing to own that they were abolitionists now publicly and privately avow themselves such and say slavery must die," observed an antislavery northerner shortly before hostilities began. Further, the North contained a dynamic element of persons, not self-defined as abolitionists, who nevertheless agreed that the welfare and destiny of the nation required destruction of the planters' power. The most direct means to this end, they believed, was emancipation. A group within the Republican party, reflecting both antislavery idealism and antiplanter bias, worked consistently toward that end. They joined free blacks and abolitionists in directing merciless criticism against Lincoln for what they regarded as his narrow conception of the war and his hesitancy to exploit its opportunities.

Military operations and the conduct of slaves themselves had the effect of supporting the critics' war aims rather than those of Lincoln, and in the end, his objections and reservations were swept aside. Despite official rationale and political exigency, the Civil War inevitably undermined slavery. But ideology and policy had less to do with promoting this result than did slaves and the army itself, and the result would have been much the same even had Lincoln and the North not possessed an antislavery reputation well known to many slaves.

Abraham Lincoln and the Emancipation Proclamation

James M. McPherson

James M. McPherson, a Pulitzer-Prize winning Civil War historian and Princeton University professor, describes the events that led President Abraham Lincoln to issue the Emancipation Proclamation on January 1, 1863. Lincoln, who personally opposed slavery, had previously hesitated in taking such a step because of political and constitutional concerns. However, as the Civil War dragged on, abolishing slavery in the Confederacy emerged as an attractive way of furthering the Union war effort. McPherson writes that although the decision to issue the Emancipation Proclamation had limited legal impact—its declarations of freedom applied only to slaves in parts of the Confederacy not under control of the Union army—it still marked a turning point that transformed the Civil War into a war against slavery.

President Abraham Lincoln hated slavery, but before the Civil War he believed he had no constitutional power to interfere with the institution in the Southern states. Then, when war broke out, the slaves became the property of the Union's enemies, and as commander in chief of the United States armed forces and with his wartime power to take away the enemy's property, the president now had the right to free the slaves. Still, for political reasons, Lincoln hesitated.

Four slave states—Kentucky, Maryland, Missouri and Delaware—had remained loyal to the Union, and Lincoln feared that hasty action against slavery might drive them into the Confederacy. Also, the president at first hoped that

Excerpted from *Marching Toward Freedom*, by James McPherson. Copyright ©1965, 1967, 1991 by James McPherson. Reprinted with the permission of Facts On File, Inc.

the war would be short and that the Confederate states could quickly be persuaded to return to the Union. Because they would never come voluntarily if the government declared an intention to abolish slavery, Lincoln was reluctant in the early months of the war to do anything that could be interpreted as unfriendly to slavery.

Even as late as August 1862, in a letter to newspaper editor Horace Greeley, who had urged Lincoln to free the slaves, the president stated, "My paramount object *is* to save the Union, and is *not* either to save or destroy slavery.... What I do about slavery, and the colored race, I do because I believe it helps to save the Union; and what I forbear, I forbear because I do *not* believe it would help to save the Union."

Views of Frederick Douglass

But many in the North, both white and black, thought the Union could not be saved without overthrowing slavery. One of the most articulate abolitionists was Frederick Douglass, an orator and editor who became the most prominent African-American of the Civil War period. A former slave who had escaped North, self-educated and now in a position of eminence, Douglass' words carried weight. From the beginning of the war, he wrote dozens of editorials and speeches asserting that slavery was the cause of the conflict and that victory was impossible without emancipation. After the fall of Fort Sumter, Douglass wrote in his newspaper, *Douglass' Monthly:*

> At last our proud Republic is overtaken. Our National Sin has found us out ... Slavery has done it all ... We have sown the wind, only to reap the whirlwind ... Could we write as with lightning, and speak as with the voice of thunder, we should write and cry to the nation, REPENT, BREAK EVERY YOKE, LET THE OPPRESSED GO FREE, FOR HEREIN ALONE IS DELIVERANCE AND SAFETY!
> ... Fire must be met with water, darkness with light, and war for the destruction of liberty must be met with war for the destruction of slavery ... This war with the slaveholders can never be brought to a desirable termination until slavery, the

guilty cause of all our national troubles, has been totally and forever abolished.

One of the best arguments of Douglass and other abolitionists was that slavery was a source of strength to the Confederacy. Slaves worked in the fields and factories; slaves dug trenches and drove wagons for the Confederate army. Without their labor, the South would collapse, and the North could win the war. A proclamation of emancipation, said Douglass, would cripple the South by encouraging slaves to flee their masters and come over to the Northern side where freedom awaited them.

> The slaveholders . . . boast that the slave population is a grand element of strength, and that it enables them to send and sustain a stronger body of rebels to overthrow the Government that they could otherwise do if the whites were required to perform the labors of cultivation; and in this they are unquestionably in the right, provided the National Government refuses to turn this mighty element of strength into one of weakness . . . Why? Oh! why, in the name of all that is national, does our Government allow its enemies this powerful advantage? . . . The very stomach of this rebellion is the negro in the condition of a slave. Arrest that hoe in the hands of the negro, and you smite rebellion in the very seat of its life . . . The negro is the key of the situation—the pivot upon which the whole rebellion turns . . . Teach the rebels and traitors that the price they are to pay for the attempt to abolish this Government must be the abolition of slavery . . . Henceforth let the war cry be down with treason, and down with slavery, the cause of treason.

As soon as Union forces occupied the border states and invaded the Confederacy, slaves from the surrounding countryside, sensing that the Northern army meant freedom, began to come into Union lines. But, as fugitives, they presented Northern generals with a problem. Should they be returned to their masters under the terms of the Fugitive Slave Law of 1850, or not? Some generals returned them, but in most cases their masters were Confederates and to return property to rebels seemed foolish. The Fugitive Slave Law could hardly be applied to slaveholders who had seceded from the United States.

Contraband of War

General Benjamin F. Butler went to the heart of the matter. Butler commanded a Union army base at Fortress Monroe, near Hampton, Virginia. In May 1861 three fugitive slaves who had escaped from a Confederate labor battalion entered the base. Butler, a former lawyer, labeled them "contraband of war" (enemy property subject to seizure) and gave them shelter and work with the Union army. By the end of July, there were almost 1,000 such "contrabands" at Fortress Monroe and many hundreds at other Union camps.

On August 6, the United States Congress passed a Confiscation Act providing for the seizure of all property, including slaves, used "in aid of the rebellion." However, the bill applied only to those slaves who had actually worked on Confederate military fortifications and naval vessels. It did not *emancipate* such slaves—it merely provided for their seizure as enemy property. Nevertheless, it was an important step: In spite of the Lincoln administration's efforts to keep slavery as an issue out of the war, the fugitive contrabands, by their own actions, were making it impossible.

Another way of dealing with the fugitives who flocked to Union lines was tried by General John C. Frémont, a former Republican presidential candidate and now commander of the Union forces in Missouri. On August 30, 1861, he issued a proclamation declaring that the slaves of every Confederate in the state were free. Black people and many white people in the North applauded, but Lincoln was afraid the proclamation would "alarm our Southern Union friends and turn them against us." So, on September 11, the president modified Frémont's order in such a way that it freed only a few slaves in Missouri.

Blacks were disappointed, and some criticized the president bitterly. But Harriet Tubman, the former slave whose secret trips into the South before the war to help other slaves escape had made her the "Moses" of her people, was hopeful that Lincoln would see the light. "God's ahead ob Massa Linkum," she said at the end of 1861, as reported by a white abolitionist in a letter to a friend that tried to capture Tubman's dialect.

> God won't let Massa Linkum beat de South till he do de right ting. Massa Linkum he great man, and I'se poor nigger; but dis nigger can tell Massa Linkum how to save de money and de young men. He do it by setting de niggers free. S'pose dar was awful' big snake down dar, on de floor. He bite you. Folks all skeered, cause you die. You send for doctor to cut de bite; but snake he rolled up dar, and while doctor dwine it, he bite you agin. De doctor cut out dat bite; but while he dwine it, de snake he spring up and bite you agin, and so he keep dwine, till you kill him. Dat's what Massa Linkum orter know.

In 1862, the government finally began to attack the "snake" of slavery. Congress passed a bill to abolish slavery in the territories and a second Confiscation Act declaring all slaves of Confederate masters "forever free" as soon as they entered Union lines. On April 16, 1862, Congress abolished slavery in the District of Columbia. The next day, a black resident of Washington wrote joyfully to a friend in Baltimore:

> This indeed has been a happy day to me sights have I witnessed that I never anticipated one of which I will relate The Chambermaid at Smith's (my former place) . . . is a slave so this morning I went there to inform her of the passage of the Bill when I entered The cook and another Slave woman who has a slave son were talking relative to the Bill expressing doubts of its passage & when I entered they perceived that something was ahead and emeadiately asked me "Whats the news?" The Districts free says I pulling out the "National Republican" and reading its editorial when I had finished the chambermaid had left the room sobbing for joy. The slave woman clapped her hands and shouted, left the house saying "let me go and tell my husband that Jesus has done all things well" While the cook who is free retired to another room to offer thanks for the blessing sent. Should I not feel glad to see so much rejoicing around me? Were I a drinker I would

get on a Jolly spree today but as a Christian I can but kneel
in prayer and bless God for the privilege I've enjoyed this
day . . . Would to God that the Law applied also to Baltimore
but a little patience and all will be well.

The Emancipation Proclamation

In the summer of 1862 Lincoln began to think about issuing
an emancipation proclamation. Several reasons had brought
him to this position. His former hope that a short and easy
war would show the Confederates their mistake and persuade them to return to the Union had not been fulfilled.
Things had been going badly for the Northern armies; they
had suffered major defeats at the First Battle of Bull Run in
July 1861, the Seven Days' Battles in June and July 1862 and
the Second Battle of Bull Run in August 1862. The prospect
of weakening the Confederacy and at the same time
strengthening the Union by emancipating the slaves and encouraging them to come over to the Union side was thus
more attractive now than at the beginning of the war.

The inconsistency of fighting a government based on
slavery without striking against slavery was also becoming
more obvious each day. The Confederacy hoped to enlist
European support for its cause, and Lincoln believed that an
emancipation proclamation might discourage England and
France from aiding the South, by showing that the North
was fighting for liberty as well as Union. Finally, more and
more Northerners were becoming convinced—by the
deaths of friends and relatives in the war—that slavery was
vicious as well as immoral and that emancipation was the
best way to win the war and secure a peace based on justice.

But Lincoln did not want to issue his proclamation in the
midst of Northern defeat, when it might be interpreted as
"our last *shriek* on the retreat." He waited until after the
Union victory at the Battle of Antietam on September 17,
1862, and then, on September 22, he issued a preliminary
Emancipation Proclamation. The final proclamation came
on January 1, 1863. By virtue of his wartime power as commander in chief, the president proclaimed all slaves in the rebellious Southern states "thenceforward, and forever free."

Black People Celebrate

Black people hailed the Emancipation Proclamation with joy. All over the North they held meetings of celebration on that first day of January 1863. One such meeting took place in the Israel Bethel Church in Washington, D.C. The pastor of the church was Henry M. Turner, freeborn black who had migrated from his native South Carolina to Baltimore and finally to Washington. He became a leader in the black community and was eventually elected a bishop in the African Methodist Episcopal Church. He was still living on January 1, 1913, the 50th anniversary of the Emancipation Proclamation, and at that time he gave his recollections of the events in Washington 50 years earlier.

Seeing such a multitude of people in and around my church, I hurriedly went up to the office of the first paper in which the proclamation of freedom could be printed, known as the "Evening Star," and squeezed myself through the dense crowd that was waiting for the paper. The first sheet run off with the proclamation in it was grabbed for by three of us, but some active young man got possession of it and fled. The next sheet was grabbed for by several, and was torn into tatters. The third sheet from the press was grabbed for by several, but I succeeded in procuring so much of it as contained the proclamation, and off I went for life and death. Down Pennsylvania Avenue I ran as for my life, and when the people saw me coming with the paper in my hand they raised a shouting cheer that was almost deafening. As many as could get around me lifted me to a great platform, and I started to read the proclamation. I had run the best end of a mile, I was out of breath, and could not read. Mr. Hinton, to whom I handed the paper, read it with great force and clearness. While he was reading every kind of demonstration and gesticulation was going on. Men squealed, women fainted, dogs barked, white and colored people shook hands, songs were sung, and by this time cannons began to fire at the navy-yard, and follow in the wake of the roar that had for some time been going on behind the White House . . . Great processions of colored and white men marched to and fro and passed in front of the White House and congratulated President Lincoln on his proclamation. The President came to the window and made responsive bows, and thousands told him, if he would come out of that palace, they would hug him to death . . . It was indeed a time of times, and a half time, nothing like it will ever be seen again in this life.

The proclamation actually freed no slaves: the slaves in the slave states loyal to the Union, and in the portions of the Confederacy under control of the Union army, were not included in Lincoln's proclamation. And it could obviously have no immediate effect in parts of the South still under Confederate control. This led some critics to jeer at the Emancipation Proclamation as a mere scrap of paper. But it was more than that. It was a declaration by the president of the United States that the North was no longer fighting only for Union; it was now fighting for the establishment of a new Union without slavery. The course of the war after January 1, 1863, and the final Northern victory put the proclamation in force, and on January 31, 1865, Congress passed the Thirteenth Amendment to the Constitution abolishing slavery *throughout* the United States. President Lincoln played a crucial role in persuading Congress to pass the Thirteenth Amendment. The amendment was ratified by the necessary three-fourths of the states 10 months later.

On February 4, 1865, blacks and whites in Boston celebrated congressional passage of the Thirteenth Amendment at a mass meeting. Several speakers entertained and inspired the crowd, and the celebration ended with the Reverend Mr. Rue, pastor of a Negro Methodist church, singing the hymn "Sound the Loud Timbrel." On the second chorus a few members of the audience seated near the platform began to sing along with Mr. Rue, and in each succeeding chorus more and more of the huge throng joined in, swelling the refrain to triumphant heights of joyfulness. A white member of the audience, William Lloyd Garrison Jr., described the meeting in a letter to his wife:

It was a scene to be remembered—the earnestness of the singer, pouring out his heartfelt praise, the sympathy of the audience, catching the glow & the deep-toned organ blending the thousand voices in harmony. Nothing during the evening brought to my mind so clearly the magnitude of the act we celebrated, its deeply religious as well as moral significance than "Sound the loud timbrel o'er Egypt's dark sea, Jehovah has triumphed, His people are free."

How Slaves Responded to Their Emancipation

Leon F. Litwack

Leon F. Litwack is a history professor at the University of California at Berkeley. His critically acclaimed book *Been in the Storm So Long: The Aftermath of Slavery*, excerpted here, draws heavily on interviews with former slaves (including many done in the 1930s by the Federal Writers' Project), diaries of slaveholders, and other primary sources in examining how slaves and their owners reacted to the end of slavery. Litwack argues that freed slaves displayed a wide range of responses to the news of their emancipation, including joy, skepticism, sorrow, shock, and uncertainty about their future.

Where the master assembled the blacks to tell them they were no longer his slaves, the reactions he provoked gave rise to the legendary stories of a "Day of Jubilo," in which crowds of ecstatically happy blacks shouted, sang, and danced their way into freedom. Large numbers of former slaves recalled no such celebration. Although not entirely myth, the notion of a Jubilee, with its suggestion of unrestrained, unthinking black hilarity, tends to neglect if not demean the wide range and depth of black responses to emancipation, including the trauma and fears the master's announcement produced on some plantations. The very nature of the bondage they had endured, the myriad of experiences to which they had been exposed, the quality of the ties that had bound them to their "white folks," and the ambivalence which had suffused those relationships were all bound to make for a diverse and complex reaction on the day the slaves were told they no longer had any masters or mistresses.

Capturing nearly the full range of responses, a former South Carolina slave recalled that on his plantation "some were sorry, some hurt, but a few were silent and glad." From the perspective of the mistress of a Florida household, "some of the men cried, some spoke regretfully, [and] only two looked surly and had nothing to say." Although celebrations seldom followed the master's announcement, numerous blacks recalled taking the rest of the day off, if only to think through the implications of what they had been told. Still others, like Harriett Robinson, remembered that before the master could even finish his remarks, "over half them niggers was gone." But the slaves on an Alabama plantation stood quietly, stunned by the news. "We didn' hardly know what he means," Jenny Proctor recalled. "We jes' sort of huddle 'round together like scared rabbits, but after we knowed what he mean, didn' many of us go, 'cause we didn' know where to of went." None of them knew what to expect from freedom and they interpreted it in many different ways, explained James Lucas, a former slave of Jefferson Davis, who achieved his freedom at the age of thirty-one.

> Dey all had diffe'nt ways o' thinkin' 'bout it. Mos'ly though dey was jus' lak me, dey didn' know jus' zackly what it meant. It was jus' somp'n dat de white folks an' slaves all de time talk 'bout. Dat's all. Folks dat ain' never been free don' rightly know de *feel* of bein' free. Dey don' know de meanin' of it. Slaves like us, what was owned by quality-folks, was sati'fied an' didn' sing none of dem freedom songs.

How long that sensation of shock or incredulity lasted would vary from slave to slave. "The day we was set free," remembered Silas Shotfore, "us did not know what to do. Our Missus said we could stay on the place." But his father made one decision almost instantly: no matter what they decided to do, they would do it somewhere else.

Suspicious as they might be of the white man's pronouncements, some blacks were initially skeptical, thinking it might all be a ruse, still another piece of deception calculated to test their fidelity. With that in mind, some thought it best to feign remorse at the announcement, while others needed to determine the master's veracity and sought confirmation elsewhere, often in the nearest town, at the local office of the Freedmen's Bureau, or on another plantation. When his master explained to him that he was now a free man, Tom Robinson refused to believe him ("You're jokin' me, I says") until he spoke with some slave neighbors. "I wanted to find out if they was free too. I just couldn't take it all in. I couldn't believe we was all free alike."

Sorrow and Confusion

Although most slaves welcomed freedom with varying degrees of enthusiasm, the sense of confusion and uncertainty that prevailed in many quarters was not easily dispelled. The first thought of sixteen-year-old Sallie Crane of Arkansas was that she had been sold, and her mistress's reassurance that she would soon be reunited with her mother did little to comfort her. "I cried because I thought they was carrying me to see my mother before they would send me to be sold in Louisiana." The impression deliberately cultivated by some masters that the Yankees intended to sell freed slaves to Cuba to help defray war costs may have had some impact. No matter what they were told, a former North Carolina slave recalled of the master's announcement, he and his mother were simply too frightened to leave the premises. "Jes' like tarpins or turtles after 'mancipation. Jes' stick our heads out to see how the land lay."

Nor did some slaves necessarily welcome the news when they fully understood its implications for their own lives. The sorrow which some displayed was not always pretense. To those who were reasonably satisfied with their positions and the relations they enjoyed with the white family, freedom offered no immediate cause for rejoicing. "I was a-farin' pretty well in de kitchen," Aleck Trimble remarked. "I didn' t'ink I eber see better times dan what dem was, and I ain't." That was how Mollie Tillman also recalled the advent of freedom, since, as she boasted, "I warn't no common eve'y-day slave," and her mistress refused to let her work in the fields. "I wuz happy den, but since 'mancipation I has jes' had to scuffle an' work an' do de bes' I kin." To Moses Lyles, a former South Carolina slave, emancipation undermined the mutual dependency upon which slavery had rested and neither class benefited from the severance of those ties. "De nigger was de right arm of de buckra [white man] class. De buckra was de horn of plenty for de nigger. Both suffer in consequence of freedom."

Standing on the porch of the Big House and watching her fellow slaves celebrate their emancipation, Sara Brown wondered why they thought the event worthy of such festivities. "I been free all de time," she thought. This insistence that they were already as free as they wanted to be repeated an old article of faith which some slaves had recited almost habitually in antebellum days when northern visitors pressed them on the subject of slavery. Disillusionment and "hard times" in the post-emancipation period helped to keep this perception of slavery alive. But for certain ex-slaves, the attachments went much deeper, and neither "good times" nor a bountiful freedom would most likely have altered the relationships and position they had come to cherish. To some of the strong-willed "mammies," whose dominance in the white household was seldom questioned and whose pride and self-respect remained undiminished, emancipation threatened to disrupt the only world and the only ties that really mattered to them and they clung all the more stubbornly to the past. Even death would not undo such relationships, as some of them anticipated a reunion in an all-white heaven.

> Who says I'se free? I warn't neber no slabe. I libed wid qual'ty an' was one ob de fambly. Take dis bandanna off? No, 'deedy! dats the las' semblance I'se got ob de good ole times. S'pose I *is* brack, I cyan't he'p it. If mah mammy and pappy chose for me ter be brack, I ain't gwine ter be lak some white folks I knows an' blame de Lord for all de 'flictions dat comes 'pon 'em. I'se put up wid dis brackness now, 'cordin' to ol' Mis's Bible, for nigh on ter ninety years, an' t'ank de good Lord, dat eberlastin' day is mos' come when I'll be white as Mis' Chloe for *eber mo'*! [Her mistress had died some years before.] What's dat, honey? How I knows I'se gwine ter be

white? Why, honey, I'se s'prised! Do you s'pose 'cause Mammy's face is brack, her soul is brack too? Whar's yo' larnin' gone to?

Many of the freed slaves who viewed emancipation apprehensively readily confessed that they had escaped the worst aspects of bondage. "I ain't never had no mother 'ceptin' only Mis' Patsey," a Florida freedwoman remarked, "an' I ain't never felt lak' a bond slave what's been pressed—dat's what dem soldiers say we all is."

Fear of the Unknown

The mixed emotions with which slaves greeted their freedom also reflected a natural fear of the unknown, along with the knowledge that "they's allus 'pend on Old Marse to look after them." For many blacks, this was the only life they had known and the world ended at the boundaries of the plantation. To think that they no longer had a master or mistress, while it brought exuberance and relief to many, struck others with dismay. "Whar we gwine eat an' sleep?" they demanded to know. And realizing they could not depend on the law or on other whites for protection, who would now stand between them and the dreaded patrollers and "po' buckra"? After hearing of their freedom, Silas Smith recalled, "de awfulest feeling" pervaded the slave quarters that night as they contemplated a future without masters or mistresses. "You felt jes' like you had done strayed off a-fishing and got lost." Fifteen years after emancipation, Parke Johnston, a former Virginia slave, vividly recalled "how wild and upset and *dreadful* everything was in them times."

> It came so sudden on 'em they wasn't prepared for it. Just think of whole droves of people, that had always been kept so close, and hardly ever left the plantation before, turned loose all at once, with nothing in the world, but what they had on their backs, and often little enough of that; men, women and children that had left their homes when they found out they were free, walking along the road with no where to go.

Since emancipation threatened to undermine the mutual obligations implicit in the master-slave relationship, some freed blacks responded with cries of ingratitude and betrayal that matched in fury the similar reactions of white families to the wartime behavior of certain slaves. When Yankee soldiers told an elderly South Carolina slave that she no longer had a master or mistress, the woman responded as though she had been insulted: "I ain' no free nigger! I *is* got a marster an' mistiss! Dee right dar in de great house. Ef you don' b'lieve me, you go dar an' see." Like so many of the older slaves, this woman felt that her services and devotion to the "white folks" over many years had more than fulfilled her part of the relationship. For the family to abandon her now and deprive her of the security, care, and protection she clearly thought she had earned would be, in her view, the rankest form of ingratitude. On a plantation in South Carolina, the oldest black on the place reacted with downright indignation when his former master read the terms of a proposed labor contract; indeed, few blacks expressed the idea of mutual obligations more clearly:

> Missis belonged to him, & he belonged to Missis, & he was not going to leave her. . . . Massa had brought him up here to take care of him, & he had known when Missis' grandmother was born & she was 'bliged to take care of him; he was going to die on this place, & he was not going to do any work either, except make a collar a week.

A Sense of Dependency

The uncertainties, the regrets, the anxieties which characterized many of the reactions to emancipation underscored that pervasive sense of dependency—the feeling, as more than one ex-slave recalled, that "we couldn't do a thing without the white folks." Slavery had taught black people to be slaves—"good" slaves and obedient workers. "All de slaves knowed how to do hard work," observed Thomas Cole, who had run away to enlist in the Union Army, "but dey didn't know nothin' 'bout how to 'pend on demselves for de livin'." Of course, the very logic and survival of the "peculiar institution" had demanded that nothing be done to prepare slaves for the possibility of freedom; on the contrary, they had been taught to feel their incapacity for dealing with its immense responsibilities. Many years before the war, a South Carolina jurist set forth the paternalistic ideal when he advised that each slave should be taught to view his mas-

---

Whites and Blacks React to Freedom

Historian Michael Perman examines the differences between white and black responses to the abolition of slavery in the South.

No longer the property of others, former slaves now owned themselves. They had the power to make independent choices, and they wanted whites to acknowledge it. Because of this, there was surprisingly little retaliation against former masters through physical violence or through destruction of property and arson. Acceptance of their autonomy, rather than reprisal for their previous lack of it, seemed to be the freedmen's overriding concern. But, to the whites, any act of self-assertion was resented as impudence and ingratitude. Former owners, in particular, regarded this independence as defiance and a threat to their sense of mastery. They could not understand how their former charges had suddenly lost their servility. It was impossible to believe, and even more difficult to explain, that blacks, whose supposed innate dependence and inability to fend for themselves had justified their enslavement in the first place, could have discovered these new notions themselves. Therefore, they had to have been indoctrinated by Yankee soldiers or someone else. But, wherever these upstart opinions had come from, southern whites interpreted every act of insubordination as a sign of impending social chaos or of the inevitability of insurrection. To the former masters, the conclusion seemed inescapable; they had lost control. . . .

Although both races found freedom a new and untried experiment, they of course differed markedly in their attitude toward it. Blacks welcomed it, whereas whites resented and resisted it.

Michael Perman, *Emancipation and Reconstruction 1862–1879*. Arlington Heights, IL: Harlan Davidson, 1987.

ter as "a perfect security from injury. When this is the case, the relation of master and servant becomes little short of that of parent and child." The testimony of former slaves suggests how effectively some masters had been able to inculcate that ideal and how the legacy of paternalism could paralyze its victims."

Nor did Federal policies or programs in the immediate aftermath of emancipation address themselves to this problem. Whatever the freedman's desire or capacity for "living independently," he would in scores of instances be forced to remain dependent on his former masters. It was precisely through such dependency, a North Carolina planter vowed, that his class of people would be able to reestablish on the plantations what they had ostensibly lost in emancipation, "until in a few years I think everything will be about as it was."

No Longer Concealing Emotions

Upon hearing of their freedom, some slaves instinctively deferred to the traditional source of authority, advice, sustenance, and protection—the master himself. Now that they were no longer his slaves, what did he want them to do? Few freed blacks, however, no matter how confused and apprehensive they may have been, were altogether oblivious to the excitement and the anticipation that this event had generated. At the moment of freedom, masses of slaves did not suddenly erupt in a mammoth Jubilee but neither did they all choose to be passive, cowed, or indifferent in the face of their master's announcement. Outside of the prayer meetings and the annual holiday frolics, plantation life had afforded them few occasions for free expression, at least in the presence of their "white folks." If only for a few hours or days, then, many newly emancipated slaves dropped their usual defenses, cast off their masks, and gave themselves the rare luxury of acting out feelings they were ordinarily expected to repress.

Once they understood the full import of the master's words, and even then perhaps only after several minutes of stunned or polite silence, many blacks found they could no longer contain their emotions. More importantly, they felt no need to do so. "That the day I shouted," was how Richard Carruthers of Texas recalled his emancipation. Booker T. Washington stood next to his mother during the announcement; many years later, he could still vividly recall how she hugged and kissed him, the tears streaming down her face, and her explanation that she had prayed many years for this day but never believed she would live to see it. Freedom took longer to reach Bexar County, Texas, where the war had hardly touched the lives and routines of the slave. But Felix Haywood, who worked as a sheepherder and cowpuncher, recalled how "everybody went wild" when they learned of freedom. "We all felt like horses and nobody had made us that way but ourselves. We was free. Just like that, we was free."

New Versions of Spirituals

If neither words nor prayers conveyed the appropriate emotions, the newly freed slaves might draw on the traditional spirituals, whose imagery easily befitted an occasion like emancipation. The triumph had come in this world, not in the next. The exuberance and importance of such a moment also inspired updated versions of the spirituals and songs especially composed for the occasion. Out in Bexar County, Felix Haywood heard them sing:

Abe Lincoln freed the nigger
With the gun and the trigger;
And I ain't goin' to get whipped any more.
I got my ticket,
Leavin' the thicket,
And I'm a-headin' for the Golden Shore!

Harriett Gresham, who had belonged to a wealthy planter in South Carolina, remembered hearing the guns at Fort Sumter that inaugurated the war, as well as the song that sounded the death of slavery:

No slav'ry chains to tie me down,
And no mo' driver's ho'n to blow fer me.
No mo' stocks to fasten me down,
Jesus break slav'ry chain, Lord.
Break slav'ry chain, Lord,

Break slav'ry chain, Lord,
Da Heben gwinter be my home.

"Guess dey made 'em up," Annie Harris said of many of the songs she heard in those days, "'cause purty soon ev'ybody fo' miles around was singin' freedom songs."

Although the classic version of the Jubilee featured large masses of people, some newly freed slaves only wanted to be alone at this moment. Neither fear of the master nor deference to his feelings entirely explains this preference. Overwhelmed by what they had just heard, some needed a momentary solitude to reflect on its implications and to convince themselves that it had really happened, while others simply preferred to express themselves with the least amount of inhibition. Lou Smith recalled running off and hiding in the plum orchard, where he kept repeating to himself, "I'se free, I'se free; I ain't never going back to Miss Jo." After hearing of his freedom, an elderly Virginia black proceeded to the barn, leaped from one stack of straw to the other, and "screamed and screamed!" Although confined to bed, Aunt Sissy, a crippled Virginia slave, heard the celebration outside, limped out the door, and then simply stood there praying. "Wouldn't let nobody tetch her, wouldn't set down. Stood dere swayin' fum side to side an' singin' over an' over her favorite hymn."

Oh, Father of Mercy
We give thanks to Thee
We give thanks to Thee
For thy great glory.

Like Aunt Sissy, many slaves viewed their deliverance as a sign of divine intervention. God's will had been heeded, if belatedly, and in this act lay final proof of His omnipresence. Few expressed it more eloquently than the Virginia black woman who looked upon emancipation as something approaching a miracle. "Isn't I a free woman now! De Lord can make Heaven out of Hell any time, I do believe." In addressing his Nashville congregation, a black preacher interpreted emancipation as a result of his people having kept the faith, even when it appeared as though there was no hope and that the Lord had forsaken them.

We was all like de chil'en of Israel in Egypt, a cryin' and cryin' and a gronin' and gronin', and no Moses came wid de Lord's word to order de door broke down, dat we might walk t'rough and be free. Now de big ugly door is broke down, bress de Lord, and we know de groans of de captive is heard. Didn't I tell you to pray and not to faint away, dat is not to doubt, and dat He who opened de sea would deliber us sure, and no tanks to de tasker massas, who would nebber let us go if dey could only hab held on to us? But dey couldn't—no dey couldn't do dat, 'cause de Lord he was wid us, and wouldn't let us be 'pressed no more. . . .

Hopes of Slave Owners

Even as many slaves reveled in their newly proclaimed freedom, few of them made any attempt to humiliate or unduly antagonize their newly dispossessed owners. Appreciating this fact, some masters and mistresses felt both grateful and immensely relieved. "Whilst glad of having freedom," Grace Elmore said of her servants, "they have never been more attentive or more respectful than now, and seem to wish to do all in their power to leave a pleasant impression." That the newly emancipated slaves had largely confined their release of emotion to a few relatively harmless celebrations encouraged some planters to think they could ease through the transition from bondage to freedom with a minimum of concession and change. Once the initial excitement subsided, they fully expected that economic necessity if not the "old ties" and attachment to the "home" would leave their blacks little choice but to carry on much as they had before the war. "We may still hope for a future I think," a prominent Alabaman confided to his journal. Since on many plantations and farms the day after freedom very much resembled the days that had preceded the master's announcement, such confidence appeared to be well founded. Even where a Jubilee atmosphere had prevailed, the blacks were no less appreciative of the immense problems they faced in acting on their new status. Like the other slaves on her Texas plantation, Annie

Hawkins had shouted for joy; nevertheless, she recalled, none of them made any move to leave "for fear old Mistress would bring us back or the pateroller would git us."

What masters and mistresses perceived as blacks fulfilling obligations learned under the tutelage of slavery might have been viewed differently by the former slaves themselves. In agreeing to stay until the planted crops had been harvested or until their assigned tasks in the household had been completed, many field hands and servants not only confirmed the freedom of choice now available to them but also exhibited a dignity and self-respect commensurate with their new status. Several of Grace Elmore's servants promised to give sufficient notice before leaving so as to enable their mistress to make other arrangements. The DeSaussure family of Charleston lost every servant but the nurse, and she agreed to stay only "as a favor until they could hire white servants." Few freed slaves, however, thought it necessary to emulate the attentiveness of a South Carolina woman who prepared to leave the family she had served for thirty-six years; before departing to join her husband and son, she made certain that all the clothes had been washed, she distributed gifts to the white children, and she left two of her children behind to wait on the family.

Despite the debilitating effects of dependency and the confusion which persisted over the precise nature of their new status, the freedmen were neither helpless, easily manipulated, nor frightened into passivity. Although some still deferred to the advice of the old master, many did not. During slavery, they had often survived only by drawing on their own inner resources, their accumulated experience, and the wisdom of those in their own ranks to whom they looked for leadership and counsel. Upon being told of their freedom, the blacks on many plantations retired to their quarters to discuss the announcement, what if any alternatives were now open to them, and the first steps they should take to test their freedom. On a plantation in Georgia, for example, where the owner had asked his former slaves to remain until they finished the current crop, they discussed his proposal for the next several days before reaching a common decision.

"They wasn't no celebration 'round the place," William Hutson recalled, "but they wasn't no work after the Master tells us we is free. Nobody leave the place though. Not 'til in the fall when the work is through."

The possibilities that suddenly presented themselves, the kinds of questions that freedom posed, the sheer magnitude of this event in their lives could not always be readily absorbed. Recounting his own escape to freedom, more than two decades before the war, William Wells Brown never forgot the strange sensations he experienced: "The fact that I was a freeman—could walk, talk, eat and sleep as a man, and no one to stand over me with the blood-clotted cowhide— all this made me feel that I was not myself." For the newly emancipated blacks, however, most of whom chose to remain in the same regions in which they had been slaves, the problems they faced were far different and more formidable than those which had confronted the fugitives upon reaching the North. Experiencing her first days of freedom, a Mississippi woman voiced that prevailing uncertainty as to how to give meaning to her new status: "I used to think if I could be free I should be the happiest of anybody in the world. But when my master come to me, and says—Lizzie, you is free! it seems like I was in a kind of daze. And when I would wake up in the morning I would think to myself, Is I free? Hasn't I got to get up before daylight and go into the field to work?"

Defining Freedom

The uncertainties plagued both blacks and whites. Under slavery, the boundaries had been clearly established and both parties understood them. But what were the proper boundaries of black freedom? What new forms would the relationship between a former slave and his former master now assume? How would the freed blacks be expected to interact with free whites? Neither the blacks nor the whites were altogether certain, though they might have pronounced views on such matters. Now that black freedom had been generally acknowledged, it needed to be defined. The state legislatures, the courts, and the Federal government offered some direction. But freedom could ultimately be defined only in the day-to-day lives and experiences of the people themselves. "De day of freedom," a former Tennessee slave recalled, the overseer came out into the fields and told them that they were free. "Free how?" they asked him, and he replied, "Free to work and live for demselves." In the aftermath of emancipation, the newly freed slaves would seek to test that response and answer the question for themselves.

Reconstruction: The Aftermath of Emancipation and Civil War

David W. Blight

The term "Reconstruction" refers to the process of re-building the United States and reintegrating the southern states following the Civil War, especially during the years between 1865 and 1877. The overthrow of slavery raised significant new issues for the nation during this time. These included what sort of political and civil rights former slaves possessed, what role the federal government should play in securing these rights, and how the South could adjust its economy from one based on slavery to one based on free labor. David W. Blight, professor of history and black studies at Amherst College in Massachusetts, provides a brief recapitulation of this era of American history. He discusses the "Black Codes" written by southern states to restrict the rights of blacks, the political reforms enacted by Radical Republicans in Congress to help former slaves, and the rise of the sharecropping system that replaced slavery as the source of agricultural labor in the South. The end of slavery was only the beginning of a long road toward full and equal citizenship for former slaves and their descendants, he concludes.

In its immediate context the meaning of the Civil War for African Americans had no more poignant illustration than the fall of Richmond, the capital of the Confederacy, in the first week of April 1865. Black troops were among the first Union forces to occupy the city, and the freed population welcomed them in what the black newspaper correspondent, T. Morris Chester, called 'a spectacle of jubilee.' Jubilant

Excerpted from "The Age of Emancipation," by David W. Blight in *A History of the African American People* (New York: Smithmark, 1995). Reprinted with the permission of Salamander Books Ltd.

black folk welcomed President Lincoln when he visited Richmond on 4 April, only two days after Confederate evacuation. Chester reported that the freedpeople formed a 'great concourse of American citizens of African descent' as Lincoln strode through the streets of Richmond. Such revolutionary transformations were cause for explosions of hope and joy.

For most blacks, Reconstruction began with emancipation. As the war lurched to its devastating conclusion across the South, black men and women began to defy old symbols of bondage and seek new identities. They were helped immeasurably by a host of private, northern freedmen's aid societies which provided food, supplies, schooling, and assistance in the transition to free labor. By the last months of the war, the federal government established the Bureau of Refugees, Freedmen, and Abandoned Lands (the Freedmen's Bureau), the first such agency of public social uplift in American history. Many freedpeople embraced new names, and insisted on being addressed as 'Mrs.' or 'Mr.' Thousands of black women removed themselves from field labor, devoting themselves to the security and cohesion of their families. Nuclear families survived slavery, but not without a terrible legacy recorded in slave traders' profits, and stories of long-lost kin. Although the vast majority of the freedpeople would end up living in their old places in time, many moved about in demonstration of their freedom. In these revolutionary circumstances, extraordinary hopes could flourish. A whole black Virginia regiment spent the final winter of the war in a freedmen's school learning to read and write. One of its sergeants wrote home in March 1865: 'Surely this is a mighty and progressive age in which we live.' The world of southern planters had been destroyed, an entire social order crushed by war. Southern whites understood their predicament. Some took out their frustration in random violence against the freedpeople, while others faced reality stoically and accepted a new order.

Radical Republicanism

No change was more apparent than the new relationship blacks now had with the American nation state, with *politics* it-

self. By right and by blood, African Americans now insisted
that they were part of the polity. For the first several years of
Reconstruction, the leaders of the Republican Party agreed,
although, during the period known as 'Presidential Reconstruction' (1865–7), they were thwarted by Lincoln's succes-
sor, Andrew Johnson of Tennessee. Motivated by racist beliefs
and the doctrine of states' rights, Johnson believed Reconstruction should preserve 'the Union as it was, the Constitution as it is.' He did not view emancipation as a victory, but as
an unfortunate, if necessary, result of defeating the Confederacy. Johnson opposed black suffrage and the extension of citizenship rights to blacks; he especially resisted the aim of
some Radical republicans to redistribute land to the freedpeople. Johnson attempted to *restore* the ex-Confederate
states to the Union at the end of 1865, with very little of
Southern society *reconstructed*. The 'Johnson governments'
included the notorious 'Black Codes,' laws written across the
South in 1865 restricting the freedmen's economic options
and mobility, and utterly denying them political or civil
rights. Designed as labor controls and plantation discipline,
such laws were clear evidence of white Southerners' refusal to
accept the deeper meanings of emancipation.

Whether the Civil War had truly fomented a Second
American Revolution depended on the fateful debates over
the place of black civil, political, and economic liberty in a
restored Union. America's national history and the actual
lives of black folks were never more interdependent. Out-
raged at the Black Codes, and led by Radicals Thaddeus
Stevens of Pennsylvania and Charles Sumner of Massachusetts, northern Republicans in Congress seized control of
Reconstruction policies during 1866–7. What ensued was an
unprecedented Constitutional struggle between Congress
and President over the function of the federal government
and the meaning of the war. The Radical Republicans produced a blueprint for Reconstruction. Their ideology was
grounded in the idea of an activist federal government, a re-
definition of American citizenship that guaranteed equal political rights for black men, and a faith in free labor. The
Radicals greatly expanded federal authority, and they envi-

sioned Reconstruction as a process of 'remaking' a nation by remaking the defeated South. Their cardinal principle was *equality before the law,* which in 1866 they enshrined in the 14th Amendment, expanding citizenship to all those born in the US without regard to race. That same year Congress also renewed the Freedmen's Bureau, and passed the first civil rights act in American history.

The southern states' rejection of the 14th Amendment, Johnson's repeated vetoes of Reconstruction measures, as well as his repudiation at the polls in the Congressional elections of 1866, gave the Radicals increased control over federal policy. In 1867 Congress divided the ex-Confederate states into five military districts, and made black suffrage a condition of readmission to the Union. By 1870 all ex-Confederate states had rejoined the Union, and in most, the Republican Party, built as a coalition of 'carpetbaggers' (northerners who moved South during Reconstruction), 'scalawags' (native southerners who gave allegiance to the new order), and black voters held the reins of state governments. Indeed, black voters were the core constituency of southern Republicanism and the means to power. In February 1869, Congress passed the 15th Amendment, a limited guarantee of equal suffrage which forbade states from denying the right to vote on grounds of race or previous condition of servitude. But the amendment was silent on the 11 northern states that still denied the vote to blacks; it also ignored women's suffrage, and most importantly, did nothing to stop future enactment of inequitable qualifications tests. Despite these limitations, many northerners saw the 15th Amendment as a final act of Reconstruction, and black leaders had little choice but to make the most of a halfway victory.

Black Leaders

Perhaps the most remarkable revolution during Radical Reconstruction was the emergence of a group of black politicians at nearly every level of government. Consisting of many free-born, northern-educated ministers, former soldiers, and activists (although some ex-slaves as well), over 600 black men served in state legislatures and 16 served in

Congress during Reconstruction (22 served in Congress between 1869 and 1901). At the state and local level these men helped to establish public school systems, more equitable taxation, bargaining mechanisms between laborers and planters, and economic development.

Political mobilization in southern black communities was a stunning achievement in 1867–8. The Union Leagues, originally founded as northern patriotic clubs during the Civil War, became the nexus of a remarkable political awakening. Blacks attended meetings and rallies where Republican newspapers were read aloud, and speeches were delivered by dozens of black itinerant lecturers. Sometimes work stoppages and strikes were born in Union League activities. Through this season of great hope, southern blacks, who had never witnessed an abolitionist meeting or read an anti-slavery newspaper like their northern cousins, now wrapped themselves in the heritage of the Declaration of Independence as well as recollections of slavery, enjoyed a freedom of expression they had only previously dreamed of, and claimed, as did an Alabama meeting, 'exactly the same rights, privileges and immunities as are enjoyed by white men—we ask nothing more and will be content with nothing less . . . The law no longer knows white nor black, but simply men.' On such principles are democratic societies built. But the days of power and security for blacks in Reconstruction politics were all too short.

Southern Redemption

In 1868, black votes were crucial to the election of Republican Ulysses S. Grant to the Presidency. Across the South, radical state constitutions provided a legal basis for the new order. But Reconstruction policies, and all the new aspirations that blacks had hitched to them, depended directly upon federal enforcement. 'These constitutions and governments,' declared a Charleston, South Carolina opposition newspaper, 'will last just as long as the bayonets which ushered them into being . . .' That year the Ku Klux Klan launched a campaign of political violence and terror directed at black and white Republicans. During Grant's first term in office, a legal and military campaign against the Klan was undertaken that was temporarily effective, but only after such groups had committed hundreds of murders in their effort to re-establish conservative white control of southern politics.

During the 1870s the power of the Radical Republicans waned dramatically. Driven by an ideology of laissez-faire government and economic expansion (especially in the wake of the depression of 1873), a postwar northern disinterest in social issues, and a desire to leave the South to its own devices, the federal government *retreated* from Reconstruction. In this context, aided by violence and terrorism, a white counterrevolution, known as 'southern redemption,' occurred through the resurgent Democratic Party. The final retreat, and the collapse of Reconstruction, came in the disputed Presidential election of 1876. Only three states, South Carolina, Florida, and Louisiana, remained under tenuous Republican Party control. Due to corruption and intimidation, the election returns in those states were fiercely disputed, leading to a late-hour national political compromise giving the Republican Rutherford B. Hayes the Presidency in return for acquiescence in Democratic Party control ('home rule') of the remaining southern states. This sectional compromise, reached under threats of marching troops and a new disunion, brought an irrevocable end to Reconstruction in spring 1877.

These events had dire consequences for African Americans. Frederick Douglass had anticipated such results at least as early as 1875. In a speech in Washington, DC, he reflected upon the nation's impending celebration of the centennial of American independence. The nation, Douglass feared, would 'lift to the sky its million voices in one grand Centennial hosanna of peace and good will to all the white race . . . from gulf to lakes and from sea to sea.' Douglass looked back upon 15 years of unparalleled change for his people, worried about the hold of white supremacy on America's historical consciousness, and asked the core question in the nation's struggle over the memory of the Civil War and emancipation: 'If war among the whites brought peace and liberty to the blacks, what will peace among the whites bring?' Answers to Douglass's poignant question would determine the character of American race relations in the late nineteenth century. The ultimate tragedy of the era was that, while the sections reconciled, the races divided.

The Birth of Sharecropping

Some of the deepest legacies of slavery were the beliefs among whites that without compulsion, blacks would not work, and that they had no essential need for education. From the Day of Jubilee into the 1890s, as the postfreedom generation came of age, southern blacks proved these notions wrong; and they did so in the face of a pervasive popular culture that made the 'old time plantation Negro' the central figure of minstrelsy and popular literature. What freedpeople most wanted during Reconstruction was land; the lack of land redistribution became the most enduring failure of the era. The freedpeople faced diminishing economic choices, but not before they left ample testimony to their heroic quest for land and literacy. By 1869 the Freedmen's Bureau alone had created some 4,000 schools attended by 250,000 people. At a freedmen's meeting in the heady days of 1866 in Virginia, an ex-slave named Bayley Wyatt left this eloquent statement of the labor theory of value:

> We now as a people desires to be elevated, and we desires to do all we can to be educated . . . I may state to all our friends, and to all our enemies, that we has right to the land where we are located. For why? I tell you. Our wives, our children, our husbands, has been sold over and over again to purchase the land we now locate upon; for that reason we have a divine right to the land . . .

Wyatt's understanding of the natural rights tradition notwithstanding, most blacks would lose the tug-of-war between the white planters' desire for labor control and the freedpeople's demands for mobility and land.

From early contracts working by 'task' and for wages, to renting arrangements that blacks came to resist because of the South's chronic cash scarcity, the sharecropping system was born as a compromise between landowners and farmers.

Freedmen accepted, even sought, tenancy because it appeared to provide a degree of autonomy over their economic lives. Sharecroppers generally worked on 'halves,' giving half of their cotton crop to the landowner, keeping the rest for their own maintenance. But this system evolved into debt dependency for most sharecroppers. Gone were slavery and the huge plantations of the antebellum period; gang labor no longer existed except in some sugar-growing districts. But a new institution—the rural furnishing merchant—now stymied hopes for self-sufficiency. The merchant at the crossroads general store now monopolized credit, forcing the sharecropper to pay in crops for his family's supplies. From season to season, most tenants found themselves deeper in debt to the man at the store. Such were the roots of the persistent post-Civil War poverty that engulfed black and white southerners. Although they were 50 percent of the southern population, by 1900 blacks owned just over 2 percent of farms. . . .

The postfreedom generation picked cotton, wrote history and novels, built colleges, edited newspapers, believed in America and was betrayed by it. . . .

Born at the end of Reconstruction, an old sharecropper named Nate Shaw observed:

> Time passes and the generations die. But the condition of the people that's livin today aint now like it's goin to be for the people that comes after us. I can't say exactly what the future way of life will be, but I has a idea. My color, the colored race of people on earth, goin to shed theirselves of these slavery ways. But it takes many a trip to the river to get clean.

Shaw peered into the human condition and into the challenge of African-American life in the second half of the nineteenth century.

Chapter 5

Was the Civil War Necessary to End Slavery?

Turning Points
Points
IN WORLD HISTORY

War Was Not Necessary to End American Slavery

Jeffrey Rogers Hummel

A question that is still debated by historians is whether America could have ended slavery without the violent and costly Civil War. Jeffrey Rogers Hummel, an economics and history professor at Golden Gate University in San Francisco, suggests that American slavery could have been stopped by other means. Citing the experiences of the British West Indies and Brazil, where slavery was abolished without war, Hummel argues that President Abraham Lincoln could have let southern states peaceably secede in 1861 and still have laid the groundwork for slavery's eventual demise. An independent Confederacy that shared a long border with a free United States would have found it very difficult to prevent slaves from running away or rebelling.

As an excuse for civil war, maintaining the State's territorial integrity is bankrupt and reprehensible. Slavery's elimination is the only morally worthy justification. The fact that abolition was an unintended consequence in no way gainsays the accomplishment. "The nineteenth century was preeminently the century of emancipations," explains [historian] C. Vann Woodward. Small-scale emancipations began in the northern states during the previous century, and chattel slavery was not ended in coastal Kenya until 1907. But starting with the British colonies in 1833 and finishing with Brazil in 1888, over six million slaves achieved some kind of freedom in the Western Hemisphere. Four million were blacks in the United States. "The emancipation experience of the South," Woodward concludes, "dwarfs all others in scale and magnitude."

Yet this justification holds only if war was indeed necessary. No abolition was completely peaceful, but the United States and Haiti are just two among twenty-odd slave societies where violence predominated. The fact that emancipation overwhelmed such entrenched plantation economies as Cuba and Brazil suggests that slavery was politically moribund anyway. An ideological movement that had its meager roots in the eighteenth century eventually eliminated everywhere a labor system that had been ubiquitous throughout world civilizations for millennia. Historical speculations about an independent Confederacy halting or reversing this overwhelming momentum are hard to credit.

Lincoln's Options

When Lincoln took the presidential oath in 1861, letting the lower South secede in peace was a viable antislavery option. At the moment of Lincoln's inauguration the Union still retained more slave states than had left. Radical abolitionists, such as William Lloyd Garrison, had traditionally advocated northern secession from the South. They felt that this best hastened the destruction of slavery by allowing the free states to get out from under the Constitution's fugitive slave provision. Passionately opposing slavery and simultaneously favoring secession are therefore quite consistent. Yet hardly any modern account of the Union's fiery conflagration even acknowledges this untried alternative.

Revisionist Civil War historians at one time argued that slavery was *economically* doomed. Economists have subjected that claim to searching scrutiny, discovering in fact that American slavery was profitable and expanding. But as [historian] Eric Foner has perceptively noted, "plantation slavery had always been both a political and economic institution. It could not have existed without a host of legal and coercive measures designed to define the status of the black laborer and prevent the emergence of competing modes of social organization." In the United States these measures included restrictions on manumission, disabilities against free blacks, compulsory slave patrols, and above all fugitive slave laws.

Slavery was doomed *politically* even if Lincoln had permitted the small Gulf Coast Confederacy[1] to depart in peace. The Republican-controlled Congress would have been able to work toward emancipation within the border states, where slavery was already declining. In due course the Radicals[2] could have repealed the Fugitive Slave Law of 1850. With chattels fleeing across the border and raising slavery's enforcement costs, the peculiar institution's final destruction within an independent cotton South was inevitable.

Even future Confederate Vice-President Alexander Stephens had judged "slavery much more secure in the Union than out of it." Secession was a gamble of pure desperation for slaveholders, only attempted because the institution clearly had no political future within the Union. The individual runaway both helped provoke secession—northern resistance to fugitive recapture being a major southern grievance—and ensured that secession would be unable to shield slavery in the end. Back in 1842, Joseph Rogers Underwood, representing Kentucky in the House of Representatives, warned his fellow Southerners that "the dissolution of the Union was the dissolution of slavery." Why? "Just as soon as Mason and Dixon's line and the Ohio river become the boundary between independent nations, slavery ceases in all the border states. How could we retain our slaves, when they, in one hour, one day, or a week at furthest, could pass the boundary?" Once across, the slave could "then turn round and curse his master from the other shore." Nor would the peculiar institution's collapse stop at the border states. "Do you not see that sooner or later, this process would extend itself farther and farther south, rendering slave labor so precarious and uncertain that it could not be depended upon; and consequently a slave would become almost worthless; and thus the institution itself would gradually, but certainly, perish?"

1. the seven states that seceded prior to the outbreak of hostilities in Fort Sumter: South Carolina, Georgia, Louisiana, Mississippi, Florida, Alabama, and Texas   2. Republicans in Congress who strongly opposed slavery and supported black civil rights

Overthrow of Slavery in Brazil

Just such a process later accelerated the demise of slavery in Brazil. This slave economy was in 1825 the New World's second largest, holding in bondage only slightly fewer than the American South. Yet even before Brazil's abolition, manumission caused free blacks to exceed slaves in total numbers, with an estimated half those manumissions through self-purchase. By 1850 free blacks were 43 percent of the population, making a large constituency opposed to slavery. Although the government instituted gradual emancipation in 1871, the law freed only slaves born after its enactment, and only when they reached the age of twenty-one. Brazil also established a tax fund to purchase the freedom of those to whom the law did not apply, but during its operation three times as many purchased their own freedom or were granted manumission.

Brazilian abolitionists meanwhile succeeded in outlawing slavery in the northeastern state of Ceará in 1884. An underground railroad immediately came into existence. Planters retaliated with a fugitive slave law, but the law was widely evaded. The state of Amazonas and many cities joined Ceará. Slavery rapidly disintegrated in the coffee growing region of São Paulo. The value of slaves fell by 80 percent despite the fact that none was slated to be liberated through gradual emancipation. Finally in 1888 the government accepted a *fait accompli* and decreed immediate and uncompensated emancipation. The total number of slaves had already declined from two and a half million, or 30 percent of the population in 1850, to half a million, or less than 3 percent.

"Slavery could not last if the slaves had freedom within arm's length," recalled American abolitionist Moncure Conway. Slavery in the Cape Colony of southern Africa, for instance, depended upon the transportation of blacks from Mozambique and Madagascar and of east Indians. The so-called Hottentots, indigenous to the area, were nearly impossible to keep enslaved because they could escape too easily. Civil War runaways so weakened the peculiar institution that the Confederacy itself turned toward emancipating and arming blacks. Slavery thus neither explains nor justifies

Northern suppression of secession. The Union war effort reduces, in the words of Conway, to "mere manslaughter."

Comparing Civil War with Slave Insurrection

Brazilian abolitionists had also encouraged resistance by distributing arms to the slaves. An independent Confederacy still faced the specter of John Brown, who merely wished to bring the revolutionary right of secession down to the plantation. The massive uprising that Brown, Lysander Spooner, and David Walker each hoped for[3] would obviously have resulted in much loss of life, but worth speculation is whether it could ever have approached the Civil War's unmatched toll: one dead soldier for every six freed slaves. The war took nearly as many lives as the total number of slaves liberated without bloodshed in the British West Indies. Those who complacently accept this as a necessary sacrifice for eliminating an evil institution inexplicably blanch at the potential carnage of slave revolts.

Violence ultimately ended slavery, but violence of a very different nature. Rather than revolutionary violence wielded by bondsmen themselves from the bottom up, a violence that at least had the potential to be pinpointed against the South's minority of guilty slaveowners, the Civil War involved indiscriminate State violence directed from the top down. Nor would an insurgency's economic devastation likely have reached the war's $6.6 billion cost (in 1860 prices), about evenly divided between the two sides. The North's portion alone was enough to buy all slaves and set up each family with forty acres and a mule. John Brown's plan had the added advantage of actively mobilizing blacks in their own liberation. The social institutions that the revolutionaries would have ineluctably created could have altered the subsequent history of the southern race relations. On what consistent grounds can anyone find war between two governments morally superior to slave rebellion?

3. Abolitionist Brown led an abortive slave uprising in Virginia in 1859. Spooner, a white Boston abolitionist, published plans to incite and assist slave uprisings in the 1850s. Walker was a free black who wrote a pamphlet in 1828 calling for black revolution.

The Significance of America's Civil War and Abolition of Slavery in World History

Robert W. Fogel

Robert W. Fogel is director of the Center for Population Economics at the University of Chicago and the author of several influential books on American slavery. In contrast to Jeffrey Rogers Hummel, author of the preceding viewpoint, Fogel concludes that a peaceful abolition of slavery in the American South was impossible at the time the Civil War began. He goes on to argue that the Confederacy's defeat in the Civil War and the end of slavery in the United States had significant global ramifications; a victorious Confederacy would have strengthened the forces of slavery and aristocracy and demoralized antislavery and democracy reform movements worldwide.

For more than a century historians have been engaged in an intense debate about the causes of the Civil War. Although some scholars have held that slavery was *the* cause, others have developed complex analyses that draw distinctions between immediate and ultimate causes and that explore a variety of ways other than war that could have settled or at least contained the issue of slavery. They have also analyzed a wide range of economic, political, and cultural issues between the sections other than slavery that promoted antagonisms and that rival slavery (some believe they dominate it) as an explanation for the war. Among the most nagging of the moral questions to emerge from these debates is the one posed by David M. Potter, who, until his death in 1971, was one of the most respected historians of his generation.

In totaling up the balance sheet of the Civil War, Potter

concluded: "Slavery was dead; secession was dead; and six hundred thousand men were dead." So one soldier died for six slaves who were freed and for ten white Southerners who were kept in the Union. In the face of so bloody a war, a "person is entitled to wonder," said Potter, "whether the Southerners could have been held and the slaves could not have been freed at a smaller per-capita cost." When he posed this problem it was still widely believed that slavery was an economically moribund system and the proposition that economic forces would eventually have solved the problem of slavery was tenable. Even so, there was a question of how soon. And if not, there was a question of when, if ever, southern slaveholders would have peacefully acceded to any scheme for emancipation, no matter how gradual, no matter how full the proffered compensation.

Prospects for Peaceful Abolition

Whatever the opportunity for a peaceful abolition of slavery along British lines before 1845, it surely was nonexistent after that date. To southern slaveholders, West Indian emancipation was a complete failure. It provided undeniable proof, if any was needed, of the malevolent designs that the abolitionists and their allies harbored for their class. They could plainly see that the economy of the West Indies was in shambles, that the personal fortunes of the West Indian planters had collapsed, and that the assurances made to these planters in 1833 to obtain their acquiescence to compensated emancipation were violated as soon as the planters were reduced to political impotency. Given such an assessment of the consequences of compensated emancipation, a peaceful end to slavery could only have been achieved if economic forces made slaves worthless or, more compelling, an absolute drain on the income of their owners.

From the mid-1840s on, however, the slave economy of the South was vigorous and growing rapidly. Whatever the pessimism of masters during the economic crises of 1826–1831 and 1840–1845, during the last half of the 1840s and most of the 1850s they foresaw a continuation of their prosperity and, save for the political threat from the North, numerous opportunities for its expansion. The main thrust of cliometric research[1] has demonstrated that this economic optimism was well-founded; it has also undermined the competing thesis that slavery was gradually expiring of its own internal economic contradictions. Although he presented it in a political rather than an economic context, [historian Kenneth] Stampp's rejoinder to Potter is equally germane here. A "person is also entitled to ask," he said, "how many more generations of black men should have been forced to endure life in bondage in order to avoid its costly and violent end."

After the [1860] election of Lincoln the choices open to northern foes of slavery no longer included the moderate strategy—which was to restrict and gradually undermine the slave economy as the British abolitionists had done between 1812 and 1833, and as the Brazilian abolitionists were able to do in the 1880s. Once the cotton states of the South moved on to the secessionist path, peaceful restoration of the Union was no longer possible merely by returning to the status quo of c. 1850, even if the rights of slaveholders everywhere below 36°30' and of their property rights in fugitives were embodied in new, irrevocable amendments to the Constitution, as was proposed in the Crittenden Resolutions.[2] The majority of the Senate and House members from these states rejected all such compromises. They were convinced that northern hostility to slavery precluded a union that would promote the economic, political, and international objectives that had become predominant among politicians of the cotton South. As the votes for the delegates to the state convention indicated, by early 1861 majority opinion in the deep South held that a future in the Union "promised nothing but increasingly galling economic exploitation by the dominant section and the rapid reduction of the South to political impotence."

So the central moral problem of the Civil War is not the

---

1. applying economic and statistical methods to the study of history   2. Senator John J. Crittenden of Kentucky introduced several resolutions in December 1860 in an effort to placate southern concerns about preserving slavery and thus prevent secession.

one posed by Potter but the one posed in Stampp's response to him. By early 1861 maintenance of peace required not merely northern acquiescence to the status quo of c. 1850, but acquiescence to the existence of an independent confederacy dedicated to the promotion of slavery. It follows that assessment of the dilemma posed by Stampp requires more than weighing the sin of slavery against the sin of war. It requires also a consideration of the likely chain of events that would have unfolded if the South had been unshackled from northern restraint and allowed to become a worldwide champion of slavery and of aristocratic republicanism.

What Would Have Happened?

Consideration of what might have happened if the Confederate states had been allowed to secede peacefully is an excursion into beliefs about a world that never existed. Even if these beliefs are based on patterns of behavior during the years leading up to the war, patterns of behavior that provide a reasonable basis for prediction, the best predictions are necessarily shrouded in uncertainty and open to debate. Yet there is no way of dealing with the moral issues of the Civil War that avoids these "counterfactual propositions" (as philosophers call them). Every historian who has set out to deal with the causes of the Civil War (certainly all those who have debated its necessity or avoidability) has implicitly or explicitly presumed what would have happened to slavery if some events had unfolded in a way that was different from the actual course. Indeed, much of the voluminous literature on the causes of the Civil War is nothing more or less than a marshaling of evidence on the events leading up to the Civil War that is dictated by different visions of this counterfactual world.

Peaceful secession, I believe, would not only have indefinitely delayed the freeing of U.S. slaves but would have thwarted the antislavery movement everywhere else in the world. It would also very likely have slowed down the struggle to extend suffrage and other democratic rights to the lower classes in Europe, and it might have eroded whatever rights had already been granted to them in both Europe and

North America. Since the forces of reaction everywhere would have been greatly encouraged, and those of democracy and reform demoralized, it is likely that the momentum for liberal reform would have been replaced by a drive for aristocratic privilege under the flags of paternalism and the preservation of order.

Such a vision of events may seem fantastic to those accustomed to the rhetoric and conventions of modern (plebeian) democracy. We live in a world in which the underprivileged regularly contend for power: abroad, through labor and socialist parties; at home, through such influential organizations as the AFL-CIO, NOW, and the Rainbow Coalition.[3] However, during the 1850s and 1860s democracy as we now know it, and lower-class rights generally, hung in the balance throughout the Western world. In Great Britain the great majority of workers were disfranchised, trade unions were illegal, strikes were criminal acts, and quitting a job without an employer's permission was a breach of contract punishable by stiff fines and years of imprisonment. The legacy of serfdom was heavy in Portugal, Spain, Italy, eastern Prussia, Russia, Hungary, the Balkans, Turkey, and much of South America, while slavery flourished in Cuba, Brazil, Surinam, Africa, the Middle East, and numerous other places. Even in the North, strikes were proscribed, property qualifications for voting were widespread until the 1820s (and were still enforced against free blacks in New York and other states in the 1860s), and vagrancy laws were a powerful club against workers. The movement for the disfranchisement of the foreign born was partially successful in some northern states during the 1850s, and in Virginia a referendum to reinstitute a property qualification for voters was approved on the eve of the Civil War.

The fact that the liberals who dominated politics in the North and in Britain rejected slavery as a solution to the

---

3. The American Federation of Labor-Congress of Industrial Organizations (AFL-CIO) is one of the nation's oldest and largest labor union organizations. The National Organization for Women (NOW), founded in 1966, is a prominent women's rights group. The "Rainbow Coalition" refers to political supporters of the 1984 and 1988 presidential bids of black civil rights leader Jesse Jackson.

menace posed by an unconstrained lower-class "rabble" does not mean that they were oblivious to the menace. Reformers such as Lord [Thomas B.] Macaulay remained adamant in the opinion that the franchise had to be restricted to men of property and that a large police force and army were needed to keep the lower classes in check. Even such a celebrated champion of the propertyless masses as [newspaper publisher] Horace Greeley supported the use of military force to put down strikes.

Potential Power of the Confederacy

If the Confederacy had been allowed to establish itself peacefully, to work out economic and diplomatic policies, and to develop international alliances, it would have emerged as a major international power. Although its population was relatively small, its great wealth would have made it a force to be reckoned with. The Confederacy would probably have used its wealth and military power to establish itself as the dominant nation in Latin America, perhaps annexing Cuba and Puerto Rico, Yucatán, and Nicaragua as well as countering Britain's antislavery pressures on Brazil. Whether the Confederacy would have sought to counter British antislavery policies in Africa or to form alliances with the principal slave-trading nations of the Middle East is more uncertain, but these would have been options.

The Confederacy could have financed its expansionist, proslavery policies by exploiting the southern monopoly of cotton production. A 5¢ sales tax on cotton not only would have put most of the burden of such policies on foreign consumers, but would have yielded about $100 million annually during the 1860s—50 percent more than the entire federal budget on the eve of the Civil War. With such a revenue the Confederacy could have emerged as one of the world's strongest military powers, maintaining a standing army several times as large as the North's, rapidly developing a major navy, and conducting an aggressive foreign policy. Such revenues would also have permitted it to covertly or overtly finance aristocratic forces in Europe who were vying with democratic ones for power across the Continent.

Shrewd manipulation of its monopoly of raw cotton would have permitted the Confederacy to reward its international friends and punish its enemies. Embargoes or other restrictions on the sale of raw cotton could have delivered punishing blows to the economies of England and the Northeast, where close to 20 percent of the nonagricultural labor force was directly or indirectly engaged in the manufacture and sale of cotton textiles. The resulting unemployment and losses of wealth would have disrupted both the labor and capital markets in these regions, and probably speeded up the emergence of a large textile industry in the South. The West would also have been destabilized economically, since the decline of the Northeast would have severely contracted the market for western agricultural products. As the Confederacy shifted more of its labor into manufacturing, trade, and the military, it would probably have developed an increasing deficit in food, making it again a major market for the grain, dairy, and meat surpluses of the Northwest.

Such economic developments would have generated strong political pressures in the North for a modus vivendi with the Confederacy. Northern politics would have been further complicated by any border states, such as Maryland, Kentucky, and Missouri, that might have remained inside the Union. Attempts to appropriate their slave property would have run a high risk of further secessions. The Republicans not only would have borne the responsibility for the economic crisis created by the rise of the Confederacy, but would have lost the plank on which the party had risen to power. With the bulk of slaveowners prohibited from entry into northern territories because of secession, the claim that the victory by the Republican party was the only way of saving these lands for free labor would have been an empty slogan to farmers and nonagricultural workers who were suffering from the effects of a severe and extended depression. Moreover, the failure of the North to act against the slaveholders who remained within the Union would have undermined its credibility with democratic forces abroad. Such developments would probably have delivered both a lasting blow to antislavery politics and an enormous fillip to nativist politics.

I do not maintain that the preceding sketch of what might have happened in the absence of a civil war is the only plausible one. However, it is a credible sketch of the likely train of events, one that is consistent with what we now know about the capacity of the slave economy of the South as well as with current knowledge of the political crosscurrents in the South, the North, and the rest of the world. At the very least, it points to reasons for doubting that there was a happy, relatively costless solution to the moral dilemma posed by Stampp.

I have not, it should be emphasized, put forward the gloomiest view of the alternative to the Civil War. The preceding sketch suggests an indefinite but more or less peaceful continuation of slavery. It would not be difficult to make a case for the proposition that peaceful secession would merely have postponed the Civil War and that the delay would have created circumstances far more favorable to a southern victory. In that case aristocratic proslavery forces would have gained unchallenged control of the richest and potentially the most powerful nation in the world. Such an outcome not only would have greatly increased the likelihood of rolling back the movement for working-class rights everywhere, but might have led to a loss of human lives far greater than the toll of the Civil War.

What the Civil War Achieved

As pacifists, [abolitionist William Lloyd] Garrison and his followers had to confront the dilemma posed by a violent confrontation with the Confederacy. They reluctantly came to the conclusion that bloody as it might be, the Civil War was the only realistic way of ridding the world of slavery. [Unitarian clergyman] William E. Channing, who had hoped against hope that slavery could be ended by moral suasion alone, explained why the destruction of slavery was the moral imperative of his age. "Slavery must fall," he said, "because it stands in direct hostility to all the grand movements, principles, and reforms of our age, because it stands in the way of an advancing world."

What the Civil War achieved, then, was more than just

inflated wealth for northern capitalists and "half" freedom for blacks ("the shoddy aristocracy of the North and the ragged children of the South"). It preserved and reinforced conditions favorable to a continued struggle for the democratic rights of the lower classes, black and white alike, and for the improvement of their economic condition, not only in America but everywhere else in the world. The fall of slavery did not usher in the millennium, it produced no heaven on earth, but it vitalized all the grand movements, principles, and reforms of Channing's age and of our own.

Discussion Questions

Chapter 1: Origins of American Slavery

1. What differences does Daniel C. Littlefield say existed between slavery in traditional African societies and slavery as it developed in the West Indies and in British North America? What accounts for these differences? Which forms of slavery does he consider most inhumane? Why?

2. Why were the English settlers of the Chesapeake colonies of Virginia and Maryland slow to create a slave society, according to John B. Boles? What factors ultimately led to the rise of a slave society in the southern colonies?

3. In what respects did slave laws and customs differ between northern and southern colonies, according to Donald R. Wright? How does he account for those differences?

Chapter 2: Slavery and the American Revolution

1. What actions does Peter Tolchin say were taken by the nation's Founding Fathers to restrict or abolish slavery during and immediately after the American Revolution? What general consensus on slavery emerged? Did the Constitution represent a victory for slave supporters or opponents, according to Tolchin?

2. Why did slavery perish in the northern states but not in the southern states, according to Gary B. Nash? Does he portray the nation's early leaders less favorably (from an antislavery perspective) than they appear in Peter Tolchin's account? Explain.

Chapter 3: A House Divided: American Slavery in the Antebellum Era

1. What important principle concerning the powers of Congress did the Missouri Compromise establish, according to Roger L. Ransom? Why, in his opinion, was the Missouri Compromise so successful in relieving national tensions over slavery?

2. According to Nathaniel Weyl and William Marina, what was the central achievement and legacy of John C. Calhoun? Why did he, and many Southerners, believe that continued territorial ex-

pansion of slavery was so important? Explain.

3. Why did many Southerners object so strongly to abolitionist literature, in the view of William W. Freehling? What made the views expressed by "South Carolina extremists" so threatening to national unity, in his view?

4. How does Ronald Takaki characterize the relationship between slave and master in the antebellum South? How could concerns about slave rebellion described by Takaki affect North/South slavery divisions that are described in the other viewpoints in this chapter? Explain.

5. How did the slaveholding class rely on the federal government to protect their property, according to James Oakes? Why, in his view, did this reliance come to be a serious problem for slaveholders?

6. John Hope Franklin and Albert A. Moss Jr. argue that if slavery did not exist, the disputes between North and South in the 1850s could have been resolved without war. What arguments do they make to support this contention? In your view, what events of the 1850s—that the authors describe—stem solely or almost solely from the slavery issue? Explain.

Chapter 4: Civil War and the End of American Slavery

1. What actions did slave and free blacks take during the Civil War, according to Merton L. Dillon? What made slave resistance so effective in the Civil War?

2. How did blacks respond to news of the Emancipation Proclamation, according to James M. McPherson? Why does he believe it to be a turning point in the history of American slavery?

3. What uncertainties and questions does Leon F. Litwack argue were created by the abolition of slavery in the United States? How might this explain the wide emotional range of responses of slaves to their liberation?

4. David W. Blight writes that many of the contentious issues of the Reconstruction era rose from the question of what place former slaves had in American society. What were some of the fundamental differences concerning slaves between President Andrew Johnson and the Radical Republicans in Congress? Why did the weakening of Radical Republican influence in the 1870s have dire consequences for African Americans?

Chapter 5: Was the Civil War Necessary to End Slavery?

1. Abraham Lincoln could have let the Southern states secede in 1861, preventing war and even ultimately ending slavery in those states, contends Jeffrey Rogers Hummel. Do you believe, as he did, that Lincoln made the wrong choice? Defend your answer.

2. Roger Fogel employs a "counterfactual" scenario, trying to envision what might have happened had the South won the American Civil War. Do you think such an exercise is useful in assessing certain historical questions? Why or why not?

3. Fogel and Hummel have differing opinions as to whether America could have abolished slavery without the Civil War. After reading both viewpoints, which do you believe presents the more convincing argument? What other viewpoints in this volume might be used to support either Fogel's or Hummel's conclusions?

Appendix of Documents

Document 1: Early Virginia Slave Laws

Slavery as a legal institution did not officially exist in the colony of Virginia when the first Africans arrived there in 1619. Blacks apparently were viewed as equivalent to white indentured servants (which were far more numerous), bound for a set number of years of servitude. However, over time Virginia developed a system in which blacks became the lifetime property of the owner. The following are excerpts from some of colonial Virginia's first laws establishing slavery; these statutes codified social practices that were probably already established at the time the laws were enacted.

Run-aways, Act CII, March, 1661–62

. . . *Bee it therefore enacted* that all runaways . . . shalbe lyable to make satisfaction by service . . . double their times of service soe neglected and if the time of their running away was in the crop or the charge of recovering them extraordinary the court shall lymitt a longer time of service . . . and in case any English servant shall run away in company of any negroes who are incapable of making satisfaction by addition of a time, *it is enacted* that the English soe running away in the company with them shall at the time of service to their owne masters expired, serve the masters of the said negroes for their absence soe long as they should have done by this act if they had not beene slaves, every christian in company serving his proportion; and if the negroes be lost or dye in such time of their being run away, the christian servants in company with them shall by proportion among them, either pay fower [four] thousand five hundred pounds of tobacco and caske or fower [four] yeares service for every negroe soe lost or dead.

Negro womens children to serve according to the condition of the mother, Act XII December 1662

WHEREAS *some doubts have arrisen whether children got by Englishmen upon a negro women should be slave or ffree, Be it therefore enacted* . . . that all children borne in this country shall be held bond or free only according to the condition of the mother, *And* that if any christian shall committ ffornication with a negro man or women, hee or shee soe offending shall pay double the ffines imposed by the former act.

An act declaring that baptisme of slaves doth not exempt them from bondage, Act 11 September, 1667

WHEREAS some doubts have arisin whether children that are slaves by birth, and by the charity and piety of their owners made pertakers of the blessed sacrament of baptisme, should by vertue of their baptisme be made ffree; *It is enacted* . . . that the conferring of baptisme doth not alter the condition of the person as to his bondage or ffreedome; that diverse masters, ffreed from this doubt, may more carefully endeavour the propagation of christianity by permitting . . . slaves . . . to be admitted to that sacrament.

An act about the casuall killing of slaves., Act I October, 1669

WHEREAS the only law in force for the punishment of refractory servants resisting their master, mistris or overseer cannot be inflicted upon negroes, nor the obstinacy of many of them by other than violent meanes supprest, *Be it enacted* . . . if any slave resist his master . . . and by the extremity of the correction should chance to die, that his death shall not be accompted ffelony, but the master . . . be acquit from molestation, since it cannot be presumed that prepensed malice . . . should induce any man to destroy his owne estate.

An act for preventing Negro Insurrections, Act X, June, 1680

WHEREAS the frequent meeting of considerable numbers of negroe slaves under pretence of feasts and burialls is judged of dangerous consequence . . . *Bee it enacted* . . . it shall not be lawfull for any negroe or other slave to carry or arme himselfe with any club, staffe, gunn, sword or any other weapon of defence or offence, nor to goe or depart from of his masters ground without a certificate from his master, mistris or overseer, . . . if any negroe or other slave shall presume to lift up his hand in opposition against any christian, . . . [he shall] receive thirty lashes on his bare back well laid on. *And* . . . if any negroe or other slave shall absent himself from his masters service and lye hid and lurking in obscure places, comitting injuries to the inhabitants, and shall resist any . . . lawfull authority . . . it shalbe lawfull . . . to kill the said negroe or slave . . .

William Waller Hening, ed., *The Statutes at Large; Being a Collection of All the Laws of Virginia from the First Session of the Legislature, in the Year 1619.* 13 vols. Richmond, VA: Samuel Pleasants, 1809–1823. Quoted in Paul Finkelman, *The Law of Freedom and Bondage: A Casebook.* New York: Oceana, 1986, pp. 15–18.

Document 2: A Quaker Protest of Slavery

Such opposition to American slavery as did exist in colonial times was often initiated by members of the Society of Friends (Quakers), a Protestant sect. The following is taken from a 1693 pamphlet, one of the earliest pieces of antislavery literature written in America. Although its author, George Keith, was disowned by the Quakers for his agitation against slavery, he formed his own group of "Christian Quakers" to continue his activities.

*Keith's arguments on why true Christians should not hold slaves for life
were circulated and quoted by later antislavery writers.*

*Some Reasons and Causes of our being against keeping of Negroes for
Term of Life.*

First, Because it is contrary to the Principles and Practice of the
Christian Quakers to buy Prize or stollen Goods, which we bore a
faithful Testimony against in our Native Country; and therefore it
is our Duty to come forth in a Testimony against stollen Slaves, it
being accounted a far greater Crime under *Moses's* Law than the
stealing of Goods: for such were only to restore four fold, *but he
that stealeth a Man and selleth him, if he be found in his hand, he shall
surely be put to Death,* Exod. 21. 16. Therefore as we are not to buy
stollen Goods, (but if at unawares it should happen through Ignorance, we are to restore them to the Owners, and seek our Remedy of the Thief) no more are we to buy stollen Slaves; neither
should such as have them keep them and their Posterity in perpetual Bondage and Slavery, as is usually done, to the great scandal of
the *Christian Profession.*

Secondly, Because Christ commanded, saying, *All things whatsoever ye would that men should do unto you, do ye even so to them.* Therefore as we and our Children would not be kept in perpetual
Bondage and Slavery against our Consent, neither should we keep
them in perpetual Bondage and Slavery against their Consent, it
being such intollerable Punishment to their Bodies and Minds,
that none but notorious Criminal Offendors deserve the same. But
these have done us no harm; therefore how inhumane is it in us so
grievously to oppress them and their Children from one Generation to another.

Thirdly, Because the Lord hath commanded, saying, *Thou shalt
not deliver unto his Master the Servant that is escaped from his Master
unto thee, he shall dwell with thee, even amongst you in that place which
he shall chuse in one of thy Gates, where it liketh him best; thou shalt oppress him,* Deut. 23. 15. 16. By which it appeareth, that those which
are at Liberty and freed from their Bondage, should not by us be
delivered into Bondage again, neither by us should they be oppressed, but being escaped from his Master, should have the liberty
to dwell amongst us, where it liketh him best. Therefore, if God
extend such Mercy under the legal Ministration and Dispensation
to poor Servants, he doth and will extend much more of his Grace
and Mercy to them under the clear Gospel Ministration; so that
instead of punishing them and their Posterity with cruel Bondage
and perpetual Slavery, he will cause the Everlasting Gospel to be

preached effectually to all Nations, to them as well as others; *And the Lord will extend Peace to his People like a River, and the Glory of the Gentiles like a flowing Stream; And it shall come to pass, saith the Lord, that I will gather all Nations and Tongues, and they shall come and see my Glory, and I will set a sign among them, and I will send those that escape of them unto the Nations, to Tarshish, Pull and Lud that draw the Bow to Tuball and Javan, to the Isles afar off that have not heard my Fame, neither have seen my Glory, and they shall declare my Glory among the Gentiles,* Isa. 66.12–18.

Fourthly, Because the Lord hath commanded, saying, *Thou shalt not oppress an hired Servant that is poor and needy, whether he be of thy Brethren, or of the Strangers that are in thy Land within thy Gates, least he cry against thee unto the Lord, and it be sin unto thee; Thou shalt neither vex a stranger nor oppress him, for ye were strangers in the Land of AEgypt,* Deut. 24. 14, 15. Exod. 12 . 21. But what greater Oppression can there be inflicted upon our Fellow Creatures, than is inflicted on the poor Negroes! they being brought from their own Country against their Wills, some of them being stollen, others taken for payment of Debt owing by their Parents, and others taken Captive in War, and sold to Merchants, who bring them to the *American* Plantations, and sell them for Bond Slaves to them that will give most for them; the Husband from the Wife, and the Children from the Parents; and many that buy them do exceedingly afflict them and oppress them, not only by continual hard Labour, but by cruel Whippings, and other cruel Punishments, and by short allowance of Food, some Planters in *Barbadoes* and *Jamaica*, 'tis said, keeping one hundred of them, and some more, and some less, and giving them hardly any thing more than they raise on a little piece of Ground appointed them, on which they work for themselves the seventh days of the Week in the after-noon, and on the first days, to raise their own Provisions, to wit, Corn and Potatoes, and other Roots, &c. the remainder of their time being spent in their Masters service; which doubtless is far worse usage than is practised by the *Turks* and *Moors* upon their Slaves. Which tends to the great Reproach of the *Christian Profession*; therefore it would be better for all such as fall short of the Practice of those *Infidels*, to refuse the name of a *Christian*, that those *Heathen* and *Infidels* may not be provoked to blaspheme against the blessed Name of Christ, by reason of the unparallel'd Cruelty of these cruel and hard hearted pretended Christians: Surely the Lord doth behold their Oppressions & Afflictions, and will further visit for the same by his righteous and just Judgments, except they break off their sins by Repentance, and their Iniquity by shewing Mercy to these poor afflicted, tormented miserable Slaves!

Fifthly, Because Slaves and Souls of Men are some of the *Merchandize of Babylon* by which the Merchants of the Earth are made Rich; but those Riches which they have heaped together, through the cruel Oppression of these miserable Creatures, will be a means to draw Gods Judgments upon them; therefore, *Brethren,* let us hearken to the Voice of the Lord, who saith, *Come out of Babylon, my People, that ye be not partakers of her Sins, and that ye receive not her Plagues: for her Sins have reached unto Heaven, and God hath remembered her Iniquities; for he that leads into Captivity shall go into Captivity,* Rev. 18. 4, 5. & 13. 10.

George Keith, "An Exhortation and Caution to Friends concerning the buying or keeping of Negroes," reprinted in *Pennsylvania Magazine of History and Biography,* 13 (1889): 266–70. Reprinted in Roger Bruns, ed., *Am I Not a Man and a Brother: The Antislavery Crusade of Revolutionary America, 1688–1788.* New York: Chelsea House, 1977, pp. 7–8.

Document 3: The Natural Rights Argument Against Slavery

James Otis, a Boston lawyer and early leader of popular opposition to British rule in Massachusetts, helped develop and spread the argument that American colonists had "natural rights" that were being violated by arbitrary British policies. In the following passage from his 1764 pamphlet The Rights of the British Colonies Asserted and Proved, *Otis extends his arguments on natural rights to blacks held in slavery.*

In order to form an idea of the natural rights of the colonists, I presume it will be granted that they are men, the common children of the same Creator with their brethren of Great Britain. Nature has placed all such in a state of equality and perfect freedom to act within the bounds of the laws of nature and reason without consulting the will or regarding the humor, the passions, or whims of any other man, unless they are formed into a society or body politic. . . .

The colonists are by the law of nature freeborn, as indeed all men are, white or black. . . . Does it follow that 'tis right to enslave a man because he is black? Will short curled hair like wool instead of Christian hair, as 'tis called by those whose hearts are as hard as the nether millstone, help the argument? Can any logical inference in favor of slavery be drawn from a flat nose, a long or a short face? Nothing better can be said in favor of a trade that is the most shocking violation of the law of nature, has a direct tendency to diminish the idea of the inestimable value of liberty, and makes every dealer in it a tyrant, from the director of an African company to the petty chapman in needles and pins on the unhappy coast. It is a clear truth that those who every day barter away other men's liberty will soon care little for their own.

James Otis, *The Rights of British Colonies Asserted and Proved.* Boston: 1764. Reprinted in Roger Bruns, ed., *Am I Not a Man and a Brother: The Antislavery Crusade of Revolutionary America, 1688–1788.* New York: Chelsea House, 1977, pp. 103–104.

Document 4: Slaves Petition for Freedom

During the American Revolution, black slaves in America sent several public petitions against slavery to state and local governments, in many cases echoing arguments on freedom and human rights used by Revolutionary leaders to justify independence from Great Britain. The following example of such a petition was addressed to the legislative assembly of Connecticut in May 1779.

To the Honbl. General Assembly of the State of Connecticut to be held at Hartford on the Second Thursday of Instant May [1779]— The Petition of the Negroes in the Towns of Stratford and Fairfield in the County of Fairfield who are held in a State of Slavery humbly sheweth—

That many of your Petitioners, were (as they verily believe) most unjustly torn, from the Bosom of their dear Parents, and Friends, and without any Crime, by them committed, doomed, and bound down, to perpetual Slavery; and as if the Perpetrators of this horrid Wickedness, were conscious (that we poor Ignorant Africans, upon the least Glimering Sight, derived from a Knowledge of the Sense and Practice of civilized Nations) should Convince them of their Sin, they have added another dreadful Evil, that of holding us in gross Ignorance, so as to render Our Subjection more easy and tolerable. may it please your Honours, we are most grievously affected, under the Consideration of the flagrant Injustice; your Honours who are nobly contending, in the Cause of Liberty, whose Conduct excites the Admiration, and Reverence, of all the great Empires of the World; will not resent, our thus freely animadverting, on this detestable Practice; altho our Skins are different in Colour, from those whom we serve, Yet Reason & Revelation join to declare, that we are the Creatures of that God, who made of one Blood, and Kindred, all the Nations of the Earth; we perceive by our own Reflection, that we are endowed with the same Faculties with our masters, and there is nothing that leads us to a Belief, or Suspicion, that we are any more obliged to serve them, than they us, and the more we Consider of this matter, the more we are Convinced of our Right (by the Laws of Nature and by the whole Tenor of the Christian Religion, so far as we have

been taught) to be free; we have endeavoured rightly to understand what is our Right, and what is our Duty and can never be convinced that we were made to be Slaves. Altho God almighty may justly lay this, and more upon us, yet we deserve it not, from the hands of Men. we are impatient under the grievous Yoke, but our Reason teaches us that it is not best for us to use violent measures, to cast it off; we are also convinced, that we are unable to extricate ourselves from our abject State; but we think we may with the greatest Propriety look up to your Honours, (who are the fathers of the People) for Relief. And we not only groan under our own burden, but with concern, & Horror, look forward, & contemplate, the miserable Condition of our Children, who are training up, and kept in Preparation, for a like State of Bondage, and Servitude. We beg leave to submit, to your Honours serious Consideration, whether it is consistent with the present Claims, of the united States, to hold so many Thousands, of the Race of Adam, our Common Father, in perpetual Slavery. Can human Nature endure the Shocking Idea? can your Honours any longer Suffer this great Evil to prevail under your Government: we entreat your Honours, let no considerations of Publick Inconvenience deter your Honours from interposing in behalf of your Petitioners; we ask for nothing, but what we are fully persuaded is ours to Claim. we beseech your Honours to weigh this matter in the Scale of justice, and in Your great Wisdom and goodness, apply such Remedy as the Evil does require; and let your Petitioners rejoice with your Honours in the Participation with your Honours of that inestimable Blessing, *Freedom* and your Humble Petitioners, as in Duty bound shall ever pray &c.
dated in Fairfield the
11th Day of May A D 1779—

prime a Negro man
servant to Mr.
Vam A. Sturge
of Fairfield
his
Prince   X   a Negro man
mark
servant of Capt. Stephen Jenings
of Fairfield—

Signed in Presence of   in Behalf of themselves and
Jonth Sturges.   the other Petitioners

Herbert Aptheker, *A Documentary History of the Negro People in the United States.* Vol. 1. New York: Carol Publishing, 1990, pp. 10–12.

Document 5: Gradual Emancipation in Rhode Island

In February 1784 Rhode Island passed a law providing for the gradual abolition of slavery, one of several northern states to do so in the years during and immediately following the American Revolution. Rhode Island's emancipation law, excerpted below, applied only to children born after March 1, 1784. Other portions of the bill not reprinted here permitted voluntary manumission of adult slaves and the continued participation in the slave trade by Rhode Island slave traders outside the state. The first federal census counted 948 slaves living in the state in 1790.

An ACT authorizing the manumission of Negroes, Mulattos and others, and for the gradual abolition of slavery.

Whereas all men are entitled to life, liberty and the pursuit of happiness, and the holding mankind in a state of slavery, as private property, which has gradually obtained by unrestrained custom and the permission of the laws, is repugnant to this principle, and subversive of the happiness of mankind, the great end of all civil government:

Be it therefore enacted by this General Assembly, and by the authority thereof it is enacted, That no person or persons, whether Negroes, Mulattos or others, who shall be born within the limits of this State, on or after the first day of March, A.D. 1784, shall be deemed or considered as servants for life, or slaves; and that all servitude for life, or slavery of children, to be born as aforesaid, in consequence of the condition of their mothers, be and the same is hereby taken away, extinguished and forever abolished.

And whereas humanity requires, that children declared free as aforesaid remain with their mothers a convenient time from and after their birth; to enable therefore those who claim the services of such mothers to maintain and support such children in a becoming manner, *It is further enacted by the authority aforesaid,* That such support and maintenance be at the expence of the respective towns where those reside and are settled: *Provided however,* That the respective Town-Councils may bind out such children as apprentices, or otherwise provide for their support and maintenance, at any time after they arrive to the age of one year, and before they arrive to their respective ages of twenty-one, if males, and eighteen, if females.

And whereas it is the earnest desire of this Assembly, that such children be educated in the principles of morality and religion, and instructed in reading, writing and arithmetic: *Be it further enacted by the authority aforesaid,* That due and adequate satisfaction be made as aforesaid for such education and instruction. And for ascertaining the allowance for such support, maintenance, education and instruction, the respective Town-Councils are hereby required to adjust and settle the accounts in this behalf from time to time, as the same shall be exhibited to them: Which settlement so made shall be final; and the respective towns by virtue thereof shall become liable to pay the sums therein specified and allowed.

And be it further enacted by the authority aforesaid, That all persons held in servitude or slavery, who shall be hereafter emancipated by those who claim them, shall be supported as other paupers, and not at the separate expence of the claimants, if they become chargeable; provided they shall be between the ages of twenty and forty years, and are of sound body and mind; which shall be judged of and determined by the Town-Councils aforesaid.

John P. Kaminski, *A Necessary Evil? Slavery and the Debate over the Constitution.* Madison, WI: Madison House, 1995, pp. 28–29.

Document 6: The Constitutional Convention Debates the Slave Trade

The role of the national government in regulating the slave trade was among the most controversial topics discussed by the 1787 Constitutional Convention, as seen in the following excerpts from notes to the debates by Virginia delegate (and future president) James Madison. Section 9 of Article I of the Constitution was ultimately approved as follows: "The Migration or Importation of such Persons as any of the States now existing shall think proper to admit, shall not be prohibited by the Congress prior to the Year one thousand eight hundred and eight, but a Tax or duty may be imposed on such Importation, not exceeding ten dollars for each Person."

JULY 23

Elbridge Gerry [delegate from Massachusetts] moved that the proceedings of the Convention for the establishment of a National Government (except the part relating to the Executive), be referred to a Committee to prepare and report a Constitution conformable thereto.

Charles Cotesworth Pinckney [delegate from South Carolina] reminded the Convention that if the Committee should fail to insert some security to the Southern States against an emancipation of slaves, and taxes on exports, he should be bound by duty to his State to vote against their Report.

The appointment of a Committee as moved by Mr. Gerry was Agreed to. . . .

AUGUST 6

John Rutledge [delegate from South Carolina] delivered in the Report of the Committee of Detail as follows: a printed copy being at the same time furnished to each member. . . .

Article VII, section 4. No tax or duty shall be laid by the Legislature [i.e., Congress] on articles exported from any State; nor on the migration or importation of such persons as the several States shall think proper to admit, nor shall such migration or importation be prohibited. . . .

AUGUST 16

Luther Martin (Md.) proposed to vary the Section 4, article VII so as to allow a prohibition or tax on the importation of slaves. In the first place as five slaves are to be counted as 3 free men in the apportionment of Representatives; such a clause would leave an encouragement to this traffic. In the second place slaves weakened one part of the Union which the other parts were bound to protect: the privilege of importing them was therefore unreasonable. And in the third place it was inconsistent with the principle of the revolution and dishonorable to the American character to have such a feature in the Constitution.

Mr Rutledge did not see how the importation of slaves could be encouraged by this Section. He was not apprehensive of insurrections and would readily exempt the other States from the obligation to protect the Southern against themselves.—Religion and humanity had nothing to do with this question. Interest alone is the governing principles with nations. The true question at present is whether the Southern States shall or shall not be parties to the Union. If the Northern States consult their interest, they will not oppose the increase of Slaves which will increase the commodities of which they will become the carriers.

Oliver Ellsworth [delegate from Connecticut] was for leaving the clause as it stands. Let every State import what it pleases. The morality or wisdom of slavery are considerations belonging to the States themselves. What enriches a part enriches the whole, and the States are the best judges of their particular interest. The old confederation had not meddled with this point, and he did not see any greater necessity for bringing it within the policy of the new one.

Charles Pinckney [South Carolina delegate and second cousin of Charles Cotesworth Pinckney]. South Carolina can never receive the plan if it prohibits the slave trade. In every proposed extension of the powers of the Congress, that State has expressly and watchfully excepted that of meddling with the importation of negroes. If the States be all left at liberty on this subject, South Carolina may perhaps by degrees do of herself what is wished, as Virginia and Maryland have already done.

AUGUST 22

Mr. [Roger] Sherman [delegate from Connecticut] was for leaving the clause as it stands. He disapproved of the slave trade; yet as the States were now possessed of the right to import slaves, as the public good did not require it to be taken from them, and as it was expedient to have as few objections as possible to the proposed scheme of Government, he thought it best to leave the matter as we find it. He observed that the abolition of Slavery seemed to be going on in the U.S. and that the good sense of the several States would probably by degrees complete it. He urged on the Convention the necessity of despatching its business.

George Mason [delegate from Virginia]. This infernal traffic originated in the avarice of British Merchants. The British Government constantly checked the attempts of Virginia to put a stop to it. The present question concerns not the importing States alone but the whole Union. The evil of having slaves was experienced during the late war. Had slaves been treated as they might have been by the Enemy, they would have proved dangerous instruments in their hands. But their folly dealt by the slaves, as it did by the Tories. He mentioned the dangerous insurrections of the slaves in Greece and Sicily; . . . Maryland and Virginia he said had already prohibited the importation of slaves expressly. North Carolina had done the same in substance. All this would be in vain if South Carolina and Georgia be at liberty to import. The Western people are already calling out for slaves for their new lands, and will fill that Country with slaves if they can be got through South Carolina and Georgia.

Slavery discourages arts and manufactures. The poor despise labor when performed by slaves. They prevent the immigration of Whites, who really enrich and strengthen a country. They produce the most pernicious effect on manners. Every master of slaves is born a petty tyrant. They bring the judgment of heaven on a Country. As nations can not be rewarded or punished in the next world they must be in this. By an inevitable chain of causes and effects providence punishes national sins, by national calamities. He lamented that some of our Eastern brethren had from a lust of gain embarked in this nefarious traffic. As to the States being in possession of the Right to import, this was the case with many other rights, now to be properly given up. He held it essential in every point of view that the General Government should have power to prevent the increase of slavery.

Mr Ellsworth. As he had never owned a slave could not judge of the effect of slavery on character: He said however that if it was to be considered in a moral light we ought to go farther and free those already in the Country.—As slaves also multiply so fast in Virginia and Maryland that it is cheaper to raise than import them, whilst in the sickly rice swamps foreign supplies are necessary, if we go no farther than is urged, we shall be unjust towards South Carolina and Georgia. Let us not intermeddle. As population increases poor laborers will be so plenty as to render slaves useless. Slavery in time will not be a speck in our Country. Provision is already made in Connecticut for abolishing it. And the abolition has already taken place in Massachusetts. As to the danger of insurrections from foreign influence, that will become a motive to kind treatment of the slaves.

Charles Pinckney. If slavery be wrong, it is justified by the example of all of the world. He cited the case of Greece, Rome and other ancient States; the sanction given by France, England, Holland and other modern States. In all ages one-half of mankind have been slaves. If the Southern States were let alone they will probably of themselves stop importations. He would himself as a Citizen of South Carolina vote for it. An attempt to take away the right as proposed will produce serious objections to the Constitution which he wished to see adopted.

General [Charles Cotesworth] Pinckney declared it to be his firm opinion that if himself and all his colleagues were to sign the Constitution and use their personal influence, it would be of no avail towards obtaining the assent of their Constituents. South Carolina and Georgia cannot do without slaves. As to Virginia she will gain by stopping the importations. Her slaves will rise in value, and she has more than she wants. It would be unequal to require South Carolina and Georgia to confederate on such unequal terms. . . . He contended that the importation of slaves would be for the interest of the whole Union. The more slaves, the more produce to employ the carrying trade; the more consumption also, and the more of this, the more of revenue for the common treasury. He admitted it to be reasonable that slaves should be dutied like other imports, but should consider a rejection of the clause as an exclusion of South Carolina from the Union. . . .

Mr. Gerry thought we had nothing to do with the conduct of the States as to Slaves, but ought to be careful not to give any sanction to it.

John Dickinson (Del.) considered it as inadmissible on every principle of honor and safety that the importation of slaves should be authorized to the States by the Constitution. The true question was whether the national happiness would be promoted or impeded by the importation, and this question ought to be left to the National Government not to the States particularly interested. If England and France permit slavery, slaves are at the same time excluded from both those Kingdoms. Greece and Rome were made unhappy by their slaves. He could not believe that the Southern States would refuse to confederate on the account apprehended; especially by the General Government. . . .

John Langdon (N.H.) was strenuous for giving the power to the General Government. He could not with a good conscience leave it with the States who could then go on with the traffic, without being restrained by the opinions here given that they will themselves cease to import slaves.

General Pinckney thought himself bound to declare candidly that he did not think South Carolina would stop her importations of slaves in any short time, but only stop them occasionally as she now does. He moved to commit the clause that slaves might be made liable to an equal tax with other imports which he thought right and which would remove one difficulty that had been started.

Mr Rutledge. If the Convention thinks that North Carolina, South Carolina and Georgia will ever agree to the plan, unless their right to import slaves be untouched, the expectation is vain. The people of those states will never be such fools as to give up so important an interest.

John P. Kaminski, *A Necessary Evil? Slavery and the Debate over the Constitution.* Madison, WI: Madison House, 1995, pp. 55, 58–61.

Document 7: Runaway Slave Advertisements

A revealing source of information on slavery for historians is the newspaper advertisements placed by slave owners seeking the capture and return of runaway slaves. The following notices first appeared in the (Savannah) Georgia Gazette *in 1789.*

Savannah *Georgia Gazette,* June 4, 1789.
R A N   A W A Y ,
From the subscriber, some time about the middle of May last past,

TWO NEGRO FELLOWS, TOM and JULY, and A NEGRO WENCH, PHOEBE.

Tom is about 38 years old, five feet five inches high, country born, well made and thick set, commonly wears his beard long on his chin, and has a scar on one of his arms occasioned by a shot; he is a very artful fellow, well known in and about Savannah, and generally passes by the name of Tom Ports.

July, a tall black slim fellow, middle aged, of the Angola country, speaks very bad English, and has lost several of his fore teeth.

Phoebe, a well made likely young wench, about five feet six inches high, country born, and of a yellowish complexion.

A reward of EIGHT DOLLARS will be paid for Tom, and FOUR for each of the others, to any person who will secure them in the gaol of Savannah, so that the subscriber may get them again; and all persons are hereby warned and forbid, upon their peril, to secrete, harbour, or carry away, the said negroes, as they will be prosecuted with the utmost rigour of the law.

JOSEPH GIBBONS jun.

Savannah *Georgia Gazette*, April 9, 1789.

RUN AWAY

From Mrs. Miller's, on Ogechee Neck, a fortnight ago, A NEGRO BOY, named HERCULES, country born, about 17 years of age, five feet three or four inches high, of a black complexion. It is supposed he is harboured in that neighbourhood. Whoever delivers him to me, or to the Warden of the Work-house in Savannah, shall be entitled to a reward of THREE DOLLARS; and, on proof of his being harboured, a further reward of TWO GUINEAS will be paid.

RAYMOND DEMERE.

Savannah *Georgia Gazette*, April 16, 1789.

RAN AWAY,

From the subscriber's plantation, in Richmond county, on Saturday the 4th instant,

TWO NEGRO FELLOWS: ARMER, about 20 years old and five feet high, has lost his right great toe, and branded on his shoulder, but do not recollect the letters branded with, walks waddling, took with him when he went away a white negro cloth jacket with a black cape to it, negro cloth overalls, felt hat, oznabrig shirt, and a blanket: ALECK, about 26 years old, about five feet six or seven inches high, speaks broken and fast, took with him when he went away a white negro cloth jacket with a black cape to it, one pair black breeches, one pair nankeen ditto, one white shirt, two felts hats, and a blanket. It is probable they will make for Savannah, as the latter was lately purchased there, and had a wife in town. Any person that will secure them in Savannah gaol, or deliver them to Dalziel Hunter, in Augusta, or to the subscriber, shall receive TWENTY DOLLARS and all reasonable charges.

THOMAS GRAVES.

Savannah *Georgia Gazette*, August 13, 1789.

R A N   A W A Y ,

A LIKELY country born MULATTO FELLOW, named Lazarus, about 23 years old, with a bushy head of hair, 5 feet 8 or 9 inches high, well made, speaks good English, and may probably endeavour to pass for free. Should he return of his own accord he will be forgiven, but otherwise TEN DOLLARS will be paid by the subscriber to any person who will apprehend and bring the said fellow to Savannah, and lodge him in gaol. Any person harbouring said fellow may depend upon being prosecuted with the utmost rigour.

I HAVE FOR SALE, As likely a SAMBO FELLOW, about 22 years of age, as any in the country; and a very valuable WENCH, cook, washer, and ironer; that I will sell low for cash.

JOHN M'CULLOCH.

Savannah *Georgia Gazette*, October 22, 1789.
Ten Pounds Reward.

Absented herself about three weeks ago, A NEGRO WOMAN, named DUMBA, but very probably will call herself BELLA, of the Angola country, aged about 35 years, 5 feet 2 or 3 inches high, slim made, has her country marks on her temples, is sensible and very artful, and may attempt to pass for a free woman. She has of late been much addicted to liquor, and when under its influence is very noisy and troublesome. Having many acquaintances in Georgia it is supposed she will endeavour to get there. All Masters of vessels and others are cautioned from carrying her away; and I hereby promise a reward for information by whom she is harboured; if by a white person, ten pounds sterling, and if by a black, five pounds, on conviction of the offender; also two guinea to any one who will deliver her to the Master of the Workhouse.

ALEXANDER INGLIS.

Lathan A. Windley, comp., *Runaway Slave Advertisements: A Documentary History from the 1730s to 1790*. Vol. 4. Westport, CT: Greenwood, 1983.

Document 8: The Fairfax Plan for Gradual Emancipation and African Colonization

The first published plan for the general emancipation of all American slaves was written by Fernando Fairfax, a wealthy Virginia planter who owned slaves. Fairfax argued that any emancipation plan must include provisions for resettling free blacks in Africa.

This subject has afforded, in conversation, a wide field for argument, or rather, speculation, both to the friends and opposers of emancipation. Whilst the former plead natural right and justice, which are considered as paramount to every other consideration: the latter insist upon policy, with respect both to the community and to those who are the objects proposed to be benefited: the one party considers liberty as a natural right, which we cannot, without injustice, withhold from this unhappy race of men: the other, at the same time that it admits these principles, opposes a general emancipation, on account of the inconveniencies which would result to the community and to the slaves themselves, and which, consequently, would render it impolitic; besides the injustice which would be done to individuals by a legislative interference (without voluntary consent) in private property, which had been acquired and possessed under the laws of the country. But no practicable scheme has yet been proposed, which would unite all these principles of justice and policy, and thereby remove all ground for opposition: all that has hitherto been offered to the public upon this subject, has been addressed, rather to the feelings, than to the cool and deliberate judgment. The following plan is therefore submitted, without apology, since it is only intended to suggest the idea, which may be improved by some abler hand.

It seems to be the general opinion, that emancipation must be gradual; since, to deprive a man, at once, of all his right in the property of his negroes, would be the height of injustice, and such as, in this country, would never be submitted to: and the resources of government are by no means adequate to making at once a full compensation. It must therefore be by voluntary consent—consequently in a gradual manner. It is equally agreed, that, if they be emancipated, it would never do to allow them *all* the privileges of citizens: they would therefore form a separate interest from the rest of the community. There is something very repugnant to the general feelings, even in the thought of their being allowed that free intercourse, and the privilege of intermarriage with the white inhabitants, which the other freemen of our country enjoy, and which only *can* form one common interest. The remembrance of their former situation, and a variety of other considerations, forbid this privilege—and as a proof, where is the man of all those who have liberated their slaves, who would marry a son or a daughter to one of them? and if *he* would not, who would? So that these prejudices, sentiments, or whatever they may be called, would be found to operate so powerfully as to be insurmountable. And though the laws should allow these privileges, yet the same effect would still be produced, of forming a separate interest from the rest of the community; for the laws cannot operate effectually against the sentiments of the people.

If this separate interest of so great a number in the same community, be once formed, by any means, it will endanger the peace of society: for it cannot exist between two neighbouring states, without danger to the peace of each—How much less, then, between the inhabitants of the same country?

This suggests the propriety, and even necessity of removing them to a distance from this country. It is therefore proposed,

That a colony should be settled, under the auspices and protection of congress, by the negroes now within the united states, and be composed of those who already, as well as those who, at any time hereafter, may become liberated by the voluntary consent of their owners; since there are many who would willingly emancipate their slaves, if there should appear a probability of their being so disposed of, as neither to injure themselves nor the community. As an additional inducement, government may, as the resources of the country become greater, offer a reward or compensation, for emancipation. There is, however, in the mean time, a sufficient number to form a very considerable colony.

That congress should frame a plan, and appoint the proper officers for the government of the colony in its infant state, until the colonists should themselves become competent to that business.

That there should be suitable provision made for their support and defence. And

That, to forward their progress in the useful arts, and to qualify them for the business of legislation; a considerable number of those who are intended to be sent over after the first settlement, should be properly educated and instructed; and that one of the first objects should be the establishment of seminaries in the colony for a like purpose.

That the seat of this colony should be in Africa, their native climate, as being most suitable for the purposes intended. They will there be at such a distance as to prevent all the before-mentioned inconveniences of intercourse, &c. at the same time that they are situated within the neighbourhood of other nations of the same kind of people, with whom they may, after a little time, maintain the most intimate intercourse without any inconvenience. They will still have a great superiority over their neighbours, on account of their knowledge in the several useful arts, and as they gradually advance in importance, will, by their influence, diffuse this knowledge among this rude race of men. Nor ought we to consider as of little importance, the tendency that this settlement would have, to spreading a knowledge of the christian religion among so great a proportion of mankind, who are at present ignorant of it—and that too in the most effectual manner.

With respect to ourselves, we might reap every advantage that we could enjoy from the settlement of any other colony—if not more. They would require our support and protection for a short time only, with fewer supplies of necessaries than any other (from the nature of the climate). And they might soon, from their industry, and by commercial intercourse, make us ample amends for our expenses, and be enabled to live without our protection; and, after some time, to become an independent nation. But if we should gain no advantages, we should still accomplish the object intended.

Fernando Fairfax, "Plan for Liberating the Negroes Within the United States," *American Museum*, December 1790. Reprinted in Gary B. Nash, *Race and Revolution*. Madison, WI: Madison House, 1990, pp. 146–49.

Document 9: George Washington Frees His Slaves

In 1782 Virginia legally permitted slave owners to manumit (grant freedom to) their slaves. One who took advantage of this change in the law was George Washington, America's first president, who owned numerous slaves on Mount Vernon and his other estates. Washington's will, drawn up several months before his death in December 1799, freed his slaves upon the death of his wife, Martha (the will did not apply to the "dower" slaves Martha had received from her first husband's estate). Washington's act was not uncommon in Virginia and neighboring states; the free black population of Virginia grew from 1,800 in 1782 to 20,000 in 1810.

Upon the decease of my wife, it is my Will and desire that all the Slaves which I hold in *my own right*, shall receive their freedom. To emancipate them during her life, would, tho' earnestly wished by me, be attended with such insuperable difficulties on account of their intermixture by Marriages with the Dower Negroes, as to excite the most painful sensations, if not disagreeable consequences from the latter, while both descriptions are in the occupancy of the same Proprietor; it not being in my power, under the tenure by which the Dower Negros are held, to manumit them. And whereas among those who will recieve freedom according to this devise, there may be some, who from old age or bodily infirmities, and others who on account of their infancy, that will be unable to support themselves; it is my Will and desire that all who come under the first and second description shall be comfortably cloathed and fed by my heirs while they live; and that such of the latter description as have no parents living, or if living are unable, or unwilling to provide for them, shall be bound by the Court until they shall arrive at the age of twenty five years; and in cases where no record can be produced, whereby their ages can be ascertained, the judgment of the Court upon its own view of the subject, shall be adequate and final. The Negros thus bound, are (by their Masters or Mistresses) to be taught to read and write; and to be brought up to some useful occupation, agreeably to the Laws of the Commonwealth of Virginia, providing for the support of Orphan and other poor Children. And I do hereby expressly forbid the Sale, or transportation out of the said Commonwealth, of any Slave I may die possessed of, under any pretence whatsoever. And I do moreover most pointedly, and most solemnly enjoin it upon my Executors hereafter named, or the Survivors of them, to see that *this* clause respecting Slaves, and every part thereof be religiously fulfilled at the Epoch at which it is directed to take place; without evasion, neglect or delay, after the Crops which may then be on the ground are harvested, particularly as it respects the aged and infirm; Seeing that a regular and permanent fund be established for their Support so long as there are subjects requiring it; not trusting to the uncertain provision to be made by individuals. And to my Mulatto man William (calling himself William Lee) I give immediate freedom; or if he should prefer it (on account of the accidents which have befallen him, and which have rendered him incapable of walking or of any active employment) to remain in the situation he now is, it shall be optional in him to do so: In either case however, I allow him an annuity of thirty dollars during his natural life, which shall be independent of the victuals and cloaths he has been accustomed to receive, if he chuses the last alternative; but in full, with his freedom, if he prefers the first; and this I give him as a testimony of my sense of his attachment to me, and for his faithful services during the Revolutionary War.

Last Will and Testament, July 9, 1799. From George Washington, *Writings*, New York: Library of America, 1997, pp. 1,022–24, previously published in vol. 37 of *The Writings of George Washington from the Original Manuscript Sources, 1745–1799*, ed. John C. Fitzpatrick. 39 vols. Washington, DC: United States Government Printing Office, 1931–1944, beginning on p. 275.

Document 10: Defending Slavery in Missouri

In 1819, Congress debated granting statehood to the territory of Missouri and the issue of forbidding the institution of slavery there. Those against imposing slavery restrictions as a condition of statehood made two general arguments. Some held that slavery would become more humane, and perhaps even more amenable to gradual abolition, if it was allowed to spread to new territory, an idea that became known as the diffusion argument. Others offered a straightforward defense of slavery as a necessary institution for freedom and equality for all whites and as a humane institution for blacks. In the following excerpts from the debates in Congress, Senator Richard M. Johnson of Kentucky, a slave state bordering Missouri, makes both of these arguments.

Can gentlemen sincerely believe that the cause of humanity will be promoted by still confining this population [slaves] within such limits, as that their relative numbers will oppose everlasting obstacles to their emancipation? Upon the most extensive principles of philanthropy, I say, let them spread forth with the growing extent of our nation. I am sure I plead the cause of humanity. I advocate the best interests of the sons of bondage, when I entreat you to give them room to be happy; and so disperse them as that, under the auspices of Providence, they may one day enjoy the rights of man, without convulsing the empire or endangering society. . . .

Before we compel our brother to pluck the mote from his eye, it will be wise to take the beam from our own. On this occasion I cannot omit to mention my own feelings on a former occurrence. When I first came to Congress, it was with mingled emotions of horror and surprise that I saw citizens from the non-slaveholding States, as they are called—yes, and both branches of our National Legislature—riding in a coach and four, with a white servant seated before, managing the reins, another standing behind the coach, and both of these white servants in livery. Is this, said I to myself, the degraded condition of the citizen, on whose voice the liberties of a nation may depend? I could not reconcile it with my ideas of freedom; because, in the State where I received my first impressions, slaves alone were servile. All white men there are on an equality, and every citizen feels his independence. We have no classes—no patrician or plebeian rank. Honesty and honor form all the distinctions that are felt or known. Whatever may be the condition of a citizen with us, you must treat him as an equal. This I find is not so in every part of the non-slaveholding States, especially in your populous cities, where ranks and distinctions, the precursors of aristocracy, already begin to exist. They whose business it is to perform menial offices in other States, are as servile as our slaves in the West. Where is the great difference betwixt the conditions of him who keeps your stable, who blacks your boots, who holds your stirrups, or mounts behind your coach when you ride, and the slave who obeys the command of his master? There may be a nominal difference; but it would be difficult to describe its reality. In the one case it is called voluntary, because it is imposed by its own necessity, and in the other involuntary, because imposed by the will of another. Whatever difference there may be in the principle, the effects upon society are the same. The condition, in some respects, is in favor of the slave. He is supplied with food and clothing; and in the hour of sickness he finds relief. No anxious cares, in relation to age and infirmity, invade his breast. . . . [H]e dreads not the coercion of payment, nor feels the cruelty of that code which confines the white servant in prison, because the iron hand of poverty has wrested from him the means of support for his family. Though slavery still must be confessed a bitter draught, yet where the stamp of nature marks the distinction, and when the mind, from early habit, is moulded to the condition, the slave often finds less bitterness in the cup of life than most white servants. What is the condition of many, who are continually saluting our ears with cries of want, even in this city? Men, women, boys, girls, from infancy to old age, craving relief from every passenger. Are they slaves? No. Among the slaves are no beggars; no vagrants; none idle for want of employ, or crying for want of bread. Every condition of life has its evils; and most evils have some palliative; though perhaps none less than those of white menials. Yet, sir, none are more lavish of their censures against slaveholders than those lordlings with livery servants of their own complexion. . . .

I never could stand having white servants dressed in livery. No, sir, when the honest laborer, the mechanic, however poor, or whatever his employment, visits my house, it matters not what company is there, he must sit with me at my board, and receive the same treatment as the most distinguished guest; because in him I recognise a fellow citizen and an equal.

The condition of the slave is but little understood by those who are not the eye-witnesses of his treatment. His sufferings are greatly aggravated in their apprehension. The general character of the slaveholding community can no more be determined, nor should they be any more stigmatized, by a particular instance of cruelty to a slave, than the character of the non-slaveholding community by a particular instance of cruelty in a parent towards his child, a guardian to his ward, or a master to his apprentice. No man among us can be cruel to his slave without incurring the execration of the whole community.

Annals of the Congress of the United States, 1789–1824 (Washington, DC), 16th Cong., 1st sess., 1819–1820, pp. 345–59. Reprinted in Harry W. Fritz et al., *Documents Collection*. New York: Worth, 1993.

Document 11: A Call for Slave Resistance

David Walker was a free black born in Wilmington, North Carolina. In the 1820s he settled in Boston and became active in political and abolitionist circles. In 1829 he published a pamphlet, excerpted below, that was one of the first extended political tracts written by an African American. Before his death in 1830, Walker distributed copies of his pamphlet in many parts of the South through a network of black Southerners and sailors. Walker's call for militant black resistance to slavery alarmed many southern political leaders, including the governors of Georgia and North Carolina.

I do not think that we were natural enemies to each other. But the whites having made us so wretched, by subjecting us to slavery, and having murdered so many millions of us in order to make us work for them, and out of devilishness—and they taking our wives, whom we love as we do ourselves—our mothers who bore the pains of death to give us birth—our fathers & dear little children, and ourselves, and strip and beat us one before the other—chain, handcuff and drag us about like rattlesnakes—shoot us down like wild bears, before each other's faces, to make us submissive to and work to support them and their families. They (the whites) know well if we are *men*—and there is a secret monitor in their hearts which tells them we are—they know, I say, if we *are* men, and see them treating us in the manner they do, that there can be nothing in our hearts but death alone, for them; notwithstanding we may appear cheerful, when we see them murdering our dear mothers and wives, because we cannot help ourselves . . . (viz. we cannot help the whites murdering our mothers and our wives) but this statement is incorrect—for we can help ourselves; for, if we lay aside abject servility, and be determined to act like men, and not brutes—the murderers among the whites would be afraid to show their cruel heads. But 0, my God!—in sorrow I must say it, that my colour, all over the world, have a mean, servile spirit. They yield in a moment to the whites, let them be right or wrong—the reason the whites are able to keep their feet on our throats. Oh! my coloured brethren, all over the world, when shall we arise from this death-like apathy?—And be men!! You will notice, if ever we become men (I mean *respectable* men, such as other people are,) we must exert ourselves to the full. For remember, that it is the greatest desire and object of the greater part of the whites, to keep us ignorant, and make us work to support them and their families.— Here now, in the Southern and Western Sections of this country, there are at least three coloured persons for one white, why is it, that those few weak, good-for-nothing whites, are able to keep so many able men, one of whom, can put to flight a dozen whites, in wretchedness and misery? It shows at once, what the blacks are, we are ignorant, abject, servile, and mean—and the whites know it— they know that we are too servile to assert our rights as men—or they would not fool with us as they do. Would they fool with any other people as they do with us? No, they know too well that they would get themselves ruined.

From *Walker's Appeal, in Four Articles Together with a Preamble to the Coloured Citizens of the World, but in Particular, and Very Expressly to Those of the United States of America,* in *Slavery: Opposing Viewpoints,* ed. William Dudley. San Diego: Greenhaven Press, 1992, p. 129.

Document 12: An Abolitionist Manifesto

William Lloyd Garrison's first editorial for his abolitionist newspaper, the Liberator, *in January 1831, introduced Americans to his beliefs and writing style, which would help shape the abolitionist movement for the next three decades.*

During my recent tour for the purpose of exciting the minds of the people by a series of discourses on the subject of slavery, every place that I visited gave fresh evidence of the fact, that a greater revolution in public sentiment was to be effected in the free States—*and particularly in New-England*—than at the South. I found contempt more bitter, opposition more active, detraction more relentless, prejudice more stubborn, and apathy more frozen, than among slave-owners themselves. Of course, there were individual exceptions to the contrary. This state of things afflicted, but did not dishearten me. I determined, at every hazard, to lift up the standard of emancipation in the eyes of the nation, *within sight of Bunker Hill and in the birthplace of liberty.* That standard is now unfurled; and long may it float, unhurt by the spoliations of time or the missiles of a desperate foe—yea, till every chain be broken, and every bondman set free! Let Southern oppressors tremble—let their secret abettors tremble—let their Northern apologists tremble—let all the enemies of the persecuted blacks tremble.

I deem the publication of my original Prospectus unnecessary, as it has obtained a wide circulation. The principles therein inculcated will be steadily pursued in this paper, excepting that I shall not array myself as the political partisan of any man. In defending the great cause of human rights, I wish to derive the assistance of all religions and of all parties.

Assenting to the "self-evident truth" maintained in the American Declaration of Independence, "that all men are created equal, and endowed by their Creator with certain inalienable rights—among which are life, liberty, and the pursuit of happiness," I shall strenuously contend for the immediate enfranchisement of our slave population. In Park-Street Church [in Boston], on the Fourth of July, 1829, in an address on slavery, I unreflectingly assented to the popular but pernicious doctrine of *gradual* abolition. I seize this opportunity to make a full and unequivocal recantation, and thus publicly to ask pardon of my God, of my country, and of my brethren the poor slaves, for having uttered a sentiment so full of timidity, injustice, and absurdity. A similar recantation, from my pen, was published in the *Genius of Universal Emancipation*[1] at Baltimore, in September, 1829. My conscience is now satisfied.

I am aware that many object to the severity of my language; but is there not cause for severity? I *will be* as harsh as truth, and as uncompromising as justice. On this subject, I do not wish to think, or speak, or write, with moderation. No! No! Tell a man whose house is on fire to give a moderate alarm; tell him to moderately rescue his wife from the hands of the ravisher; tell the mother to gradually extricate her babe from the fire into which it has fallen;—but urge me not to use moderation in a cause like the present. I am in earnest—I will not equivocate—I will not excuse—I will not retreat a single inch—*AND I WILL BE HEARD*. The apathy of the people is enough to make every statue leap from its pedestal, and to hasten the resurrection of the dead.

It is pretended, that I am retarding the cause of emancipation by the coarseness of my invective and the precipitancy of my measures. *The charge is not true.* On this question my influence,—humble as it is,—is felt at this moment to a considerable extent, and shall be felt in coming years—not perniciously, but beneficially—not as a curse, but as a blessing; and posterity will bear testimony that I was right. I desire to thank God, that he enables me to disregard "the fear of man which bringeth a snare," and to speak his truth in its simplic-

---

1. newspaper published by Quaker abolitionist and Garrison associate Benjamin Lundy

ity and power. And here I close with this fresh dedication:

> *"Oppression! I have seen thee, face to face,*
> *And met thy cruel eye and cloudy brow;*
> *But thy soul-withering glance I fear not now—*
> *For dread to Prouder feelings doth give place*
> *Of deep abhorrence! Scorning the disgrace*
> *Of slavish knees that at thy footstool bow,*
> *I also kneel—but with far other vow*
> *Do hail thee and thy herd of hirelings base:—*
> *I swear, while life-blood warms my throbbing veins,*
> *Still to oppose and thwart, with heart and hand,*
> *Thy brutalising sway—till Afric's chains*
> *Are burst, and Freedom rules the rescued land,—*
> *Trampling Oppression and his iron rod:*
> Such is the vow I take—SO HELP ME GOD!"

William Lloyd Garrison, 1805–1879: The Story of His Life Told by His Children. Vol. 1 New York: Century, 1885, pp. 224–26. Reprinted in Irwin Unger, ed., *American Issues: A Primary Source Reader in United States History.* Englewood Cliffs, NJ: Prentice-Hall, pp. 185–86.

Document 13: A Kidnapping in Ohio

Slaves who successfully escaped to the North lived with the ever-present fear of kidnapping by agents sent by slave owners to recover their missing property. Even free blacks who were not escaped slaves were sometimes seized and sold into slavery. William Wells Brown, a former slave turned anti-slavery lecturer and writer, tells of such an incident in Ohio in an 1844 letter to Sydney H. Gay, editor of the National Anti-Slavery Standard.

I left Cadiz this morning at four o'clock, on my way for Mount Pleasant. Passing through Georgetown at about five o'clock, I found the citizens standing upon the corners of the streets, talking as though something had occurred during the night. Upon inquiry, I learned that [at] about ten o'clock at night, five or six men went to the house of a colored man by the name of John Wilkinson, broke open the door, knocked down the man and his wife, and beat them severely, and seized their boy, aged fourteen years, and carried him off into Slavery. After the father of the boy had recovered himself, he raised the alarm, and with the aid of some of the neighbors, put out in pursuit of the kidnappers, and followed them to the river; but they were too late. The villains crossed the river, and passed into Virginia. I visited the afflicted family this morning. When I entered the house, I found the mother seated with her face buried in her hands, weeping for the loss of her child. The mother was much bruised, and the floor was covered in several places with blood. I had been in the house but a short time, when the father returned from the chase of the kidnappers. When he entered the house, and told the wife that their child was lost forever, the mother wrung her hands and screamed out, "Oh, my boy! oh, my boy! I want to see my child!" and raved as though she was a maniac. I was compelled to turn aside and weep for the first time since I came into the State. I would that every Northern apologist for Slavery, could have been present to have beheld that scene. I hope to God that it may never be my lot to behold another such. One of the villains was recognized, but it was by a colored man, and the colored people have not the right of their oath in this State. This villain will go unwhipped of Justice. What have the North to do with Slavery? Ever yours, for the slave.

National Anti-Slavery Standard, November 7, 1844. Reprinted in Herbert Aptheker, *A Documentary History of the Negro People in the United States*. Vol. 1. New York: Carol Publishing, 1990, pp. 245–46.

Document 14: Comparing Slave and Free Labor

In 1847 a pamphlet attacking slavery was published anonymously in Lexington, Virginia (now West Virginia). The author was Henry Ruffner, a teacher at Washington College in Lexington and a slave owner. The "Ruffner pamphlet" was later republished in Louisville, Kentucky, and widely read in the states bordering the North. Its arguments comparing slave labor and free labor not only reveal antislavery sentiment held by many southern whites, but also presage many of the ideas that spurred the creation of the Republican Party in the 1850s.

Nowhere, since time began, have the two systems of slave labor and free labor, been subjected to so fair and so decisive a trial of their effects on public prosperity, as in these United States. Here the two systems have worked side by side for ages, under such equal circumstances both political and physical, and with such ample time and opportunity for each to work out its proper effects, that all must admit the experiment to be now complete, and the result decisive. No man of common sense, who has observed this result, can doubt for a moment, that the system of free labor promotes the growth and prosperity of States, in a much higher degree than the system of slave labor. In the first settlement of a country, when labor is scarce and dear, slavery may give a temporary impulse to improvement: but even this is not the case, except in warm climates, and where free men are scarce and either sickly or lazy: and when we have said this, we have said all experience in the United States warrants us to say, in favor of employing slave labor.

It is the common remark of all who have traveled through the

United States, that the free States and the slave States, exhibit a striking contrast in their appearance. In the older free States are seen all the tokens of prosperity: a dense and increasing population; thriving villages, towns, and cities; a neat and productive agriculture, growing manufactures and active commerce.

In the older parts of the slave States—with a few local exceptions—are seen, on the contrary, too evident signs of stagnation and positive decay: a sparse population; a slovenly cultivation spread over vast fields, that are wearing out, among others already worn out and desolate. Villages and towns, "few and far between," rarely growing, often decaying, sometimes mere remnants of what they were, sometimes deserted ruins, haunted only by owls; generally no manufactures, nor even trades, except the indispensable few; commerce and navigation abandoned, as far as possible to the people of the free States; and generally, instead of the stir and bustle of industry, a dull and dreamy stillness, broken, if broken at all, only by the wordy brawl of politics . . .

Fellow citizens, we esteem it a sad, a humiliating fact, which should penetrate the heart of every Virginian, that from the year 1790 to the present, Virginia has lost more people by emigration than all the old free States together. Up to 1840, when the last census was taken, she had lost more by nearly 300 000. She has sent—or we should rather say, she has driven from her soil—at least one third of all the emigrants, who have gone from the old States to the new. More than a third have gone from the other old slave States. Many of these multitudes who have left the slave States, have shunned the regions of slavery, and settled in the free countries of the West. These were generally industrious and enterprising white men, who found by sad experience, that a country of slaves was not the country for them. It is a truth, a certain truth, that *slavery drives free laborers—farmers, mechanics, and all, and some of the best of them too—out of the country, and fills their places with Negroes.*

What is it but slavery that makes Marylanders, Carolinians, and especially old Virginians and new Virginians fly their country at such a rate? Some go because they dislike slavery and desire to get away from it; others, because they have gloomy forebodings of what is to befall the slave States, and wish to leave their families in a country of happier prospects; others because they cannot get profitable employment among slaveholders; others, industrious and high-spirited workingmen, will not stay in a country where slavery degrades the workingman. Others go because they see that their country, for some reason, does not prosper, and that other countries, not far off, are prospering, and will afford better hopes of prosperity to themselves; others, a numerous class, who are slaveholders and cannot live without slaves, finding that they cannot live longer with them on their worn-out soils, go to seek better lands and more profitable crops, where slave labor may yet for a while enable them and their children to live.

From Herbert Aptheker, ed., *And Why Not Every Man? Documentary Story of the Fight Against Slavery in the U.S.* New York: International Publishers, 1970, pp. 153–55.

Document 15: A Slave Owner's Opinions on Abolitionists and Slavery

David Gavin owned a modest farm and a few slaves in North Carolina. The following excerpts from his diary provide information on the economics of slavery and Gavin's views on abolitionists.

Monday June 23, 1856. At Indian Field church yesterday. . . . Men, manner and things change wonderfully in this changeable world. When I was a boy twenty-five years ago it was a great thing to have made a trip to Mississippi, it took 20 days, then it became more common and took 16 days, and I came once in fourteen from the Eastern boundary. Now men and women esteem it a small matter, they take the R. Road & stage and perform the trip in 2 or 3 days, it is too tedious and slow on horseback or with a carriage. But 25 or 30 years ago few persons in this section of country were in debt and when a man contracted a debt he generally made arrangements to pay it, now the general rule is if he makes any arrangements about it, it is to avoid its payment. Negroes were then $175 & 200.00 per head by the plantation or number, men $4 & 500.00 women $3 & 400.00, now plantations or gangs are from four to six hundred dollars, men from 8 to $1100.00 & women from $6 to 800.00, cotton about the same then as now, from 8 to 11 cts per lb. I believe however, that more is made to the band for now there is little spinning done, most persons depending on buying their clothes and meat, those times 25 or 30 years it was rare for a farmer to buy either his clothes, shoes or bacon, all were made at home. Negro men then hired out for from $3 to six dollars per month now from ten to fifteen dollars per month. Our pine lands then sold for from ten to twenty five cents per acre now from one to three dollars per acre. People then went to church on foot, on horseback or in a waggon, now it is on horseback, in a buggy or carriage, with a waiting boy or boys.

July 4, 1856. To-day is the annaversary of American independence the 80th. 1776, 1 have no doubt in many parts there will be pretensions of great rejoiceings, but I cannot really rejoice for a freedom which allows every bankrupt, swindler, thef and scoundrel, traitor and seller of his vote to be placed on an equality with myself, which allows men to openly talk, plan and threaten to take away my property, threaten and abuse my person and even destroy my property with impunity. The Northern abolitionists are threatening and planning to take away or destroy the value of our slave property, and the demon democracy, by its leveling principles, universal suffrage, and numerous popular elections, homestead laws, and bribery are sapping the foundation of the rights of property in every thing.

From Michael Mullin, ed., *American Negro Slavery: A Documentary History*. Columbia: University of South Carolina Press, 1976, pp. 200–201.

Document 16: The Lincoln-Douglas Debates

In a series of seven celebrated debates, incumbent Illinois senator Stephen A. Douglas and Republican challenger Abraham Lincoln debated the future of slavery in the United States and in its western territories. The following excerpts are taken from their last debate, held in Alton, Illinois, in October 15, 1858. Douglas, the champion of "popular sovereignty"— the idea that territorial settlers should decide the slavery issue without federal interference—won the 1858 election. Lincoln, who argued that the federal government should ban slavery in the territories, gained national exposure through the debates that ultimately helped win him the presidency in 1860.

Douglas

In regard to his [Lincoln's] doctrine that this government was in violation of the law of God, which says that a house divided against itself cannot stand, I repudiated it as a slander upon the immortal framers of our Constitution. I then said, I have often repeated, and now again assert, that in my opinion our government can endure forever, divided into free and slave states as our fathers made it— each state having the right to prohibit, abolish, or sustain slavery, just as it pleases. This government was made upon the great basis of the sovereignty of the states, the right of each state to regulate its own domestic institutions to suit itself, and that right was conferred with the understanding and expectation that, inasmuch as each locality had separate interests, each locality must have different and distinct local and domestic institutions, corresponding to its wants and interests. Our fathers knew when they made the government that the laws and institutions which were well adapted to the Green Mountains of Vermont were unsuited to the rice plantations of South Carolina. They knew then, as well as we know now, that the laws and institutions which would be well adapted to the beautiful prairies of Illinois would not be suited to the mining regions of California. They knew that in a republic as broad as this, having such a variety of soil, climate, and interest, there must necessarily be a corresponding variety of local laws—the policy and institutions of each state adapted to its condition and wants. For this reason this Union was established on the right of each state to do as it pleased on the question of slavery and every other question; and the various states were not allowed to complain of, much less interfere with, the policy of their neighbors. . . .

I say to you that there is but one hope, one safety, for this country, and that is to stand immovably by that principle which declares the right of each state and each territory to decide these questions for themselves. This government was founded on that principle and must be administered in the same sense in which it was founded.

But the Abolition party really think that under the Declaration of Independence the Negro is equal to the white man and that Negro equality is an inalienable right conferred by the Almighty, and hence that all human laws in violation of it are null and void. With such men it is no use for me to argue. I hold that the signers of the Declaration of Independence had no reference to Negroes at all when they declared all men to be created equal. They did not mean Negro, nor the savage Indians, nor the Fiji Islanders, nor any other barbarous race. They were speaking of white men. They alluded to men of European birth and European descent—to white men and to none others—when they declared that doctrine. I hold that this government was established on the white basis. It was established by white men for the benefit of white men and their posterity forever and should be administered by white men and none others. But it does not follow, by any means, that merely because the Negro is not a citizen, and merely because he is not our equal, that, therefore, he should be a slave. On the contrary, it does follow that we ought to extend to the Negro race, and to all other dependent races all the rights, all the privileges, and all the immunities which they can exercise consistently with the safety of society. Humanity requires that we should give them all these privileges; Christianity commands that we should extend those privileges to them. The question then arises: What are those privileges and what is the nature and extent of them? My answer is that that is a question which each state must answer for itself. We in Illinois have decided it for ourselves. We tried slavery, kept it up for twelve years, and, finding that it was not profitable, we abolished it for that reason, and became a free state. We adopted in its stead the policy that a Negro in this state shall not be a slave and shall not be a citizen. We have a right to adopt that policy. For my part I think it is a wise and sound policy for us. You in Missouri must judge for yourselves whether it is a wise policy for you. If you choose to follow our example, very good; if you reject it, still well, it is your business, not ours. So with Kentucky. Let Kentucky adopt a policy to suit herself. If we do not like it, we will keep away from it, and if she does not like ours let her stay at home, mind her own business and let us alone. If the people of all the states will act on that great principle, and each state mind its own business, attend to its own affairs, take care of its own Negroes, and not meddle with its neighbors, then there will be peace between the North and the South, the East and the West, throughout the whole Union. Why can we not thus have peace? Why should we thus allow a sectional party to agitate this country, to array the North against the South and convert us into enemies instead of friends . . .

Lincoln

It is not true that our fathers, as Judge Douglas assumes, made this government part slave and part free. Understand the sense in which he puts it. He assumes that slavery is a rightful thing within itself—was introduced by the framers of the Constitution. The exact truth is that they found the institution existing among us, and they left it as they found it. But, in making the government, they left this institution with many clear marks of disapprobation upon it. They found slavery among them, and they left it among them because of the difficulty—the absolute impossibility—of its immediate removal. . . .

I have stated upon former occasions, and I may as well state again, what I understand to be the real issue in this controversy between Judge Douglas and myself. On the point of my wanting to make war between the free and the slave states, there has been no issue between us. So, too, when he assumes that I am in favor of introducing a perfect social and political equality between the white and black races. These are false issues, upon which Judge Douglas has tried to force the controversy. There is no foundation in truth for the charge that I maintain either of these propositions. The real issue in this controversy—the one pressing upon every mind—is the sentiment on the part of one class that looks upon the institution of slavery *as a wrong* and of another class that *does not* look upon it as a wrong. The sentiment that contemplates the in-

stitution of slavery in this country as a wrong is the sentiment of
the Republican party. It is the sentiment around which all their actions—all their arguments circle—from which all their propositions radiate. They look upon it as being a moral, social, and political wrong; and, while they contemplate it as such, they
nevertheless have due regard for its actual existence among us, and
the difficulties of getting rid of it in any satisfactory way and to all
the constitutional obligations thrown about it. Yet having a due regard for these, they desire a policy in regard to it that looks to its
not creating any more danger. They insist that it should, as far as
may be, *be treated* as a wrong, and one of the methods of treating
it as a wrong is to *make provision that it shall grow no larger.* They
also desire a policy that looks to a peaceful end of slavery at some
time as being wrong. . . .

On this subject of treating it as a wrong, and limiting its spread,
let me say a word. Has anything ever threatened the existence of
this Union save and except this very institution of slavery? What is
it that we hold most dear amongst us? Our own liberty and prosperity. What has ever threatened our liberty and prosperity save
and except this institution of slavery? If this is true, how do you
propose to improve the condition of things by enlarging slavery—
by spreading it out and making it bigger? You may have a wen or
cancer upon your person and not be able to cut it out lest you
bleed to death; but surely it is no way to cure it, to engraft it and
spread it over your whole body. That is no proper way of treating
what you regard a wrong. You see this peaceful way of dealing with
it as a wrong—restricting the spread of it, and not allowing it to go
into new countries where it has not already existed. That is the
peaceful way, the old-fashioned way, the way in which the fathers
themselves set us the example.

From *Political Debates Between Hon. Abraham Lincoln and Hon. Stephen A. Douglas, in the Celebrated Campaign of 1858,* published by Follett, Foster & Co., for the Ohio Republican State
Central Committee. Reprinted in William Dudley, ed., *Opposing Viewpoints in American History,*
vol. 1. San Diego: Greenhaven Press, 1996, pp. 252–57.

Document 17: Slavery Is the Cornerstone of the Confederacy

*In an 1861 speech describing the new secessionist constitution, Alexander
H. Stephens, a U.S. senator from Georgia who became vice president of
the Confederacy, argued that slavery was the "cornerstone" of the newly
formed Confederate States of America.*

But not to be tedious in enumerating the numerous changes for
the better, allow me to allude to one other—though last, not least.

The new constitution [of the Confederate States of America] has put at rest, *forever*, all the agitating questions relating to our peculiar institution—African slavery as it exists amongst us—the proper *status of* the negro in our form of civilization. This was the immediate cause of the late rupture and present revolution. [Thomas] Jefferson in his forecast, had anticipated this, as the "rock upon which the old Union would split." He was right. What was conjecture with him, is now a realized fact. But whether he fully comprehended the great truth upon which that rock *stood* and *stands*, may be doubted. The prevailing ideas entertained by him and most of the leading statesmen at the time of the formation of the old constitution, were that the enslavement of the African was in violation of the laws of nature; that it was wrong in *principle*, socially, morally, and politically. It was an evil they knew not well how to deal with, but the general opinion of the men of that day was that, somehow or other in the order of Providence, the institution would be evanescent and pass away. This idea, though not incorporated in the constitution, was the prevailing idea at that time. The constitution, it is true, secured every essential guarantee to the institution while it should last, and hence no argument can be justly urged against the constitutional guarantees thus secured, because of the common sentiment of the day. Those ideas, however, were fundamentally wrong. They rested upon the assumption of the equality of races. This was an error. It was a sandy foundation, and the government built upon it fell, when the "storm came and the wind blew."

Our new government is founded upon exactly the opposite idea; its foundations are laid, its corner-stone rests upon the great truth, that the negro is not equal to the white man; that slavery—subordination to the superior race—is his natural and normal condition.

This, our new government, is the first, in the history of the world, based upon this great physical, philosophical, and moral truth. This truth has been slow in the process of its development, like all other truths in the various departments of science. It has been so even amongst us. Many who hear me, perhaps, can recollect well, that this truth was not generally admitted, even within their day. The errors of the past generation still clung to many as late as twenty years ago. Those at the North, who still cling to these errors, with a zeal above knowledge, we justly denominate fanatics. All fanaticism springs from an aberration of the mind—from a defect in reasoning. It is a species of insanity. One of the most striking characteristics of insanity, in many instances, is forming correct conclusions from fancied or erroneous premises; so with the anti-slavery fanatics; their conclusions are right if their premises were. They assume that the negro is equal, and hence conclude that he is entitled to equal privileges and rights with the white man. If their premises were correct, their conclusions would be logical and just—but their premise being wrong, their whole argument fails. I recollect once of having heard a gentleman from one of the northern States, of great power and ability, announce in the House of Representatives, with imposing effect, that we of the South would be compelled, ultimately, to yield upon this subject of slavery, that it was as impossible to war successfully against a principle in politics, as it was in physics or mechanics. That the principle would ultimately prevail. That we, in maintaining slavery as it exists with us, were warring against a principle, a principle founded in nature, the principle of the equality of men. The reply I made to him was, that upon his own grounds, we should, ultimately, succeed, and that he and his associates, in this crusade against our institutions, would ultimately fail. The truth announced, that it was as impossible to war successfully against a principle in politics as it was in physics and mechanics, I admitted; but told him that it was he, and those acting with him, who were warring against a principle. They were attempting to make things equal which the Creator had made unequal. . . .

May we not, therefore, look with confidence to the ultimate universal acknowledgment of the truths upon which our system rests? It is the first government ever instituted upon the principles in strict conformity to nature, and the ordination of Providence, in furnishing the materials of human society. Many governments have been founded upon the principle of the subordination and serfdom of certain classes of the same race; such were and are in violation of the laws of nature. Our system commits no such violation of nature's laws. With us, all of the white race, however high or low, rich or poor, are equal in the eye of the law. Not so with the negro. Subordination is his place. He, by nature, or by the curse against Canaan, is fitted for that condition which he occupies in our system. The architect, in the construction of buildings, lays the foundation with the proper material—the granite; then comes the brick or the marble. The substratum of our society is made of the material fitted by nature for it, and by experience we know that it is best, not only for the superior, but for the inferior race, that it should be so. It is, indeed, in conformity with the ordinance of the Creator. It is not for us to inquire into the wisdom of his ordinances, or to question them. For his own purposes, he has made one race to differ from another.

Henry Cleveland, *Alexander H. Stephens in Public and Private.* Philadelphia: National Publishing Company, 1866, pp. 721–23. Reprinted in Irwin Unger, ed., *American Issues: A Primary Source Reader in United States History.* Englewood Cliffs, NJ: Prentice-Hall, pp. 271–73.

Document 18: A Union Major Asks Instructions Regarding Slave Refugees

The presence of fugitive slaves seeking refuge in Union army camps presented a thorny political problem for Civil War leaders. Some commanders gave them shelter and protection and employed them as "contraband of war"; others returned them to masters who could prove their loyalty to the United States; both courses of action were criticized. In November 1861 General Henry W. Halleck, commander of the Department of the Missouri, issued General Order No. 3, excluding all fugitive slaves from Union army camps because they posed a security risk. His subordinate, General Alexander S. Asboth, asked regimental commanders in his division to report on their compliance with Halleck's exclusion order. In the following letter, Major George E. Waring Jr. responds to Asboth's inquiry, arguing that the blacks in his camp have become valued workers, and that all of them have claimed to be free people and not to be fugitive slaves. In March 1862 Congress passed a law forbidding army officers from returning fugitive slaves to their masters.

Camp Halleck near Rolla Mo. Dec 19th 61
General: In obedience to the order contained in your circular (No. 2), received this day, I beg to report that on the receipt of your order No 23 communicating Gen. Order No. 3, from the Commanding General, ordering fugitive slaves to be excluded from the lines, I caused all negroes in my camp to be examined, and it was reported to me that they all stoutly asserted that they were free.

Since that time a woman employed in my own mess as cook has been claimed by one Captain Holland as the fugitive slave of his father-in-law. In compliance with your order, to that end, which he produced, she was given up to him. Since the receipt of your circular of today, I have again caused an investigation to be thoroughly made which has resulted as in the first instance.

I beg now, General, to ask for your instructions in the matter. These negroes all claim and insist that they are *free.* Some of them, I have no question, are so; others I have as little doubt have been slaves,—but no one is here to prove it, and I hesitate to take so serious a responsibility as to decide, arbitrarily, in the absence of any direct evidence, that they are such.

If I turn them away, I inflict great hardship upon them, as they would be homeless and helpless. Furthermore, such a course would occasion much personal inconvenience and sincere regret, to other officers no less than to myself. These people are mainly our servants, and we can get no others. They have been employed in this capacity for some time—long enough for us to like them as servants, to find them useful and trustworthy, and to feel an interest in their welfare.

The Commanding General, in his letter to Col. Blair, (as published in the Missouri Democrat of the 16ᵗʰ inst), says—in explanation of General order No 3.—"Unauthorized persons, black or white, free or slave, must be kept out of our camps." The negroes in my camp are employed, in accordance with the Army Regulations, as officers' servants, teamsters, and hospital attendants, and, with the exception of one little child are such as we are authorized to have in the camp. It seems to me that they are without the pale of the order and the *intention* of the Commanding General, and I trust that I may be excused for awaiting more explicit instructions before doing what may be an extra-official act—at which my private feelings revolt.

I recognize the fact that obedience to Gen. Orders No. 3 is a part of my military duty, and I shall unflinchingly comply with it in the consciousness that I am in no way responsible therefore; but I *am* personally responsible for my decision, when it is to affect the happiness and security of others.

May I ask you, General, to relieve me of this responsibility by giving me your final decision at your earliest convenience. Very Respectfully Your Obedient Servant

Geo. E. Waring, Jr.

Ira Berlin et al., eds., *Free at Last: A Documentary History of Slavery, Freedom, and the Civil War.* New York: New Press, 1992, pp. 27–29.

Document 19: The Emancipation Proclamation

On September 22, 1862, President Abraham Lincoln issued a preliminary proclamation declaring that if the Confederate states were still in rebellion at the beginning of the next year, he would, as wartime leader of the United States, declare all slaves within their borders "forever free." On January 1, 1863, he issued the following Emancipation Proclamation freeing the slaves in the Confederacy (the status of slaves in Union-controlled areas was left unchanged).

Whereas, on the twenty-second day of September, in the year of our Lord one thousand eight hundred and sixty-two, a proclamation was issued by the President of the United States, containing, among other things, the following, to wit:

"That on the first day of January, in the year of our Lord one thousand eight hundred and sixty-three, all persons held as slaves within any state or designated part of a state, the people whereof shall then be in rebellion against the United States, shall be then, thenceforward, and forever, free; and the Executive Government of the United States, including the military and naval authority thereof, will recognize and maintain the freedom of such persons, and will do no act or acts to repress such persons, or any of them, in any efforts they may make for their actual freedom.

"That the Executive will, on the first day of January aforesaid, by proclamation, designate the states and parts of states, if any, in which the people thereof, respectively, shall then be in rebellion against the United States; and the fact that any state, or the people thereof, shall on that day be in good faith represented in the Congress of the United States, by members chosen thereto at elections wherein a majority of the qualified voters of such states shall have participated, shall, in the absence of strong countervailing testimony, be deemed conclusive evidence that such state, and the people thereof, are not then in rebellion against the United States."

Now therefore, I, Abraham Lincoln, President of the United States, by virtue of the power in me vested as commander-in-chief of the army and navy of the United States, in time of actual armed rebellion against the authority and government of the United States, and as a fit and necessary war measure for suppressing said rebellion, do, on this first day of January, in the year of our Lord one thousand eight hundred and sixty-three, and in accordance with my purpose so to do, publicly proclaimed for the full period of one hundred days from the day first above mentioned, order and designate as the states and parts of states wherein the people thereof, respectively, are this day in rebellion against the United States, the following, to wit:

Arkansas, Texas, Louisiana (except the parishes of St. Bernard, Plaquemines, Jefferson, St. Johns, St. Charles, St. James, Ascension, Assumption, Terre Bonne, Lafourche, St. Mary, St. Martin, and Orleans, including the city of New Orleans), Mississippi, Alabama, Florida, Georgia, South Carolina, North Carolina, and Virginia (except the forty-eight counties designated as West Virginia, and also the counties of Berkeley, Accomac, Northampton, Elizabeth City, York, Princess Ann, and Norfolk, including the cities of Norfolk and Portsmouth) and which excepted parts are for the present left precisely as if this proclamation were not issued.

And by virtue of the power and for the purpose aforesaid, I do order and declare that all persons held as slaves within said designated states and parts of states are, and henceforward shall be, free; and that the Executive Government of the United States, including the military and naval authorities thereof, will recognize and maintain the freedom of said persons.

And I hereby enjoin upon the people so declared to be free to abstain from all violence, unless in necessary self-defense; and I recommend to them that, all cases when allowed, they labor faithfully for reasonable wages.

And I further declare and make known that such persons, of suitable condition, will be received into the armed service of the United States to garrison forts, positions, stations, and other places, and to man vessels of all sorts in said service.

And upon this act, sincerely believed to be an act of justice, warranted by the Constitution upon military necessity, I invoke the considerate judgment of mankind and the gracious favor of Almighty God.

In witness whereof, I have hereunto set my hand and caused the seal of the United States to be affixed.

Done at the city of Washington this first day of January, in the year of our Lord one thousand eight hundred and sixty-three, and of the Independence of the United States of America the eighty-seventh.

Roy P. Basler, ed., *The Collected Works of Abraham Lincoln*. Vol. 6. New Brunswick, NJ: Rutgers University Press, 1953, pp. 28–30. Reprinted in Richard Hofstadter, *Great Issues in American History, from the Revolution to the Civil War, 1765–1865*. New York: Vintage, 1958, pp. 411–13.

Document 20: Remembrances of Emancipation

In the 1930s the federal government sponsored a program in which interviewers recorded the accounts and reminiscences of elderly former slaves. The following passages provide various recollections of these men and women on learning that they were no longer slaves.

Everybody went wild. We didn't feel like anybody had done anythin' for us. We all felt like heroes, and like nobody had made us that way but ourselves. We wuz free! Just like that, we wuz free. It didn't seem to make the whites mad, either. They went right on giving us food, just the same. Nobody took our homes away. But, right off, colored folks started on the move. They seemed to want to get closer to freedom, so they'd know what it wuz—like it wuz a place or city. Me and my father stuck close as a lean tick to a sick kitten.

—FELIX HAYWOOD

When the Yankee soldiers came, the niggers run and hid under the beds, and the soldiers came and poked their bayonets under the beds and shouted, "Come on out from under there. You're free."

—DICEY THOMAS

Glory! Glory! Yes, child, de Negroes are free, an' when dey knew dat dey were free—oh, baby!—dey began to sing:

Mammy, don't yo' cook no mo',
Yo' are free, yo' are free!
Rooster, don't yo' crow no mo',
Yo' are free, yo' are free!
Ole hen, don't yo' lay no mo',
Yo' free, yo' free!

—FANNIE BERRY . . .

After the War, many soldiers came to my mistress, Mrs. Blakely, trying to make her free me. I told them I was free, but I did not want to go anywhere—that I wanted to stay in the only home that I had ever known. In a way, that placed me in a wrong attitude. I was pointed out as different. Sometimes, I was threatened for not leaving, but I stayed on.

—AUNT ADELINE

When freedom come, Marster tells us all to come to front of de house. He am standin' on de porch. He 'splains 'bout freedom and says, "You is now free and can go whar you pleases." Den, he tells us he have larned us not to steal and to be good, and we-uns should 'member dat, and if we-uns gets in trouble, to come to him and he will help us. He sho' do dat, too, 'cause de niggers goes to him lots of times, and he always helps.

Marster says dat he needs help on de place, and sich dat stays, he'd pay 'em for de work. Lots of dem stayed, but some left. To dem dat leaves, Marster gives a mule or cow, and sich, for de start. To my folks, Marster gives some land. He doesn't give us de deed, but de right to stay till he dies.

—BETTY BORMER

You ought to been behind a tree the day young Master George told me I me I was free. You would have laughed fit to kill. I was down on the farm plowing, and Master George rid up on a hoss and say, "Morning, Allen." I say, "Morning, Master George."

"Laying by the crap [crop]?" he say. "Yes, Sah," I told him. Then, he say, "Allen, you is free." I say, "What you mean, 'free'?" "The damn Yankees is freed you," he say.

I got off the plow, and he grabbed me by the arm, and pushed my sleeve up, and p'inted to my skin, and say, "Allen, my daddy give a thousand dollars in gold for that, didn't he?" "He sho' did," I told him. Then, he say, "Didn't my daddy give you to me? And didn't I put them clothes on you?" "Sho' 'nuf, you did," I say to him. Then, Master George say, "Yes, and the damn Yankees took you away from me. But them is my clothes." Then, he made like he was gonna take my clothes away from me, and we scuffled all round the field.

Then, Master George begin to laugh, and say, "Allen, I ain't gonna take your clothes. I's gonna put some better ones on you. You is free, but I want you to stay right on and tend to your mistress, like you been doing." I lived with them till after I was grown. I was in and out five or six years, 'fore I married. When I couldn't get work, I went back to them and et Old Mistress' meat and bread.

—ALLEN WILLIAMS

We went right on workin', after freedom. Old Buck Adams wouldn't let us go till dey have a man select' to go out through de country an' tell de slaves dat dey was free, now. Dat was way after de War was over. De freedom man come to our place an' read a paper what de Pres'dent had writ what said we was now free, an' he talk to us 'bout freedom an' tole us not to work no more, 'less we got paid for it.

When he had finished an' gone, old Buck Adams' wife, old Mary Adams, come out an' spoke to us. I rec'lec' what she say jes' as well as if I jes' hear her say it. She say, "Ten years from today, I'll have you all back 'gain." Yes, sir. "Ten years from today, I'll have you all back 'gain." Dat ten years been over a mighty long time, an' she ain' got us back yet, an' she is dead an' gone.

Us ain' had no time for no celebration, for dey make us git right off de place—jes' like you take an old horse an' turn it loose. You see a lot of cattle in de field eating de grass wit' a fence round dem, an' den somebody open de gate an' say, "Git!" Dat's how we was. No money, no nothin'—jes' turn' loose wit'out nothin'.

—WILLIAM MATTHEWS

I remember well how the roads was full of folks walking and walking along, when the niggers were freed. Didn't know where they was going. Just going to see about something else, somewhere else. Meet a body in the road and they ask, "Where you going?" "Don't know." "What you going to do?" "Don't know." And then sometimes we would meet a white man, and he would say, "How you like to come work on my farm?" And we say, "I don't know." And then maybe he say, "If you come work for me on my farm, when the crops is in, I give you five bushels of corn, five gallons of molasses, some ham meat, and all your clothes and vittles while you works for me." "All right! That's what I do." And then, something begins to work up here and I begins to think and to know things. And I knowed then I could make a living for my own self, and I never had to be a slave no more.

—ROBERT FALLS

James Mellon, ed., *Bullwhip Days: The Slaves Remember: An Oral History*. New York: Avon, 1988, pp. 346–48.

Chronology

1619
Twenty Africans are deposited at Jamestown, Virginia, by a Dutch frigate; whether their legal status was that of slaves or servants remains unclear.

1641
Massachusetts is the first American colony to recognize slavery officially in its laws.

1671
Maryland's legislature enacts a law holding that conversion to Christianity does not alter one's slave status.

1672
Virginia passes a law rewarding the killing of "Maroons"—runaway slaves who maintain a nomadic existence on the western frontier; between 1672 and 1864 dozens of Maroon communities are formed in the forests and swamps of South Carolina, Florida, Virginia, and other colonies and states.

1688
Quakers in Germantown, Pennsylvania, denounce slavery in America's first recorded formal protest against the institution.

1723
Virginia forbids owners to free (manumit) their slaves by law.

1739
Forty-four black slaves and thirty white colonists are killed in the Stono slave rebellion near Charleston, South Carolina.

1775–1783
The British royal governor of Virginia, Lord Dunmore, issues a proclamation in November 1775 declaring those slaves free who join "his Majesty's troops." During the Revolutionary War an estimated fifty thousand slaves escape to join the British.

1776
Thomas Jefferson drafts the Declaration of Independence; the document is adopted by the Continental Congress after passages condemning the slave trade are removed.

1777
Vermont forbids slavery in its founding state constitution.

1780
Pennsylvania passes a law to gradually abolish slavery; similar laws are passed by Rhode Island and Connecticut in 1784, New York in 1799, and New Jersey in 1804.

1782
Virginia passes a law permitting the private manumission of slaves at the owner's discretion.

1787
Congress passes the Northwest Ordinance, banning slavery in the western territory north of the Ohio River acquired from England in the Revolutionary War.

1788
The Constitution, which indirectly sanctions slavery and forbids Congress from abolishing the slave trade for twenty more years, is ratified by the states.

1791–1801
A violent slave insurrection erupts in St. Domingue (Haiti); former slave Toussaint-L'ouverture liberates the island and abolishes slavery, developments that are watched closely by Americans.

1793
Congress passes the Fugitive Slave Act, providing for the return of slaves who have escaped across state boundaries; Eli Whitney invents the cotton gin, which greatly increases the demand for slaves.

1800
Gabriel Prosser is captured and hanged after his planned slave rebellion in Virginia is betrayed and thwarted.

1807
Congress forbids the importation of slaves into the United States as of January 1, 1808.

1812–1815
The War of 1812 helps secure America's western boundaries; western settlement and slave labor enable Alabama and Mississippi to become the heart of the "Cotton Kingdom."

1816
The American Colonization Society, which seeks to return slave and free blacks to Africa, is founded.

1819
Missouri residents petition Congress for admission to the Union as a slave state.

1820
Congress passes the Missouri Compromise, admitting Missouri as a slave state and Maine as a free state; it also draws a line (at 36°30' north latitude) dividing the remaining Louisiana Territory (purchased from France in 1803) into slave and free regions.

1822
Denmark Vesey, a free black, is executed after his five-year effort to organize a slave rebellion in Charleston, South Carolina, is betrayed by an informant.

1831
William Lloyd Garrison publishes the first issue of the *Liberator*, his abolitionist newspaper, in January; in August, Nat Turner leads a slave revolt in Virginia that results in the deaths of sixty whites and more than two hundred blacks, including Turner, who is captured and executed; Southern states pass new laws to prevent future rebellions.

1833
The American Anti-Slavery Society is founded; slavery is abolished in the British Empire.

1836–1844
Congress imposes a gag rule automatically tabling all antislavery petitions and preventing discussion of the issue; it is repealed after eight years at the urging of former president John Quincy Adams.

1838
Frederick Douglass escapes from slavery to New York City, where he establishes himself as a leading black abolitionist.

1840
The abolitionist movement splits over whether to engage in political activity; the Liberty Party is founded and fields a presidential candidate.

1845
Texas is admitted to the Union as a slave state.

1846–1849
U.S. victory in the Mexican War raises the question of whether

America's newly acquired territories should permit slavery; Congressman David Wilmot introduces but fails to pass the Wilmot Proviso in 1846 banning slavery in all territory acquired from Mexico.

1849
Harriet Tubman escapes from slavery in Maryland to freedom in Philadelphia; she will return to the South nineteen times to help slaves escape via the Underground Railroad.

1850
Congress passes the Compromise of 1850; California is admitted as a free state, New Mexico and Utah are admitted as territories with the power to decide the issue on their own ("popular sovereignty"), the slave trade is abolished in Washington, D.C., and a tougher Fugitive Slave Law is passed penalizing people who interfere with the capture and return of escaped slaves.

1852
Harriet Beecher Stowe's novel *Uncle Tom's Cabin* is published.

1854
Congress passes the Kansas-Nebraska Act, organizing those territories under the principle of popular sovereignty; the law voids the 1820 Missouri Compromise by potentially permitting slavery north of the 36°30' dividing line; negative reaction to the Kansas-Nebraska Act leads to the creation of the Republican Party.

1855–1858
The Kansas territory becomes a political and military battleground over the expansion of slavery in the area.

1857
The U.S. Supreme Court in *Dred Scott v. Sandford* abrogates the Missouri Compromise line dividing slave and free territory and declares that blacks "had no rights the white man was bound to respect."

1859
John Brown leads an unsuccessful raid on the federal armory in Harpers Ferry, Virginia, hoping to start a general slave revolt.

1860
Abraham Lincoln is elected president on a platform of restricting slavery in the territories; South Carolina secedes from the Union.

1861–1865
The Civil War follows the secession of the southern states amid

concerns over the preservation of slavery; thousands of slaves escape during the conflict, are declared "contraband of war," and serve the Union war effort; an estimated 250,000 African Americans, some of whom were slaves, serve as soldiers.

January 1, 1863
President Lincoln's Emancipation Proclamation, announced in September 1862, takes effect; it frees slaves held in the Confederate states.

1865
The Thirteenth Amendment to the Constitution, abolishing slavery throughout the United States, is ratified.

For Further Research

General Studies on American Slavery

David Brion Davis, *Slavery and Human Progress.* New York: Oxford University Press, 1984.

Merton L. Dillon, *Slavery Attacked: Southern Slaves and Their Allies, 1619–1865.* Baton Rouge: Louisiana State University Press, 1990.

Paul Finkelman, ed., *Slavery and the Law.* Madison, WI: Madison House, 1997.

Robert Fogel and Stanley Engerman, *Time on the Cross: The Economics of American Negro Slavery.* Boston: Little, Brown, 1974.

William W. Freehling, *The Reintegration of American History: Slavery and the Civil War.* New York: Oxford University Press, 1994.

Eugene D. Genovese, *Roll Jordan Roll: The World the Slaves Made.* New York: Pantheon, 1974.

Vincent Harding, *There Is a River: The Black Struggle for Freedom in America.* New York: Harcourt Brace Jovanovich, 1981.

Nathan I. Huggins, *Black Odyssey: The Afro-American Ordeal in Slavery.* New York: Pantheon, 1977.

Charles Johnson, Patricia Smith, and the WGBH Series Research Team, *Africans in America: America's Journey through Slavery.* New York: Harcourt Brace, 1998.

Peter Kolchin, *American Slavery, 1619–1877.* New York: Hill and Wang, 1993.

Daniel Pratt Mannix with Malcolm Cowley, *Black Cargoes; A History of the Atlantic Slave Trade, 1518–1865.* New York: Viking Press, 1962.

Randall M. Miller and John D. Smith, eds., *Dictionary of Afro-American Slavery.* Westport, CT: Praeger, 1997.

Harry P. Owens, ed., *Perspectives and Irony in American Slavery.* Jackson: University Press of Mississippi, 1976.

Peter J. Parish, *Slavery: History and Historians.* New York: Harper & Row, 1989.

Larry E. Tise, *Proslavery: A History of the Defense of Slavery in America, 1701–1840.* Athens: University of Georgia Press, 1987.

American Slavery Before 1800

Ira Berlin, *Many Thousands Gone: The First Two Centuries of Slavery in North America*. Cambridge, MA: The Belknap Press of Harvard University Press, 1998.

Ira Berlin and Ronald Hoffman, eds., *Slavery and Freedom in the Age of the American Revolution*. Charlottesville: University Press of Virginia, 1983.

Sylvia R. Frey, *Water from the Rock: Black Resistance in a Revolutionary Age*. Princeton, NJ: Princeton University Press, 1991.

Peter Charles Hoffer, ed., *Africans Become Afro-Americans: Selected Articles on Slavery in the American Colonies*. New York: Garland, 1988.

Winthrop D. Jordan, *White over Black: American Attitudes Toward the Negro, 1550–1812*. New York: Norton, 1977.

John P. Kaminski, *A Necessary Evil? Slavery and the Debate over the Constitution*. Madison, WI: Madison House, 1995.

Edmund S. Morgan, *American Slavery, American Freedom: The Ordeal of Colonial Virginia*. New York: Norton, 1975.

Gary B. Nash, *Race and Revolution*. Madison, WI: Madison House, 1990.

William D. Piersen, *From Africa to America: African American History from the Colonial Era to the Early Republic, 1526–1790*. New York: Twayne, 1996.

Raymond Starr and Robert Detweiler, eds., *Race, Prejudice, and the Origins of Slavery in America*. Cambridge, MA: Schenkman, 1975.

Betty Wood, *The Origins of American Slavery: Freedom and Bondage in the English Colonies*. New York: Hill and Wang, 1997.

Peter H. Wood, *Black Majority: Negroes in Colonial South Carolina from 1670 Through the Stono Rebellion*. New York: Knopf, 1974.

Arthur Zilversmit, *The First Emancipation: The Abolition of Slavery in the North*. Chicago: University of Chicago Press, 1967.

American Slavery After 1800

John Ashworth, *Slavery, Capitalism, and Politics in the Antebellum Republic, 1820–1850*. New York: Cambridge University Press, 1995.

Ira Berlin, *Slaves Without Masters: The Free Negro in the Antebellum South*. New York: Pantheon, 1974.

Henrietta Buckmaster, *Flight to Freedom: The Story of the Underground Railroad*. New York: Dell, 1972.

Catherine Clinton, *The Plantation Mistress: Woman's World in the Old South*. New York: Pantheon, 1982.

William J. Cooper, *Liberty and Slavery: Southern Politics to 1860*. New York: Knopf, 1983.

LaWanda Cox, *Lincoln and Black Freedom: A Study in Presidential Leadership*. Columbia: University of South Carolina Press, 1981.

Barbara J. Fields, *Slavery and Freedom on the Middle Ground: Maryland During the Nineteenth Century*. New Haven, CT: Yale University Press, 1985.

Eric Foner, *Free Soil, Free Labor, Free Men: The Ideology of the Republican Party Before the Civil War*. New York: Oxford University Press, 1970.

Elizabeth Fox-Genovese, *Within the Plantation Household: Black and White Women of the Old South*. Chapel Hill: University of North Carolina Press, 1988.

John Hope Franklin and Loren Schweninger, *Runaway Slaves: Rebels on the Plantation, 1790–1860*. New York: Oxford University Press, 1999.

William Freehling, *Road to Disunion*. New York: Oxford University Press, 1990.

Louis S. Gerteis, *From Contraband to Freedmen: Federal Policy Toward Southern Blacks, 1861–1865*. Westport, CT: Greenwood Press, 1973.

Michael Holt, *The Political Crisis of the 1850s*. New York: Wiley, 1978.

Robert Johannsen, *Lincoln, the South and Slavery: The Political Dimension*. Baton Rouge: Louisiana State University Press, 1991.

Bruce Levine, *Half Slave and Half Free: The Roots of Civil War*. New York: Hill and Wang, 1992.

Henry Mayer, *All on Fire: William Lloyd Garrison and the Abolition of Slavery*. New York: St. Martin's Press, 1998.

James McPherson, *Abraham Lincoln and the Second American Revolution*. New York: Oxford University Press 1991.

Thomas D. Morris, *Free Men All: The Personal Liberty Laws of the North, 1780–1861*. Baltimore: Johns Hopkins University Press, 1974.

James Oakes, *Slavery and Freedom: An Interpretation of the Old South*. New York: Knopf, 1990.

David M. Potter, *The Impending Crisis, 1848–1861*. New York: Harper & Row, 1976.

Roger L. Ransom, *Conflict and Compromise: The Political Economy of Slavery, Emancipation, and the American Civil War*. New York: Cambridge University Press, 1989.

Kenneth M. Stampp, *The Peculiar Institution: Slavery in the Antebellum South*. New York: Knopf, 1956.

Robert Starobin, *Industrial Slavery in the Old South*. New York: Oxford University Press, 1970.

James B. Stewart, *Holy Warriors*. New York: Hill and Wang, 1976.

Document Collections and Primary Sources

Ira Berlin et al., eds., *Free at Last: A Documentary History of Slavery, Freedom, and the Civil War*. New York: New Press, 1992.

Ira Berlin, Marc Favreau, and Steven F. Miller, eds., *Remembering Slavery: African Americans Talk About Their Personal Experiences of Slavery and Emancipation*. New York: New Press, 1998.

John W. Blassingame, ed., *Slave Testimony: Two Centuries of Letters, Speeches, Interviews, and Autobiographies*. Baton Rouge: Louisiana State University Press, 1977.

Carol Bleser, ed., *Secret and Sacred: The Diaries of James Henry Hammond, a Southern Slaveholder*. New York: Oxford University Press, 1988.

B.A. Botkin, ed., *Lay My Burden Down: A Folk History of Slavery*. New York: Delta, 1994.

Roger Bruns, ed., *Am I Not a Man and a Brother: The Antislavery Crusade in Revolutionary America, 1688–1788*. New York: Chelsea House, 1977.

Richard Beale Davis, *William Fitzhugh and His Chesapeake World, 1676–1701: The Fitzhugh Letters and Other Documents*. Chapel Hill: University of North Carolina Press, 1963.

Elizabeth Donnan, ed., *Documents Illustrative of the History of the Slave Trade to America*. 4 vols. New York: Octagon Books, 1969.

Drew Gilpin Faust, ed., *The Ideology of Slavery: Proslavery Thought in the Antebellum South, 1830–1860*. Baton Rouge: Louisiana State University Press, 1981.

James Mellon, ed., *Bullwhip Days: The Slaves Remember, An Oral History*. New York: Avon, 1988.

Michael Mullin, ed., *American Negro Slavery: A Documentary History*. Columbia: University of South Carolina Press, 1976.

Gilbert Osofsky, ed., *Puttin' On Ole Massa*. New York: Harper & Row, 1969.

George P. Rawick, ed., *The American Slaver: A Composite Autobiography*. 39 vols. Westport, CT: Greenwood, 1972–1979.

Willie Lee Rose, ed., *A Documentary History of Slavery in North America*. New York: Oxford University Press, 1976.

Lathan A. Windley, ed., *Runaway Slave Advertisements: A Documentary History from the 1730s to 1790*. 4 vols. Westport, CT: Greenwood, 1983.

Index

abolition movement, 23–24
  Civil War goals of, 146–47
  controversial mailings from,
    105–107
  defiance of, law by, 130
  on Dred Scott decision, 132
  fear of white dissent through,
    108–10
  John Brown's raid, 132–33
  and Lincoln's election, 134
  on necessity of Civil War, 192
  northern opposition to, 110–11
  North vs. South, 111–12
  propaganda by, 125–26
  and religious converts, 104–105
  as scapegoat for southern troubles,
    107–108
  see also emancipation
Adams, John Quincy, 104–105
Africa, slavery in, 39–40
African Americans. See black slaves
African Methodist Episcopal
  Church, 154
African slave trade, 15–16, 34–35
  banning of, 84
  legislation opposing, 71–72
  and New England colonies, 62–63
  participation in, by northern
    colonies, 60–62
  voyage of, 40–42
  see also black slaves; slavery
Alabama, 86
Alvarado, Pedro de, 35
American Antislavery Society, 105
American Colonization Society, 80
American Museum (magazine), 75
American Revolution
  and emancipation, 70–71, 73
  impact on slavery, 17–21
  questions raised about slavery
    from, 68–69
American Slavery as It Is (Weld), 125
Anderson, Osborn Perry, 132–33
An Essay in Favor of Slavery (Dew),
  93
Aristotle, 99
Arkansas Territory, 85

Athenians, 99
Atlantic slave trade. *See* African slave
  trade
Ayllon, Lucas Vasquez de, 54

Bacon's Rebellion, 53
Barbados, 34, 38, 49
  slavery moving to South Carolina
    from, 54–55
Belknap, Jeremy, 77
Benjamin, Judah P., 93
Berlin, Ira, 30
Bibb, Henry, 119
Birney, James, 105
Black Codes, 173
Black Reconstruction (DuBois), 29
black slaves
  abolitionists inciting through
    mailings, 107–108
  avenues to freedom, 48–49
  celebration of Emancipation
    Proclamation by, 154–55
  as childlike and lazy, 115
  Civil War as uprising of, 137–38
  as contraband of war, 151
  defining freedom of, 169–70
  dependency on slaveholders,
    162–64
  discipline and control of, 114–15
  dual roles of docility vs. rebellion
    in, 118–20
  English switch to using, 49–50,
    51–52
  first in America, 46–48
  as happy, 115–16
  help Union army, 30–31, 141–43
    resistance by Union government,
      143–45
  influence of Emancipation
    Proclamation on, 167
  influence on Civil War, 29–31
  in North American colonies,
    42–43
  Northern European use of, 37–38
  northern free, 65–66
  population in the South, 22, 113
  population in Virginia, 75–76

racism against, 48, 52–53, 78–79
  during Reconstruction
    political leadership of, 174–75
    political rights of, 172–74
    relations with whites, 176–77
    sharecropping by, 177–78
  reproduction of, 38–39
  response to Civil War, 138–39
  response to emancipation, 171–72
    as diverse and complex, 157–58
    expression of feelings, 164–65
    fear of the unknown, 161–62
    responsibilities to slaveholders,
      167–69
    solitude, 166
    sorrow and confusion, 159–61
    viewed as divine intervention,
      166–67
    white vs. black, 163
  and Spanish domination, 35–37
  as threat to whites, 52–53
  work routine on plantations,
    113–14
  see also African slave trade; fugitive
    slaves; slavery
Blight, David W., 171
Boles, John B., 44
Brazil, 180, 183, 184
Brown, John, 132–34, 184
Brown, Sarah, 160
Brown, William Wells, 169
Bureau of Refugees, Freedmen, and
  Abandoned Lands. See Freedmen's
  Bureau
Butler, Benjamin F., 141, 144, 151

Calhoun, John C., 96–97, 109, 129
  on expansion of slavery, 27
  legacy of, 102
  philosophy of, 97–98
  political leadership of, 93
  on race and slavery, 98–100
  on social order, 101–102
Carey, Mathew, 75
Caribbean Island, 62–63
Carruthers, Richard, 165
Carter, Robert III, 70
Channing, William E., 192
Charles II, king of England, 54
Charles V, emperor of Spain, 36
Chase, Salmon P., 129
Chesapeake
  decreased supply of white servants

  in, 50–51
  switch to using black slaves in,
    49–50, 51–52
  see also North, the
Chester, T. Morris, 171, 172
Civil War, 11, 13
  abolitionist's goal of, 146–47
  achievements of, 192–93
  compared with slave insurrection,
    184
  Emancipation Proclamation's
    influence on, 155
  events leading to, 131–35
  freeing fugitive slaves during,
    151–52
  as instrumental in ending slavery,
    29
  Lincoln's hesitancy on
    emancipation through, 148–49
  politics and economy of slavery
    before, 181–82
  possibilities in absence of, 190–92
  and possibilities of peaceful
    secession, 183–90
  reasons for
    achieving emancipation, 14,
      149–51
    debate on, 185–86
    emancipation vs. saving the
      Union, 145–46
  slavery did not justify, 183–84
  slaves helping Union army in,
    141–45
  slaves' influence on, 29–31
  slave uprising through, 137–38
  state concerns over slavery during,
    139–41
  see also Reconstruction
Clay, Henry, 85, 89, 129
Cole, Thomas, 162
Colleton, John, 54
Columbus, Christopher, 35, 36
Compromise of 1850, 122, 129–30
Confederate Army, 138
  potential power of, 190–91
  shortages in, 139
Confiscation Act, 151, 152
Connecticut, 64
  see also New England
Constitution, U.S., 25–26
Constitutional Convention of 1787,
  25–26, 72–73
Copeland, John Anthony, 132–33

cotton gin, 21, 79, 94
cotton production
  influence on slavery, 21–23, 94–96
Coxe, Tench, 81
Crane, Silas, 159
Cuba, 15, 34

Davis, Jefferson, 93, 138
Declaration of Independence, 18, 97
Delaware, 20, 148
  see also Middle Colonies
Democratic Party, 176
Dew, Thomas Roderick, 93
Dillon, Merton L., 18, 137
Dissertation on Slavery (Tucker), 79
District of Columbia, 79, 152–53
Douglas, Stephen A., 129, 131
Douglass, Frederick, 149–51, 176
Douglass' Monthly (newspaper),
  149–50
Dred Scott decision, 28, 124,
  131–32
Du Bois, W.E.B., 29
Dumond, Dwight, 134
Dupre, Lewis, 79–80
Dutch West India Company, 61
Dwight, Timothy, 80, 80–81

Elmore, Grace, 167, 168
Eltis, David, 34
emancipation, 11, 13
  American Revolution and, 20–21,
    69
  in Brazil, 183, 184
  Civil War as goal of, 14, 29–31,
    149–51
  defining black freedom from,
    169–70
  during American Revolution,
    70–71, 73
  necessity of war for, 180–81
  obstacles to, 90
  pre–Civil War prospects for
    peaceful, 186–88
  proposals for gradual, 74–75,
    77–79
    failure of North to act on, 79,
      80–81
  Richmond, Virginia after, 171–72
  secession would have delayed,
    188–89
  spirituals and songs inspired by,
    165–67

see also abolition movement
Emancipation Proclamation, 29, 165
  influence on slaves, 155
  slaves celebrating, 154–55
English
  aiding southern cause, 153
  decrease in white servants available
    to, 50–51
  relations with other races, 48–49
  on slavery, 44–46, 47
  switch to using black slaves, 49–50,
    51–52
Equiano, Olaudah, 36, 37, 40

Fairfax, Ferdinando, 74
federal government
  on fugitive slaves, 122–25
  slaveholders supported by, 122
Federalist Party, 91
Fifteenth Amendment, 174
Finney, Charles Grandison,
  103–104, 111
First Battle of Bull Run, 153
Fitzhugh, George, 93
Florida, 176
Fogel, Robert W., 185
Foner, Eric, 181
France, 153
Franklin, John Hope, 128
Freedmen's Bureau, 172, 174, 177
Freehling, William W., 103
Free Soil movement, 24
  see also abolition movement
Fremont, John C., 151
Fugitive Slave Law of 1793, 123,
  125, 182
Fugitive Slave Law of 1850, 150–51
fugitive slaves, 129, 130
  conflict of laws over, 122–25
  contributed to ideological war,
    126–27
  freeing Confederate, 151–52
  narratives by, 127
  propaganda on, 125–26
  see also black slaves

Garrison, William Lloyd, 104, 105,
  138
  on celebration of Thirteenth
    Amendment, 155–56
  favoring secession, 181
  on necessity of Civil War, 146, 192
  on slaves helping Union army,

144–45
on U.S. Constitution, 26
Georgia, 84, 140
Gettysburg Address, 137
Grant, Ulysses S., 175–76
Greater Antilles, 37–38
Great Plague, 50
Greeley, Horace, 149, 190
Green, Duff, 109–10
Green, Shields, 132–33
Gresham, Harriett, 165
Grimké, Angelina, 105

Haiti, 181
see also St. Domingue
Hamilton, Robert, 145
Hammond, James Henry, 109, 111, 114–15
Harding, Vincent, 142
Harris, Annie, 166
Hawkins, Annie, 167–68
Hawkins, John, 45
Hayes, Rutherford B., 176
Hayne, Arthur P., 108
Haywood, Felix, 165
Henry, Patrick, 18
Hicks, Thomas, 144
Holy Band, 104
Hottentots, 183
Huger, Alfred, 105, 106, 107
Hummel, Jeffrey Rogers, 27, 28, 180
Hutson, William, 169

Illinois, 86
illiteracy, 107
immigration, 34, 96
see also African slave trade
Industrial Revolution, 21
interracial fornication, 52–53
interracial marriage, 53
Israel Bethel Church, 154

Jackson, Andrew, 106–107
Jamaica, 34, 42
Jefferson, Thomas, 69, 85
on abolishing slavery, 78
displacing, 93
and Missouri Compromise, 91
as slaveholder, 18
Johnson, Andrew, 173, 174
Johnson, Samuel, 18
Johnston, Parker, 161
Jones, Charles C., 143

Kansas. See Kansas-Nebraska Act of 1854
Kansas-Nebraska Act of 1854, 27–28, 130–31
Kemble, Frances A., 118
Kendall, Amos, 106, 107
Kentucky, 20, 148
Kenya, 180
Kolchin, Peter, 18, 21, 23, 28, 29–30, 68
Ku Klux Klan, 175–76

Las Casas, Bartolome de, 35–36
Latimer, George, 125
Leary, Lewis Sheridan, 132–33
legislation
abolishing slavery, 152–53
on African slave trade, 71–72
Compromise of 1850, 122, 129–30
Dred Scott case, 131–32
emancipating slaves during Revolutionary War, 70–71
enforcing racism, 52–53
fugitive slave, 26, 123–25
Kansas-Nebraska Act of 1854, 27–28, 130–31
on northern slavery, 64–65
in support of slaveholders, 121–22
see also Missouri Compromise of 1820
Lesser Antilles, 38
Levine, Bruce, 24
Lincoln, Abraham, 126
election of, 28–29, 134
on freeing Confederate slaves, 151
on goals of Civil War, 29, 145–46
hesitancy on abolishing slavery, 148–49
on reasons for Emancipation Proclamation, 165
role in Thirteenth Amendment, 155
on slaves in Union army, 143–44
literature, 125–26, 130
Littlefield, Daniel C., 34
Litwack, Leon F., 157
Locke, John, 18, 55
Logue, Sarah, 119
Loguen, J.W., 119
Louisiana, 176
Louisiana Purchase Act, 85
Louisiana Territory, 26

Lovejoy, Elijah P., 110
Lucas, James, 158
Lyles, Moses, 160

Macaulay, Thomas B., 190
Macon, Nathaniel, 90
Madison, James, 80
mailings, antislavery, 105–107
Maine, 88
Mansfield, Lord, 124
Marina, William, 92
Maryland, 20, 148
Massachusetts, 64–65
  see also New England
Mather, Cotton, 64–65
McClellan, George B., 144
McHenry, Jerry, 130
McPherson, James M., 148
Mexican-American War, 27
Middle Colonies
  participation in slave trade, 60–62
  slavery in, 59–60
  see also Delaware; New Jersey;
    New York; Pennsylvania
Middle Passage, 40–42
Mississippi, 140
Missouri. See Missouri Compromise
  of 1820
Missouri Compromise of 1820,
  26–27, 28, 87–89, 148
  achievement of, 89–91
  background to, 85–87
  unresolved issues over, 91
Monroe, James, 92–93
Moore, Glover, 88–89
Morgan, Margaret, 124–25
Moss, Albert A., Jr., 128

Nash, Gary B., 63, 74
Native Americans, 35–36, 37
Navigation Act of 1660, 53
Newby, Dangerfield, 132–33
New England
  participation in slave trade, 62–63
  slavery in, 59, 59–60
  see also Connecticut;
    Massachusetts; Rhode Island
New Hampshire. See New England
New Jersey, 71
  see also Middle Colonies
New Netherland, 61
New World
  England's labor system in, 46

Northern Europeans in, 37–39
Spanish importing slaves to, 35–36
voyage from Africa to, 40–42
see also United States
New York, 71
  see also Middle Colonies
Niven, John, 17
nonslaveholders, 116–17
North, the
  abolition movement in, 24
  anti-abolitionism in, 110–11
  class war in, 100–101
  on Compromise of 1850, 130
  emancipation during American
    Revolution in, 70–71, 73
  failure to act on emancipation
    schemes, 79, 80–81
  fear of white dissent from, 108–10
  free slaves in, 65–66
  on Missouri Compromise, 89
  plea for abolition to, 77–79
  as refuge for fugitive slaves, 26
  slave laws in, 64–65
  southern slavery vs. slavery in, 17,
    23–24
  vs. South on abolition, 111–12
  urban and rural slavery in, 63–64
  white racism in, 80–81
  see also Civil War; Middle Colonies;
    New England; Union army
Northern Europe, 37–39
Nott, Henry, 109

Oakes, James, 121
Ordinance of 1787, 84

Parish, Peter J., 22–23
Parrington, Vernon Louis, 96
Parrish, John, 79–80
Patterson, Robert, 144
Pearce, William, 119
Penn, William, 62
Pennsylvania, 11, 71
  see also Middle Colonies
Pennsylvania Abolition Society, 79,
  81
Perman, Michael, 163
Perth Amboy, 62
Pierce, Franklin, 14
Piersen, William D., 25
plantations
  sugar, 36–37, 38
  work routine on plantations,

113–14
see also cotton production
Plato, 100
Pollard, Edward, 115
Portuguese, 15, 44, 45
Potter, David M., 185–86
Prigg v. Pennsylvania, 125, 129
Proctor, Jenny, 158
Puritans, 64–65

Quakers, 62, 69, 70

racism, 52–53
  by English, 48
  in the North, 80–81
  as obstacle to abolition, 78–79,
    80–81
  during Reconstruction, 175–76
Radical Republicans, 173–74, 176
Randolph, John, 70
Ransom, Roger L., 83
Reconstruction
  beginning of, 172
  black leadership during, 174–75
  Republican Party during, 172–74
  retreat and collapse of, 175–77
  sharecropping during, 177–78
Republic, The (Plato), 100
Republican Party, 131
  as dominant, 91
  forming of, 28
  during Reconstruction, 172–74
Rhode Island, 64
  see also New England
Richmond, Virginia, 171–72
Robinson, Harriet, 158
Robinson, Tom, 159
Rolfe, John, 46, 47
Royal African Company, 41

sailors, death of, 41
Sandys, Sir Edwin, 46
Schwartz, Benjamin, 18–19
Scott, Dred, 124
Scott, Harriet, 124
Scott v. Sanford, 131–32
secession. *See* Civil War
Second Battle of Bull Run, 153
Seven Days' Battles, 153
Seward, William, 129
sharecropping, 177–78
Shaw, Nate, 178
Shotfore, Silas, 158

1696 Act for the Better Ordering
  and Governing of Negroes and
  Slaves, 56
slaveholders
  control methods over slaves,
    114–15
  doubts about slavery by, 117
  fear of slave rebellion, 117–18
  fugitive slaves destroyed political
    power of, 123, 124
  John Brown's raid against, 132–34
  reliance on government support,
    122
  slaves as deceptive to, 118–20
  slaves' dependency on, 162–64
  slaves perceived by, 115–16
  zeal of, 130
slave revolts, fear of, 22, 76, 108,
  109, 117–18
slavery
  in Africa, 39–40
  African vs. Indian, 35–37
  American Revolution's impact on,
    17–21, 68–69
  chattel vs. wage, 101–102
  Civil War destroyed, 192–93
  Civil War disruptions in, 139–41
  Civil War fought for, 134–35,
    185–86
  Constitutional Convention on,
    72–73
  cotton production's influence on,
    21–23, 94–96
  divisions over, 17, 24–25, 128–30
  efforts to end during American
    Revolution, 69–73
  expansion of, 26–29
  following U.S. Constitution,
    84–85
  four characteristics of American,
    16–17
  introduced in Americas, 15–16
  John Calhoun's philosophy on,
    97–98, 99–100
  Lincoln on, 134, 148–49
  Missouri crisis over, 85–87
    see also Missouri Compromise of
      1820
  in northern colonies, 59–60
  northern slave laws on, 64–65
  as politically and economically
    doomed, 181–82
  predating New World, 14–15

in rural and urban North, 63–64
saving the Union vs. abolishing,
    145–46
in South Carolina, 54–57
South's philosophy on, 93–94
in South vs. North, 17
under Spanish domination, 35–37
trends toward disunion over,
    130–31
and U.S. Constitution, 25–26
varying in mainland regions, 58–59
was not predetermined by English,
    44–45
whites' misgivings on, 116–17
white social unrest encouraging,
    53–54
see also abolition movement;
    African slave trade; black slaves;
    emancipation
slave ships, 36, 37, 40–42
slave trade. See African slave trade
Smith, Gerrit, 130
Smith, Lou, 166
Smith, Samuel Stanhope, 80–81
Somerset Principle, 124
songs, 165–67
South, the
    abolitionists as scapegoats for
        activities in, 107–108
    abolition movement in, 23
    antislavery mailings in, 105–107
    before the Civil War, 187
    black vs. white population in, 42
    on Compromise of 1850, 129–30
    cotton production in, 21–22,
        94–96
    emancipation in, 20–21, 70, 73
    fear of white dissent in, 108–10
    on Missouri Compromise, 89
    nonslaveholders in, 116–17
    vs. North on abolition, 111–12
    northern slavery vs. slavery in, 17,
        23–24
    on opposition to slave imports, 72
    perception of slaves in, 115
    political leadership in, 92–93
    political power in, 95–96
    slave population in, 22–23, 113
    see also Civil War; Confederate
        army; South Carolina; Virginia
South America, 15
South Carolina, 84
    anti-abolition extremism in,
        111–12
    antislavery mailings in, 105–106
    Republican control in, 176
    slavery in, 54–57
    white vs. black population in, 42
Spain, 15
    domination of New World, 35–36
    English feeling superior to, 45, 46
    Spirit of the Laws (Montesquieu), 76
spirituals, 165–67
Spooner, Lysander, 184
Stampp, Kenneth, 113, 187, 188
St. Domingue, 34, 76
Stephens, Alexander H., 93, 182
Stevens, Thaddeus, 173
Story, Joseph, 125
Stowe, Harriet Beecher, 125–26, 130
Stuart, Charles, 105
sugar plantations, 36–37, 38
Sumner, Charles, 173

Takaki, Ronald, 113
Talmadge, James, 86–87
Taney, Roger B., 132
Tappan, Benjamin, 105
Tappan, Louis, 105
Taylor, John, 93
Texas, 27
Thirteenth Amendment, 29, 155–56
Thomas, Jesse, 88
Thomas Proviso, 88–89, 90
Tillman, Mollie, 159–60
Tise, Larry, 81
tobacco cultivation, 47–48
Toombs, Robert, 93
Trimble, Aleck, 159
Tubman, Harriet, 151–52
Tucker, St. George, 75–78, 79, 90
Turner, Nat, 119–20

Uncle Tom's Cabin (Stowe), 125–26,
    130
Underwood, John Rogers, 182
Union army
    slaves as contraband of war in, 151
    slaves help, 30–31, 141–43
    resistance by Union government,
        143–45
Union government
    Civil War according to, 137
    goal of Civil War as emancipation
        vs. saving, 145–46
Union Leagues, 175

United States
African vs. European immigration
to, 34
first Africans in, 46–48
following Constitution, 84–85
number of Africans brought to, 42
slaveholders supported by
government of, 122
slavery dividing nation of, 17,
24–25, 130–31
slavery's turning points in, 11, 13
see also American Revolution; Civil
War; New World; North, the;
South, the
United States Telegraph (Green), 109

Vermont, 11
Virginia
black slaves' arrival in, 46–47
emancipation in, 20
fear of black revolts in, 76
legislating interracial fornication
in, 52–53
political philosophy out of, 93
proposal for abolition in, 74–75,
77–78
slave population in, 75–76
slavery's establishment in, 42–43
tobacco growth in, 47–48

Walker, David, 184

Washington, Booker T., 165
Washington, George
on abolishing slavery, 25
freeing of slaves by, 70
as slaveholder, 18–20
Washington, Martha, 70
Weld, Theodore Dwight, 104, 111,
125
West Indies, 47
emancipation in, 186
slave population in, 22
slaves arriving in northern colonies
from, 63
Weyl, Nathaniel, 92
whites
black slaves as threat to, 52–53
as nonslaveholders, 116–17
social unrest among, 53–54
see also racism; slaveholders
white supremacy, 176
Whitney, Eli, 21, 79, 94
Wieck, William M., 16–17
Wilmot, David, 27
Wilmot Proviso, 27
Wise, Henry A., 133
Woodward, C. Vann, 180, 181
Wright, Donald R., 15–16, 58
Wyatt, Bayley, 177

Yancey, William Lowndes, 93